Credits

Author
Jennifer Farley

Reviewers
Corey Gutch
Ben Harrison
Cristian Radu

Acquisition Editor
Wilson D'souza

Lead Technical Editor
Unnati Shah

Technical Editors
Joyslita D'Souza
Ankita Meshram
Unnati Shah
Zinal Shah

Copy Editor
Alfida Paiva

Project Coordinator
Leena Purkait

Proofreader
Chris Brown

Indexer
Hemangini Bari

Graphics
Aditi Gajjar

Production Coordinator
Nilesh R. Mohite

Cover Work
Nilesh R. Mohite

About the Author

Jennifer Farley has over 12 years experience working in the graphic and web design industry. In 2002, she became a full time educator, teaching Adobe Photoshop, Illustrator, Dreamweaver, and Design Theory. She runs her own design business, called Laughing Lion Design but now divides her time equally between teaching design and freelance illustration work.

Thanks to my husband Jason for his support and love, and for sometimes staying up very late with me while I wrote this book.

Thanks to my parents for their support and love and for introducing me to books at a very, very young age.

About the Reviewers

Corey Gutch has worked with various web technologies at Adobe Systems since 1996, and is an Adobe Certified Expert in Dreamweaver and Illustrator. He is currently the Interactive Director for creative agency Dumb Eyes, designing and developing standards-compliant websites, the Lead Instructor for the Web Design with Creative Suite certificate program at the University of Washington, and Community Manager for Adobe Muse at Adobe Systems. Along with his knowledge of Adobe products, he is proficient in authoring HTML, XHTML, CSS, PHP, and JavaScript, and working with open source frameworks such as Wordpress and Drupal. He has deep knowledge and insight into real-world web design and development scenarios with both corporate and boutique clients.

Ben Harrison is also known as Mr. Fuddlebunker of Kelso, WA. He is married to a wonderful woman, has four kids and works at Swanson Bark & Wood Products. His current responsibilities are Digital Marketing and Brand Management. He loves to play with his kids, travel with his wife, volunteer in his community, build websites in his spare time as Fuddlebunker Design, and when he has a free weekend, he plays paintball.

Cristian Radu is a technically astute IT professional with strong experience providing support to corporate clients across diverse industries, recognized for his ability to coordinate special projects, his excellent analytical and problem solving skills, and his willingness to rise to any challenges. He started his career working for small local companies then moved to large corporations.

www.PacktPub.com

Support files, eBooks, discount offers and more

You might want to visit www.PacktPub.com for support files and downloads related to your book.

Did you know that Packt offers eBook versions of every book published, with PDF and ePub files available? You can upgrade to the eBook version at www.PacktPub.com and as a print book customer, you are entitled to a discount on the eBook copy. Get in touch with us at service@packtpub.com for more details.

At www.PacktPub.com, you can also read a collection of free technical articles, sign up for a range of free newsletters and receive exclusive discounts and offers on Packt books and eBooks.

http://PacktLib.PacktPub.com

Do you need instant solutions to your IT questions? PacktLib is Packt's online digital book library. Here, you can access, read and search across Packt's entire library of books.

Why Subscribe?

- Fully searchable across every book published by Packt
- Copy and paste, print and bookmark content
- On demand and accessible via web browser

Free Access for Packt account holders

If you have an account with Packt at www.PacktPub.com, you can use this to access PacktLib today and view nine entirely free books. Simply use your login credentials for immediate access.

Table of Contents

Preface

Adobe Muse is an exciting new tool from the world's foremost software design company, which allows users to create beautiful and fully-functioning websites without writing any code. It provides graphic designers the power to use their print design skills over the Web.

This book will help web designers as well as graphic designers to master Adobe Muse quickly. It will provide step-by-step instructions that guide you through building a website with Adobe Muse.

Learning Adobe Muse will teach you how to plan, design, and publish websites using Adobe Muse. It starts by covering the tools and interface of the program and moves on to the concepts you'll need to understand for laying out your web pages. You'll learn how to format text using reusable styles, add images, create a clean navigation system, and add interactive elements such as panels and slideshows to your pages and all this without writing a single line of code!

By the end of the book you will have created a smartly designed, fully-functioning website.

What this book covers

Chapter 1, Welcome to Muse, discusses how Muse enables us to create websites without writing code. We will familiarize ourselves with the Muse workspace, its tools, panels, and the document window. We look at shortcuts for each of the tools which are well worth spending some time learning as you go.

Chapter 2, The Muse Workflow, addresses some of the challenges faced by designers creating web pages. These include making your design look good when viewed on multiple browsers at a variety of resolutions, and making it fast-loading. We look at the Muse Workflow and the steps involved in taking a website from an idea to a published website.

Chapter 3, Planning your Site, discusses some of the basic layouts used in web design. We look at the idea of wire framing using pen and paper and also how to set up a website structure and wireframe in Muse.

Chapter 4, Powerful Pages, looks at the concept of Master Pages and how we use them to apply a look-and-feel across many pages. We will learn how to add simple text onto individual web pages and how to add links. We use some of Muse's layout tools, namely guidelines, and the grid overlay to align our content.

Chapter 5, The Joy of Rectangles, teaches how to set up a flexible background rectangle. We added rectangles to our pages and manipulated their size, Fill color, and Stroke, and learned how to add effects such as drop shadows.

Chapter 6, Typography, Muse, and the Web, looks at how to add and style text on our web pages. We examine how to combine images and text wrapped together in a text frame. We discuss the importance of headings both from an organizational and SEO point of view, and we see how to add the hidden (to human visitors) metadata to our pages.

Chapter 7, Working with Images, teaches how to add images to our pages and how to manipulate them by changing their position, rotating, duplicating, and cropping them. We discussed the type of image file formats that are suitable for use on the Web and how to choose the appropriate format.

Chapter 8, Customizing with Widgets – Menus and Panels, looks at how to create a menu bar for our entire website. We style the menu, and the individual menu items which appear for each page in our website structure. We will use an Accordion panel as a way to put a large amount of text on a page without taking up too much space.

Chapter 9, More Widgets – Compositions and Slideshows, discusses Composition and Slideshow widgets, which allow us to add some very useful interactivity and functionality to our pages without as much as a hint of coding from our end. We also look at how to take code from another website (such as YouTube, Google Maps, or Twitter) and embed it into our Muse web pages.

Chapter 10, Muse, Meet the Adobe Creative Suite, examines how we can create a layered image in Photoshop and then place it as a Photoshop button in Muse. This allows us to create buttons with multiple states which is a useful way to give feedback to our web visitors. We will also see how easy it is to take an image created in another program and copy-and-paste it into Muse.

Chapter 11, Previewing and Testing your Site, looks at how to preview your page within Muse and in a browser, how to preview the entire website in a browser, and how to export the site as HTML and its associated assets. We also discuss testing and what you as the designer should be checking for, and we provide some tips on making your website mobile device friendly.

Chapter 12, Publishing Your Site, discusses how to publish and launch your website. You can publish using Adobe's own hosting with Business Catalyst or you can export your website as HTML and then upload it to a host of your choice.

What you need for this book

- Adobe Muse
- Adobe Photoshop (optional)

Who this book is for

This book is written for beginner web designers and also graphic designers who are interested in using their print design skills on the Web. It will teach you how to quickly build websites without the need to learn HTML or CSS.

Conventions

In this book, you will find a number of styles of text that distinguish between different kinds of information. Here are some examples of these styles, and an explanation of their meaning.

Code words in text are shown as follows: "You can see an example of this in the previous screenshot where the site name `Windsurf` has an asterisk beside it."

New terms and **important words** are shown in bold. Words that you see on the screen, in menus or dialog boxes for example, appear in the text like this: " Notice that the **Prototype** thumbnail shows us the content of that page."

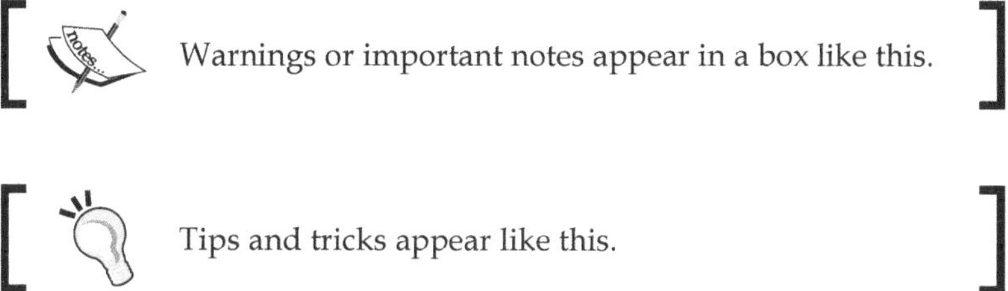

Warnings or important notes appear in a box like this.

Tips and tricks appear like this.

Reader feedback

Feedback from our readers is always welcome. Let us know what you think about this book—what you liked or may have disliked. Reader feedback is important for us to develop titles that you really get the most out of.

To send us general feedback, simply send an e-mail to feedback@packtpub.com, and mention the book title through the subject of your message.

If there is a topic that you have expertise in and you are interested in either writing or contributing to a book, see our author guide on www.packtpub.com/authors.

Customer support

Now that you are the proud owner of a Packt book, we have a number of things to help you to get the most from your purchase.

Downloading the example text and image

You can download the example text and image files for this book you have purchased from your account at http://www.packtpub.com. If you purchased this book elsewhere, you can visit http://www.packtpub.com/support and register to have the files e-mailed directly to you.

Errata

Although we have taken every care to ensure the accuracy of our content, mistakes do happen. If you find a mistake in one of our books—maybe a mistake in the text or the code—we would be grateful if you would report this to us. By doing so, you can save other readers from frustration and help us improve subsequent versions of this book. If you find any errata, please report them by visiting http://www.packtpub.com/support, selecting your book, clicking on the **errata submission form** link, and entering the details of your errata. Once your errata are verified, your submission will be accepted and the errata will be uploaded to our website, or added to any list of existing errata, under the Errata section of that title.

Piracy

Piracy of copyright material on the Internet is an ongoing problem across all media. At Packt, we take the protection of our copyright and licenses very seriously. If you come across any illegal copies of our works, in any form on the Internet, please provide us with the location address or website name immediately so that we can pursue a remedy.

Please contact us at `copyright@packtpub.com` with a link to the suspected pirated material.

We appreciate your help in protecting our authors, and our ability to bring you valuable content.

Questions

You can contact us at `questions@packtpub.com` if you are having a problem with any aspect of the book, and we will do our best to address it.

1
Welcome to Muse

Welcome friends, to Adobe Muse! As we work our way through this book, we will learn how to use Adobe's latest web design software to create eye-catching websites. All without writing any code.

Examples of some of the interesting ways in which people have used Muse include portfolio-style websites for photographers, illustrators, and designers and interactive brochure style sites for all kinds of service providers. If you would like to see some examples of how other designers have used Muse to create their websites, check out Muse Showcase at `http://www.adobe.com/products/muse/showcase.html`.

In this chapter, you will learn:

- What Muse is
- How to get around the workspace
- How to save your site
- How to select tools
- How to work with panels

What is this Muse you speak of?

Muse is a brand new offering from the software design company, Adobe. The idea behind it is to allow designers to create websites as easily as we can create layouts for print. Known as a **WYSIWYG (What You See Is What You Get)** web design tool, Muse allows us to build entire sites without worrying about HTML, CSS, JavaScript, or jQuery—all of which have the ability to leave a designer in a cold sweat.

If you are a graphic designer and have used Adobe InDesign, Illustrator, or Photoshop, you will find that you will have a certain level of familiarity with Muse. The interface is similar to others from the Adobe stable and the ability to drag-and-drop elements into your layout is what makes Muse special. You can focus on the look and feel, while Muse creates the code behind the scenes.

The following are some of Muse's features:

- **Plan, design, and publish**: Starting your website with a plan is always a good idea and that's the first step in the Muse workflow.
- **Easy layout of text and images**: You don't have to worry about adding DIV tags, Padding, and Margin attributes in order to place your design elements on the page. You can drag-and-drop where you want and precisely control your layouts.
- **Add interactivity**: Muse lets you add rollovers and button states created with the Photoshop layers. Arbitrary HTML and Muse widgets allow you to set up more advanced interactive features such as accordion panels, custom lightboxes, and menus.
- **Automatically-generated menus**: As you add pages to your site, Muse will update the navigation menus on the fly.
- **Publishing is easy**: While you focus on creating a compelling and beautifully designed site, Muse automatically generates all the HTML, CSS, and scripting required to make it function. You can publish your site from within Muse if you host it with Adobe, or you can export your site and host it with any service provider of your choice.

So let's get started.

Where to find Muse

In order to follow along and work with the program, the first step is to download the software to your computer. There are two ways to buy Muse: either by paying monthly or yearly as part of Adobe's Creative Suite, or you can just try it out as a thirty-day trial. Either way, you can download the software from `http://www.adobe.com/products/muse.html` and install it on your system. Muse is available for Mac and Windows.

The Muse workspace

A good worker knows their tools, so we're going to take a little time to find our way around the tools and panels that make up the Muse workspace.

The Muse workspace lets you plan, design, preview, and publish web pages and site assets. The toolbars and panels allow us quick access to the most common operations for creating and editing documents. Multiple documents can be displayed in the workspace and we can jump from one page to another by clicking on the tab that identifies that page.

The Welcome screen

The very first time you open Muse you will be greeted by the Welcome screen. This screen provides quick access to recently opened sites and easy creation of new sites. It also provides a direct connection to the Adobe Muse site where you can learn more about the program. A link provides information on the most current version available.

The Welcome screen will continue to appear every time you start Muse from the application icon in Windows or Mac OS. If you open a Muse file directly from a folder on your computer then the site will open without showing the Welcome Screen.

1. To disable the Welcome screen, select **Don't Show Again** and close it.
2. To re-enable the Welcome screen, enable the **Show Welcome Screen** option in the **Edit** menu.

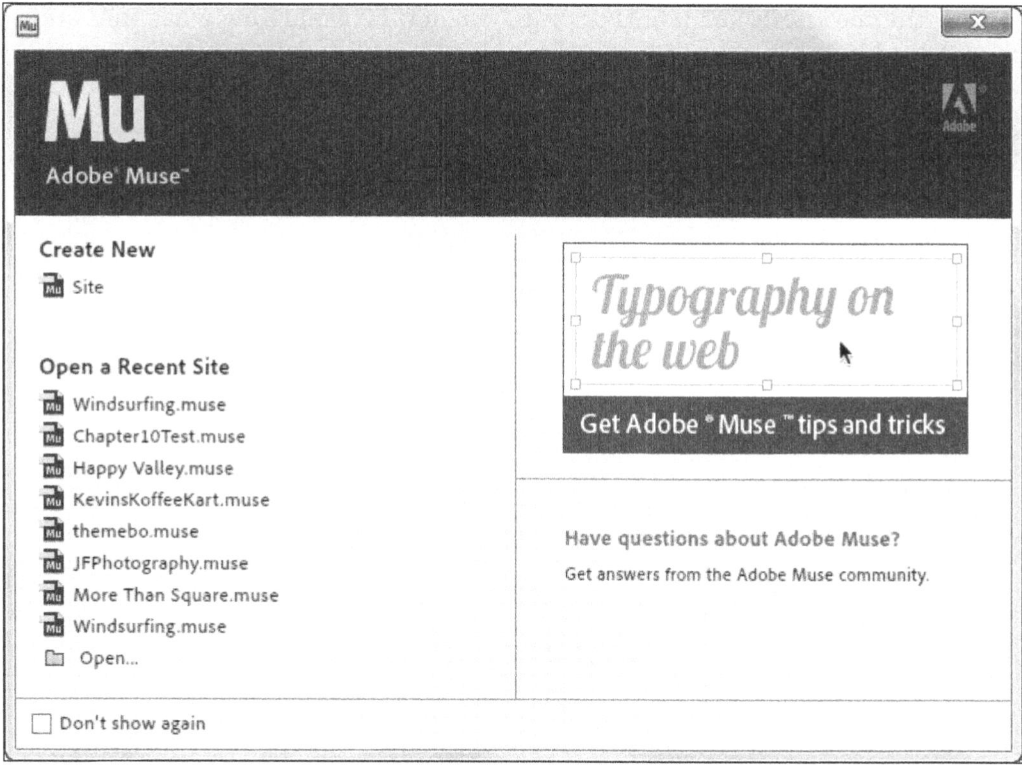

To open a recent site

Click on the site name on the left-hand side of the Welcome screen. If the site you want to work on is not listed there, click on the **Open** icon and browse through your folders to find the Muse site.

To create a new site

For creating a site, follow the given steps:

1. Click on the **Site** icon under **Create New** on the **Welcome Screen** or choose **File | New Site** from the main menu.
2. A **New Site** dialog box opens, which allows us to set up the dimensions of our site, the number of columns, and margin and padding settings.

   If you are a graphic designer used to working with units such as millimeters, centimeters, inches, points or picas, you may be wondering what units are used here. All units are in pixels as Muse is intended entirely for screen-based design work.

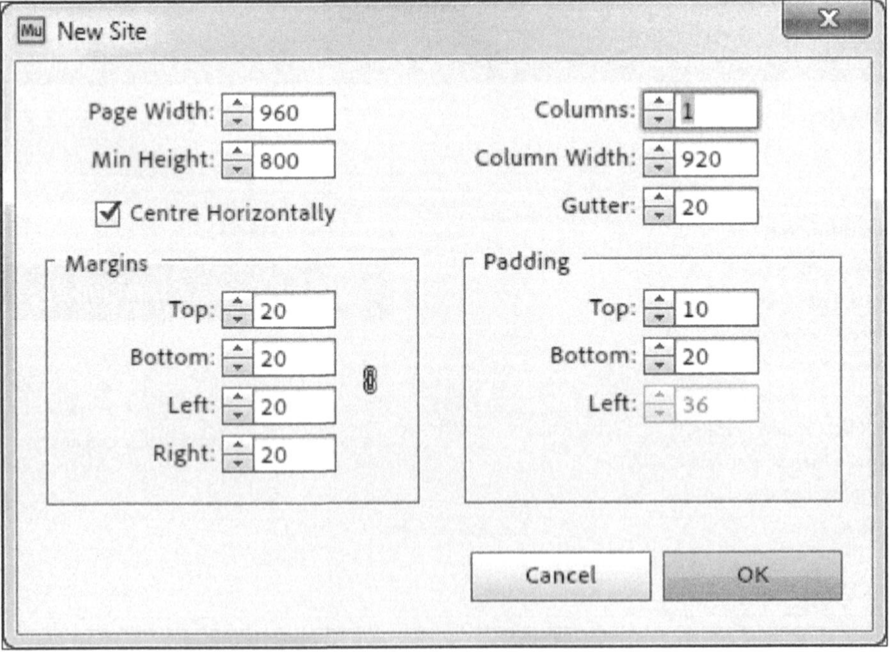

The fields in the screenshots can be described as follows:

- **Page Width**: This specifies the width of the container that will hold your web page's content.
- **Min Height**: This specifies the minimum height of your page. As you add content, your page will stretch but this value ensures each page will always have a minimum height.
- **Columns**: This specifies the number of columns that are used for guides to align objects in the design mode.
- **Column Width**: This is the width of each column.
- **Gutter**: This specifies the gap between columns.
- **Center Horizontally**: Leave this checked so that the container, which holds your web page content, sits in the centre of the user's screen regardless of their screen resolution. This is a standard practice when designing websites.
- **Margins**: This defines the space between the edge of your page container and other outer elements.
- **Padding**: This defines the space between the edge of the page container and the content inside the container.

The settings you specify in the **New Site** and **Site Properties** dialog boxes apply to all pages and master pages throughout the new site. However, you can customize properties for individual and master pages. We'll look at how to do that shortly. It is a good practice to set your site dimensions when you start a project, just as you would if you were designing for a printed page, but don't worry if you find you need to change the settings later. You can access this dialog box at any time by choosing **File | Site Properties** or by right-clicking (Windows)/*Ctrl* + clicking (Mac) the page or master page in the Plan view.

3. For this example, we'll set the **Width** as **960** pixels, **Height** as **800** pixels, all **Margins** as **20** pixels, **Top Padding** as **10** pixels, and **Bottom Padding** as **20** pixels. Type the numbers in the fields or click on the up and down arrows next to each field to increase or decrease the current values.
4. Click on **OK** to complete your initial site's setup.

Views

After clicking on **OK**, the next screen you'll see is the Plan view. The Plan view displays your site plan—an overview of how your website is organized. When you first create a new site, Muse automatically generates a Home page, also called the index page, that is linked to the Master Page design. Plan view is the default view when you open a Muse site.

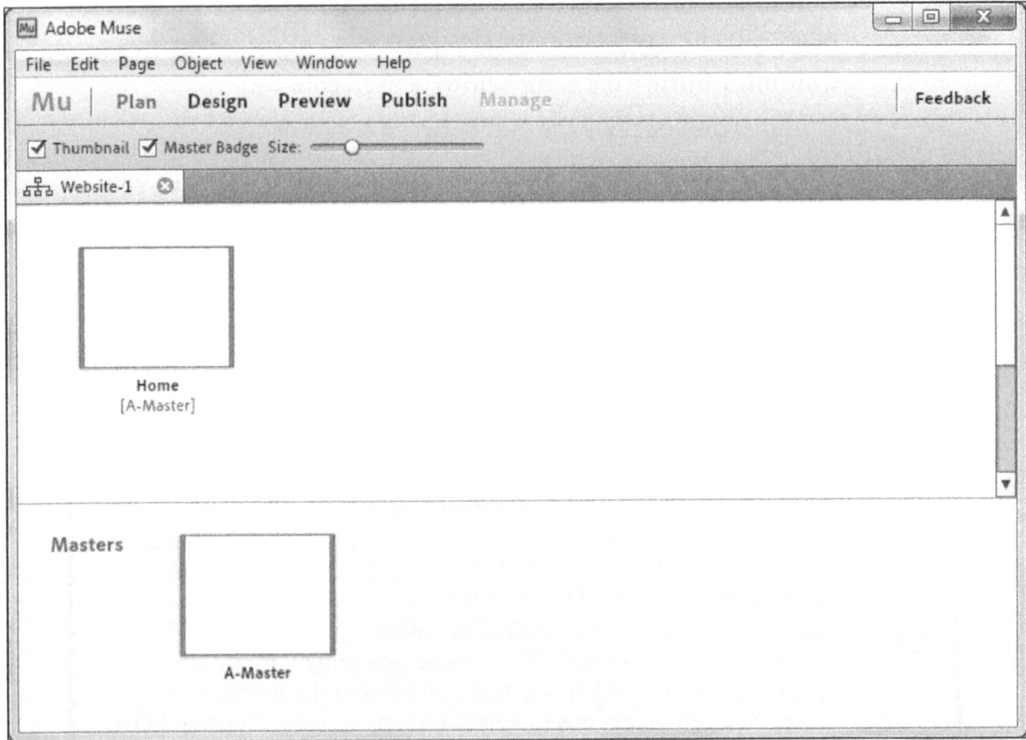

At this stage, your Plan view will only have a single page: the home page, which appears as a thumbnail on the upper section of the Plan view. Beneath that you should see your Master pages. In this case you will have one master page, named A-Master. The Master pages act as templates to share common design elements such as headers, footers and logos that are required on more than one web page.

A Muse site has five views: Plan, Design, Preview, Publish, and Manage. You can switch between any of the views by clicking the links at the top of the interface. The fourth link, Publish, opens the Sign In window which starts the publishing process. We'll talk about these views in more detail in later chapters.

Saving your site

Before we go any further it's a good idea to save our site.

1. Choose **File | Save**. The **Save Muse File As** dialog box opens. Type in a name for your site; let's call it `MyFirstWebSite.muse`.
2. Navigate to the location on your computer where you want to save your sample project and then click on **Save**.

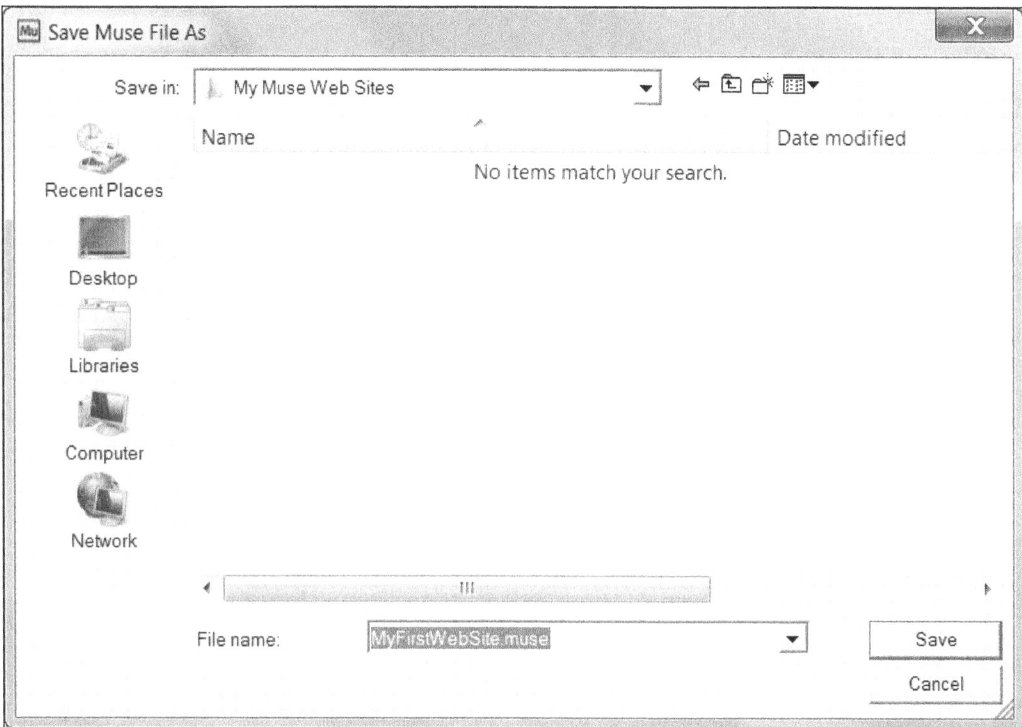

Opening a page in Design view

With our site saved, we can move into the Design view and check out the rest of the Muse workspace. While still in the Plan view, double-click on the homepage thumbnail to open that page.

You can also switch to the Design view by clicking on **Design** at the top of the **Muse** window.

The Design view is where most of the heavy lifting of the design work takes place. This is where we add our text, images, and multimedia widgets to our web page.

The Design view workspace encompasses everything you see when you open or create a new document:

- Views
- Toolbox
- Document window
- Panels
- Menus
- Control panel

With your homepage open, notice that tabs appear for your selected page and for your site plan. You can open multiple pages in Muse and each one will appear with its own tab. To jump from a page to another page or to the site plan, simply click on the page name tab.

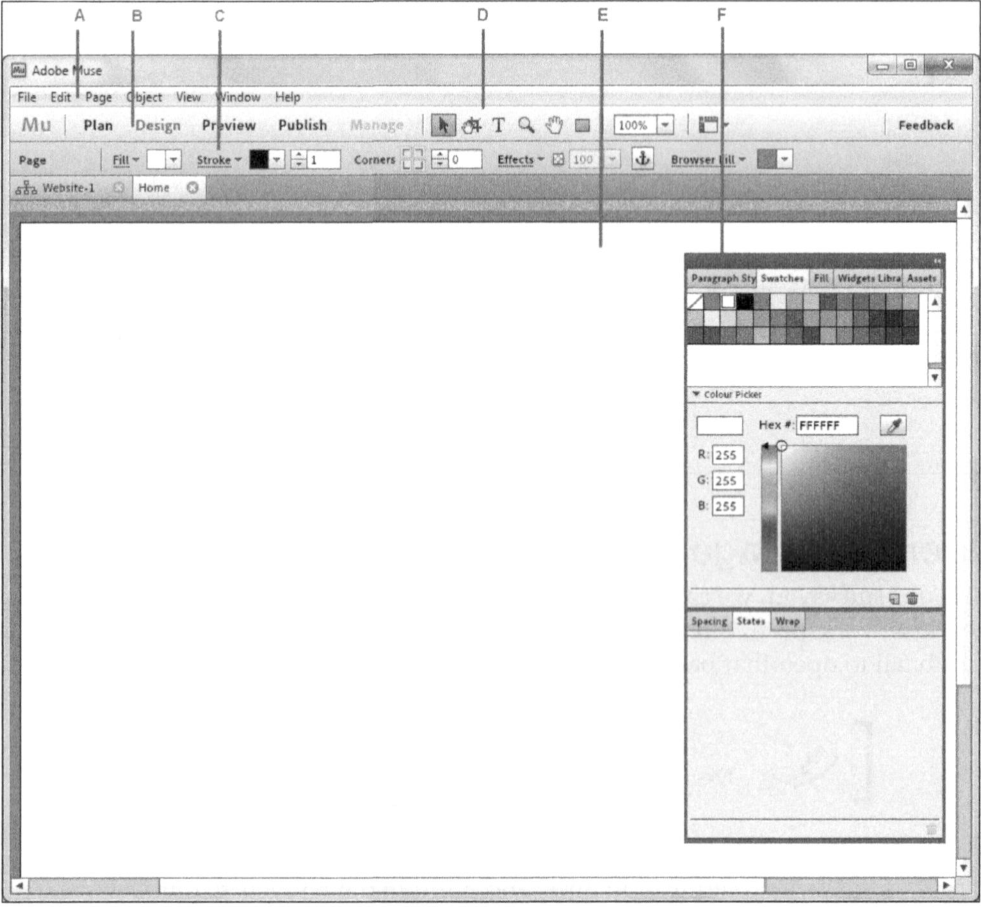

As shown in the previous screenshot, the letters indicate the different components of the Muse workspace, as follows:

- A: Menu
- B: Views
- C: Control Panel
- D: Toolbar
- E: Document window
- F: Panels

The toolbar

The toolbar contains tools for selecting objects, working with type, cropping, and drawing rectangles. It sits at the top of screen, to the right of the **Views** section. It contains some tools you may be familiar with if you've used other Adobe programs.

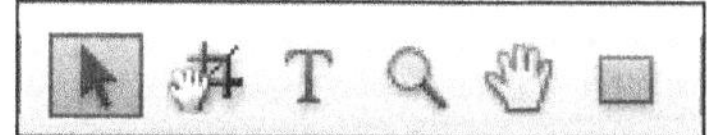

The following is a brief overview of the function of each tool:

- **Selection tool**: It lets you select objects on a page
- **Crop tool**: It lets you crop images on a page
- **Text tool**: It lets you create a text area where you can add text to a page
- **Zoom tool**: It lets you zoom in or out from the page
- **Hand tool**: It lets you pan around the page by dragging
- **Rectangle tool**: It lets you create rectangular, round rectangular, or circular objects that can be filled with colors or images

Using the tools

To use a tool, simply click on the tool using the mouse or press the appropriate shortcut key. You can find the shortcuts for each tool by positioning your mouse over the tool icon. A tool tip appears, revealing the tool's name and its shortcut. For example, follow the given steps:

1. Position your mouse over **Zoom Tool**.
2. Click on **Zoom Tool** to select it, as shown in the following screenshot:

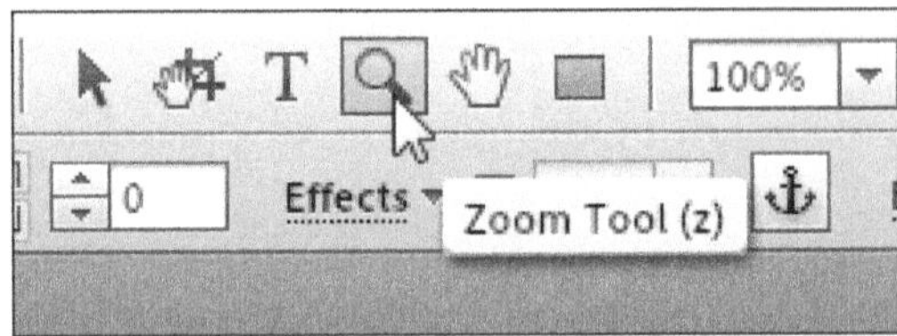

3. Roll your mouse over each of the tools and pause to see each tool's name and shortcut. Make a mental note of each shortcut.

Even at this early stage, it's worth making an effort to remember the shortcut for each one (and there are only a few tools here in comparison with other Adobe programs). You'll find that your workflow speeds up considerably as you work with one hand on your mouse and the other hand ready on the keyboard to press shortcuts.

The Control Panel

The Control Panel (**Window | Control**) gives you quick access to options and commands related to the current page item or objects you select. The Control Panel is context-sensitive, so depending on which tool you have selected or which object you have clicked in the document window, the options displayed will vary. To get more information about each option, hover over an icon or the option's label to see a tool tip.

Click on **Type Tool (T)**. Notice how the options on the Control Panel change.

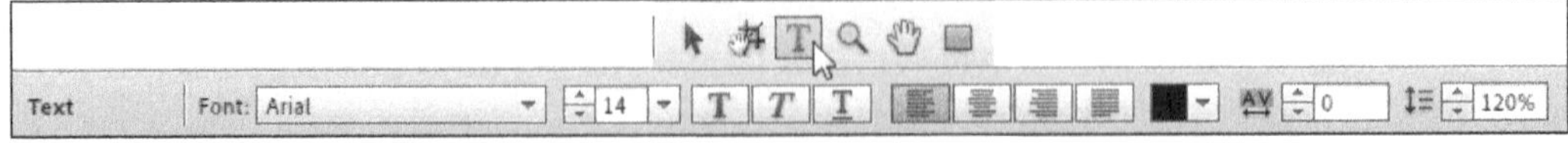

Panels

Panels give us speedy access to additional tools and features. By default, the panels sit together in a dock on the right-hand side of the screen. This is not a permanent position; the panels are actually floating and are independent of the document window. We can customize the workspace by changing each panel's location and reorganizing them to suit our own needs. In the following screenshot, the Swatches, Character Styles, and Spacing panels are currently active. By clicking on the name in any **Panel** tab, that particular panel becomes active. Unlike other Adobe software you may have used, individual panels cannot be separated; they are "stuck" together.

Click on the **Text** tab, the **Paragraph** tab, and the **Wrap** tab in order to activate them.

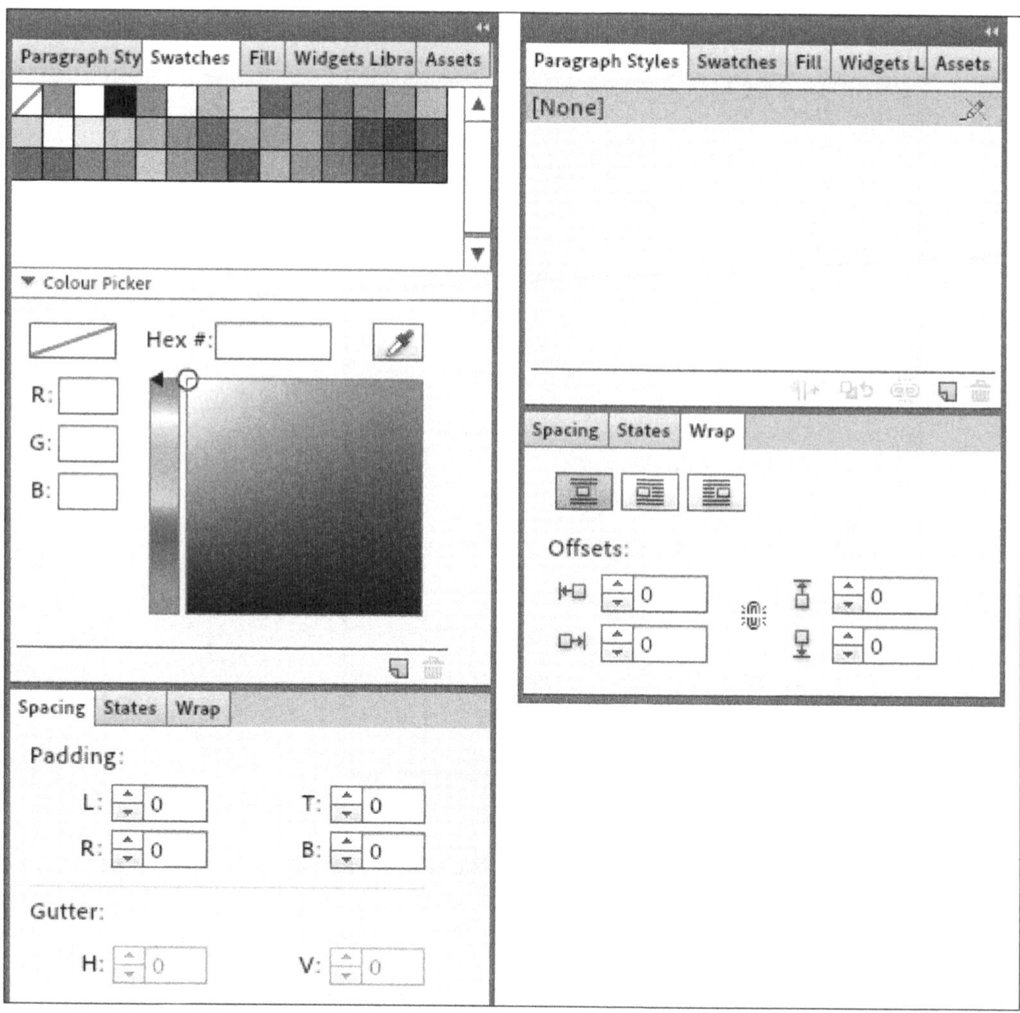

Expanding and collapsing panels

The panels take up a small chunk of the real estate on your screen, however, you may not always want them to appear fully expanded. We can reduce the amount of space they take up by collapsing them to show icons without names. The following steps show how to expand and collapse all the panels in the dock:

1. Click on the double arrow to the right of the panels' names to collapse the panel, as shown in the following screenshot:

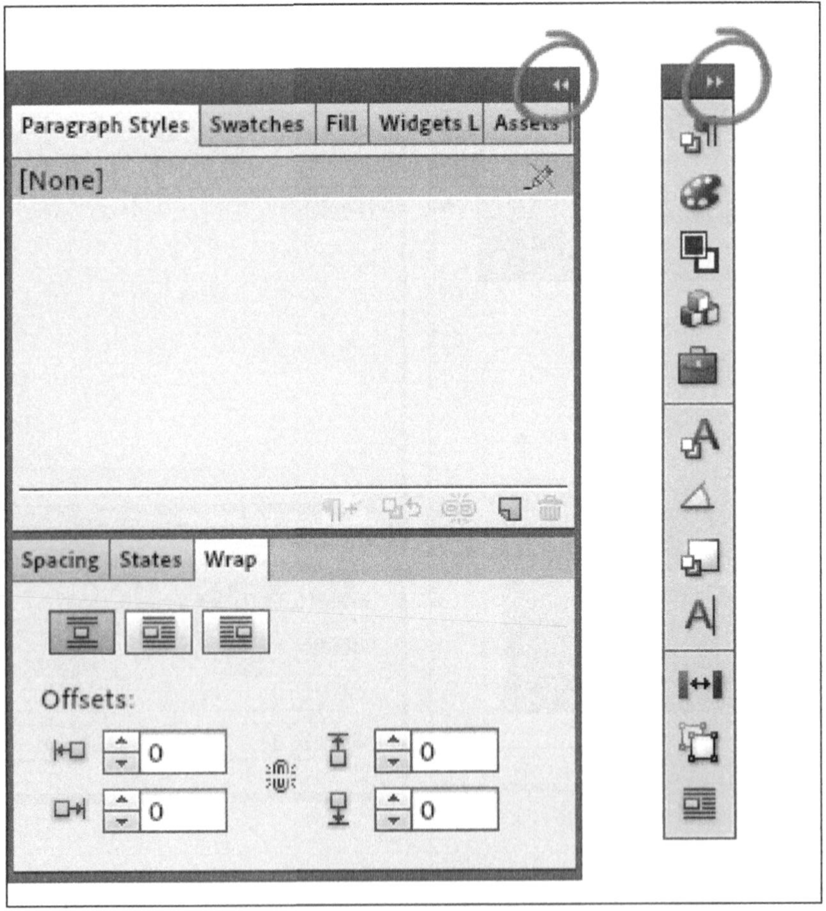

2. To expand the panels, click again on the double arrow at the top of the icons.

Another way to save space is to collapse the panels so that only the tab and panel name are visible. To do this, perform the following steps:

1. Click on the tab name. The tab itself will be highlighted but the controls and features in the panel will be hidden.

2. Click on the tab name a second time to expand the panel again.
3. To resize a panel, drag the bottom edge of the expanded panel.

Hide all panels

You may not want to see any panels while you're working on your design. To hide all the panels choose **Window** | **Hide Panels**. When you're ready, you can show them again by choosing **Window** | **Show Panels**.

Open a panel

If you can't see any particular panel in the panel groups, you can find a full list of panels under the **Window** menu. To open a panel that isn't showing in the workspace, choose **Window** | **Fill** to open the **Fill** panel.

If the panel name has a check mark under the **Window** menu, this means it is already active on the screen and that particular panel will appear highlighted in its panel group.

Rearranging panels

To move a panel into another group, drag the panel's tab. As you drag, you'll see a ghosted version of the panel and a blue highlighted drop zone appears in the group, which indicates the area where you can drop the panel. You can move a panel up or down within the dock by dragging it to the narrow blue drop zone.

As an exercise, try dragging the **Fill** panel downwards to join the group below it.

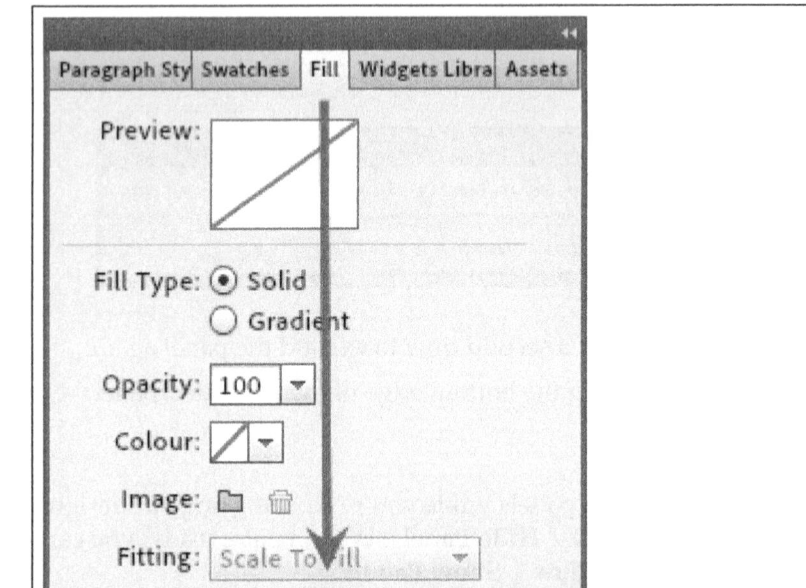

The document window

The document window is the white page in the middle of your screen and this, of course, is where all the action happens. We can see blue guidelines indicating the number of columns, the gutter size, and the margins. In the following screenshot, we can see a setup using three columns with space between them (known as the gutter) and the margin around the edge of the content area:

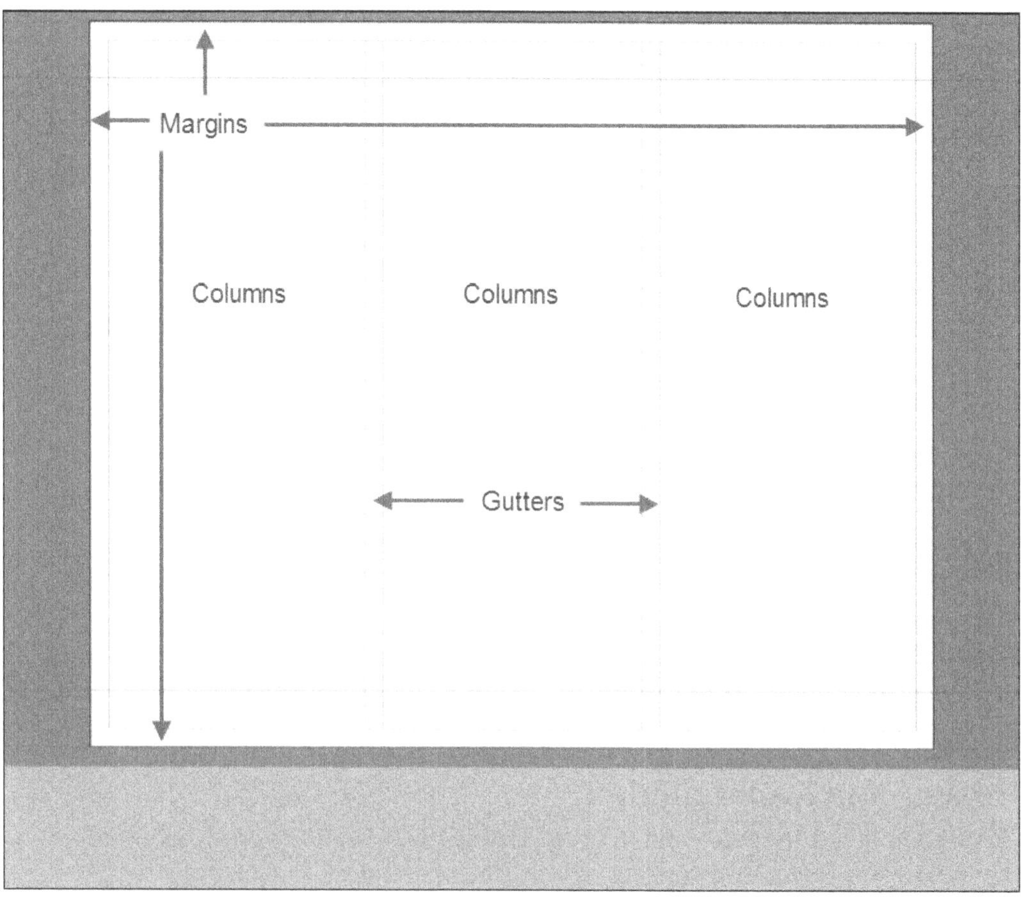

Rulers, guides, and grids

Rulers and guides are a designer's best friend, whether you are working with print or on the Web. By default, Muse displays rulers along the top and left side of the workspace. As mentioned earlier, the measurement units used are pixels. To show or hide rulers, choose **View | Show/Hide Rulers**.

Muse also displays five guides that define the page size, the header, and the footer. We haven't yet defined a header and footer height so you should see guides with handles for dragging the top of the page, the bottom of the page, and the bottom of the browser.

When you use the mouse to hover over guides along the left side of the workspace, you'll see a tool tip about the purpose and functionality of each guide.

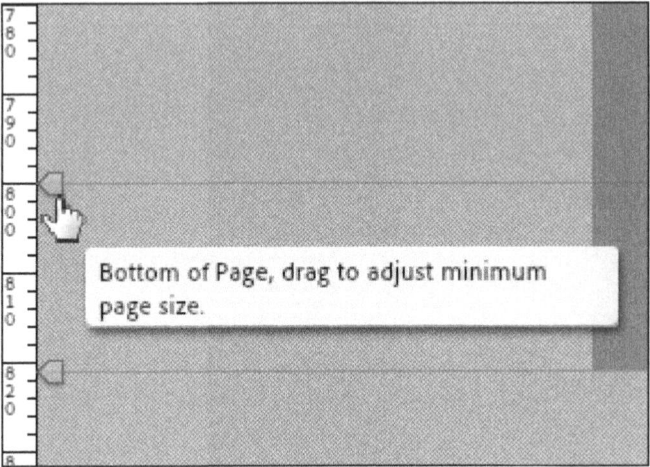

The top and two bottom guides help you to determine your overall page size. If you want to change the size of your page without going back to the **Site Properties** dialog box, you can drag the first guide up, or the fourth guide down to extend the content area of your page. To show or hide page guides, choose **View | Show/Hide Guides**.

Header and footer guides

The second and third guides on the page define the bottom of your header and the top of your footer, respectively. These guides become editable only after you have defined your header and footer in the master page. We'll discuss that in more detail in a future chapter. On normal pages, the header and footer guides are displayed for visual reference, but they cannot be dragged to a new location. To show or hide header and footer guides, choose **View | Show/Hide Header and Footer** or *Ctrl + Shift + ;/Cmd + Shift + ;*.

Grid overlay

Many people think about web design layouts in terms of columns. Three-column and two-column layouts are very popular but it's important to remember that thinking about rows and columns together gives us a grid—an important tool to help designers create elegant and attractive layouts. Muse provides a grid overlay.

To show or hide the grid overlay, choose **View | Show/Hide Grid Overlay** or press *Ctrl* + '/*Cmd* + '.

Zooming

While viewing content in the document window, it's important that we have the ability to zoom in and zoom out as we work on our design.

Changing magnification

There are a number of ways to change the magnification or zoom level. You can do any of the following:

- Select the Zoom tool (**Z**). The cursor changes to a magnifying glass with a **+** symbol inside it. Click on the document window to zoom in at the point of clicking. Keep clicking to be able to zoom into a magnification of up to **4000%**.
- To zoom out while using the Zoom tool, hold down the *Alt* key (Win)/*Option* key (Mac) while clicking. The cursor will change to a magnifying glass with a **-** symbol inside it.
- Choose the magnification level directly from the drop-down box beside the toolbar. The drop-down box offers values from **50%** to **400%** but you can type in any magnification level between **10%** to **4000%**.
- Choose **View | Zoom In** or **View | Zoom Out**.
- Use the shortcuts *Ctrl* + = (Win)/*Cmd* + = (Mac) to zoom in and *Ctrl* + - (Win)/*Cmd* + - (Mac) to zoom out.

- Use *Ctrl* + *0* (Win)/*Cmd* + *0* (Mac) to fit the page inside your window and *Ctrl* + *1* (Win)/*Cmd* + *1* (Mac) to view the page at its actual size.

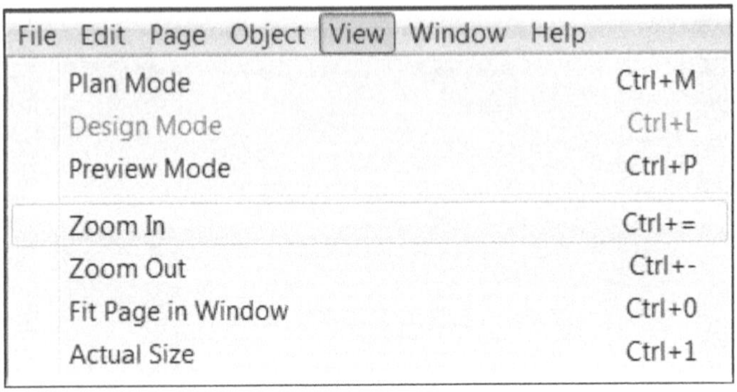

File Edit Page Object View Window Help

Plan Mode	Ctrl+M
Design Mode	Ctrl+L
Preview Mode	Ctrl+P
Zoom In	Ctrl+=
Zoom Out	Ctrl+-
Fit Page in Window	Ctrl+0
Actual Size	Ctrl+1

Undoing actions

In an ideal world, we could put together our websites without making any mistakes. Unfortunately, we do not live in that world and sometimes we need to backtrack or undo some of our actions. Thankfully, Muse allows us to step back and undo multiple actions. In fact, you are allowed to undo up to the last 20 actions. If you make a mistake you can do one of the following:

- Choose **Edit | Undo (Action)** or
- Hit *Ctrl* + *Z* (Win)/*Cmd* + *Z* (Mac)

If you want to redo something you have just undone, you can do one of the following:

- Choose **Edit | Redo (Action)** or
- Hit *Ctrl* + *Shift* + *Z* (Win)/*Cmd* + *Shift* + *Z* (Mac)

Getting help and more resources

For complete and up-to-date information about using Muse panels, tools, and other application features, visit the Adobe website. To search for information in Muse Help and support documents, as well as other websites relevant to Muse users, choose **Help | Muse Help**. You can narrow your search results to view only Adobe Help and support documents, as well.

For additional resources, such as tips and techniques and the latest product information, check out the Muse Community Feedback page at `http://forums.adobe.com/community/muse`.

Muse updates

As Adobe updates the software, you will see a message on the the Muse Welcome screen informing you there is a new version available. This message only appears when you have an active Internet connection.

Summary

In this chapter, we have discussed how Muse enables us to create websites without writing code. We have also familiarized ourselves with the Muse workspace, its tools, panels, and the document window and we looked at shortcuts for each of the tools. Remember, it is worthwhile to learn these shortcuts to speed up your workflow.

In the next chapter, we'll look at the Muse workflow, which is based on a typical web designer's workflow from the initial concept to the final website. We'll look at the steps of planning, creating, designing, and publishing.

2

The Muse Workflow

In this chapter, we'll look at the Muse workflow from the initial concept to the final website. The Muse workflow closely follows what could be described as the typical web designer's workflow, namely Planning, Creating, Previewing and Testing, and finally Publishing your site.

In this chapter we will cover:

- Differences between designing for the Web and for print
- Things to consider during the web design planning stage
- The Muse Workflow—creating a site, setting up a site plan, designing, and publishing
- Domain names and hosting

In the previous chapter, we familiarized ourselves with the Muse workspace, its toolbars, and panels. Before we jump back into Muse, let's begin by taking a look at some of the differences between designing for print and for the Web. We will look at the factors which can affect the user experience on the site which include they type of web browser used and the resolution of the user's screen.

Print workflow versus web workflow

In an ideal world, print design would retain an important pride of place forever. However, the reality is that in many parts of the world, people are finding their information and entertainment on the Web. If the audience is on the Web, designers will need to move with the times and follow suit. Making a smooth transition from paper to screen can be challenging, but that's where Muse joins the party.

Muse allows you to create websites in a similar fashion to how you create print layouts. It is aimed squarely at graphic designers and newbie designers who want to create eye-catching designs for the Web, but who don't want to learn coding in order to create a website.

In a print workflow, a graphic designer may begin their design with a pencil and paper to create a quick initial mockup. The designer would use Adobe InDesign (or something similar such as Quark Express) to lay out the page, and software such as Illustrator or Photoshop to create and edit images and graphics for the page content. Mixing it all up with a sprinkle of design know-how results in an end product that is a beautiful print creation.

The Web workflow using Muse is comparable to that of the print workflow. Regardless of the medium, it's a good idea to sketch out some ideas before turning on the computer. In five minutes you can have several sketches down on paper. It's highly unlikely you would have the same number of ideas produced in the design software in the same time. That's step one: get your ideas out of your head and onto paper. While the designer in each of us wants to create a visual masterpiece, the number one priority is to meet the needs of the visitors on the site.

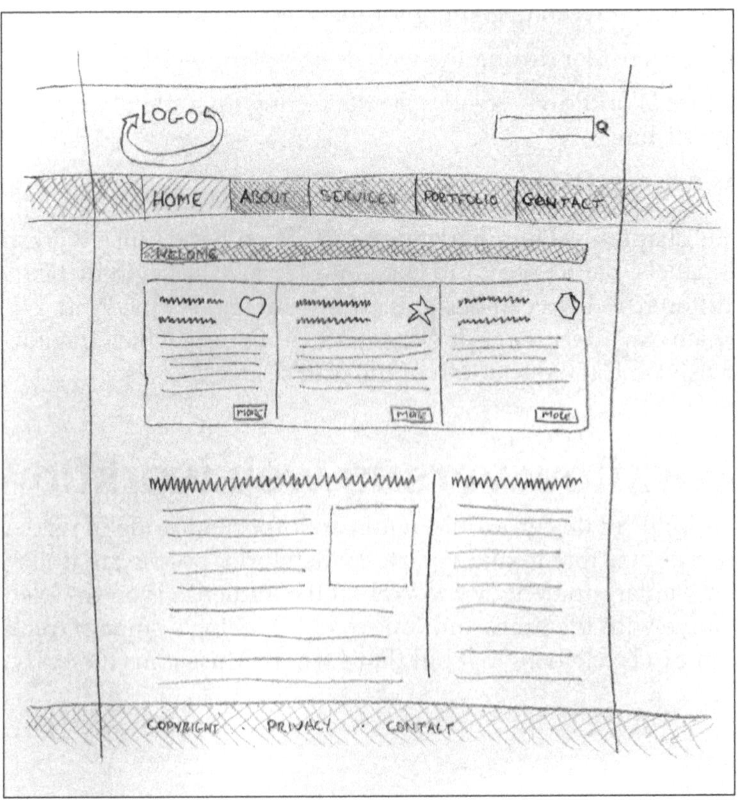

Pre-Muse planning

It's important to understand that the effort spent in researching, exploring, and planning at the early stages (before you even double-click on the Muse icon) is vitally important, so that when the time comes to fire up Muse, you'll find the workflow is straightforward and flexible. Many parameters influence how a design layout translates into an effective web design. These include the user environment, the resolution of the user's computer monitor, and to a small extent, their Internet connection speed.

Browser battles

If you've come from a print background, you'll know that part of the fun of designing for paper-based projects is the ability to choose the size and even the shape of your medium. For example, you could choose heavy stock, recycled cardboard, flimsy tissue paper, or a woven finish. Your paper design may include cut-outs, embossing, or folding. The possibilities for your paper graphic designs are many and varied. However, the one thing you can be absolutely sure of when it comes to print design is that whatever size or shape you choose will be exactly the same for everyone who looks at it. If you print on an A4 sheet of paper, we all see that piece of paper the same way. This is not the case for web design, and this is possibly the greatest challenge for web designers.

When we design for the Web, our design is viewed in the browser window. That browser may be sitting on a 28-inch monitor, a 15-inch laptop screen, or a 3-inch mobile phone screen and anything in-between. As you can imagine, this can lead to problems if we don't consider how our site will look in these setups.

There are many web browsers available, the most popular being Firefox, Internet Explorer, Safari, and Google Chrome. Each one of these display the results of the code differently, and as a result each one displays your web page differently. Most of the time, the differences are small, and as web designers we sometimes have to make small compromises to ensure that our designs look great and as similar as possible on any browser. At the time of writing, the statistics from the `w3schools.com` show the following browser usage:

Internet Explorer	Firefox	Chrome	Safari	Opera
16.7%	34.4%	41.7%	4.1%	2.2%

The data provided by W3C is collected from the W3Schools' log files and should be used as a guide only.

Resolution

We know that visitors to our site could be using any one of a wide number of browsers to view our web page. The next variable to add to the web design equation is the resolution of their computer monitors or mobile devices. A question frequently asked by web designers is "What screen resolution should we design for?".

To answer this question, it's helpful to know what is the most common screen resolution in use today. Here is the breakdown from last year according to `www.w3schools.com`. Again, this information is best used as a guide, rather than being set in stone.

Higher	1024x768	800x600	640x480	Other
85%	14%	0%	0%	1%

We can see from the table that most computer resolutions are now at 1024×768 or higher, so that is the size we should optimize our page for.

Usability expert Jacob Nielsen defines optimizing as ensuring:

> *"..your page should look and work the best at the most common size. It should still look good and work well at other sizes"*

Because many users have a screen resolution higher than 1024x768, most web designers will design their pages so that the content sits in a container that is centered on the page. A centre-aligned layout looks better on larger screens. Web designs tend to look better with an equal amount of white space on each side.

Download speed

When designing for print, there is generally no limit to the number of graphics or images you can use in the piece. It may cause a certain amount of hassle when e-mailing to the printer because of the file size, but you could put the work onto a CD or DVD and post it.

When it comes to web design, however, we need to think carefully about our use of images. Download speed is vitally important on the Internet and visitors will not wait around for a slow loading website. Google places a value on speed and takes site speed into account in their search rankings (`http://googlewebmastercentral.blogspot.com/2010/04/using-site-speed-in-web-search-ranking.html`).

Until everyone in the world has a superfast broadband connection, we must always be aware of how fast our pages load. Many users are now accessing websites using cellular data networks, which are much slower than typical Internet connections. One way to increase download speed is to use optimized image files: JPG, GIF, and PNG, which are a compromise between image quality and file size. We'll discuss these file formats in much more detail in a later chapter, but for now it's enough to remember that the speed of our website is a very important factor when planning the design and build of the site, and even has implications for search engine optimization.

Where to find more information?

So, how do we find out more about who's using what? As mentioned already, the W3C is an Internet organization whose mission is to develop web standards. In addition to providing advice and tutorials on all aspects of web design, they keep track of statistics regarding access and usage. To find out more about browsers, screen resolutions, and the operating systems of web users, check out the following links:

- `www.w3schools.com/browsers/browsers_stats.asp`: Gives information on browser statistics
- `www.w3schools.com/browsers/browsers_display.asp`: Offers (reasonably) up-to-date information on screen resolutions
- `www.w3schools.com/browsers/browsers_os.asp`: Provides a breakdown on operating systems

The Muse workflow

Muse features five distinct views or sections. These are:

- **Plan**
- **Design**
- **Preview**
- **Publish**
- **Manage**

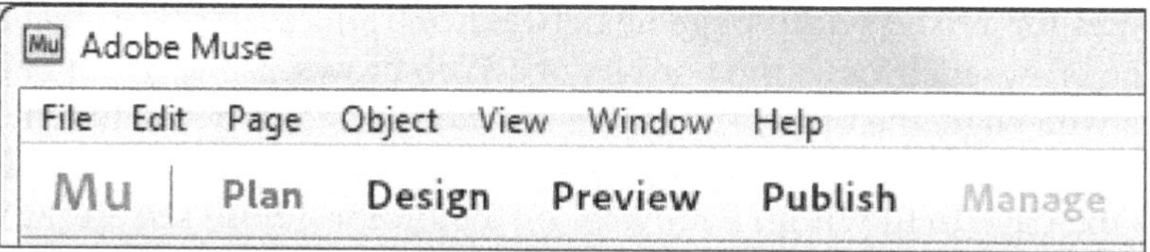

These views are a representative of the steps a designer will take when designing and building a website (without Muse). We'll take a look at each of these in turn, but let's start with a quick recap on how to create your site in Muse.

Create a site

In the first chapter we looked at the Muse interface and saw how to create a new site in Muse. Choose **File | New**. This process is very similar to creating a new document in InDesign. It creates a `.muse` file which is similar to an `.indd` (InDesign) file as it holds information about our web pages and the master pages.

We can set up the width of our page, and based on our knowledge of common screen resolutions (1024x768), the default width of 960 pixels is suitable.

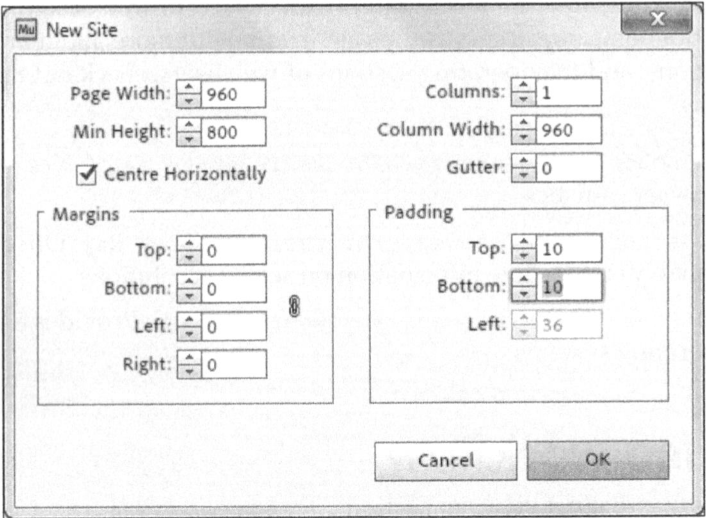

By entering a page width value we are creating a fixed width (sometimes called static width) layout. This means that the layout will not change in width even if the browser window is made narrower or wider. The alternative to fixed width is a fluid width layout. This means that the content stretches to fit the width of the browser window. At the time of writing we can only choose a fixed page width option. By default, the container holding the content is centered on the page.

Typical values for a fixed width page lie between 960 and 1010 pixels, leaving some space for the browser chrome, the borders of a Web browser, and scroll bars. When designing a web page, the browser chrome must be added to determine the width of the page. The most widely used width for a fixed-width web page is 960 pixels. That size allows the page to fit within a browser on a monitor whose screen resolution is 1024 by 768 pixels.

Why 960 instead of 1024?

Graphic designers have been using grids for layout for a far longer time than the Web has been around. The 960-based grid is used by web designers as a way to quickly prototype a layout in any number of columns: 9 x 3, 3 x 3 x 3, 4 x 4 x 4 x 4, 10 x 2 columns and so on.

In the following screenshot you can see, on the left, Nick Finck's website and on the right, the same site with the grid overlay superimposed on it. The grid helps designers align objects on the page neatly.

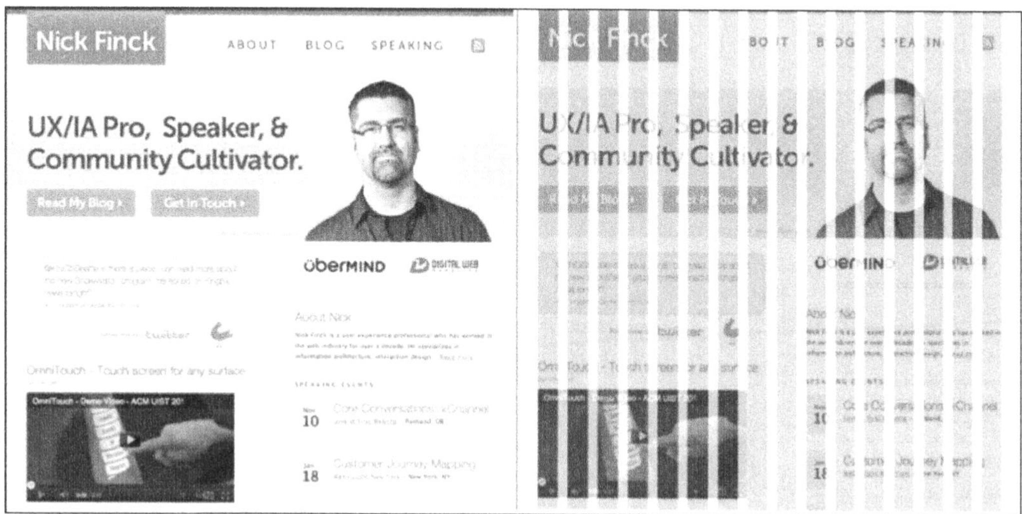

To read more about the 960 pixel based grid visit `http://960.gs/`.

Plan your site

Once you click on **OK** in the **New Site** dialog box, Muse opens the **Plan** view. When working with a page layout program such InDesign, you can set up how many pages you want. You can also set up master pages, which hold design elements or content that will appear consistently across many pages. We can do exactly the same thing in Muse. Every Muse site starts with a single thumbnail representing the home page on the top-half of the **Plan** view and a thumbnail representing a master page on the bottom-half of the Plan view. In the following screenshot you can see that we have added pages for **About**, **Services**, and **Contact**. Under the **Services** page there are three subpages called **Graphic Design**, **Web Design**, and **Illustration**.

The **Plan** view lets us easily add and organize pages by dragging-and-dropping thumbnails. A sitemap describes the way in which the pages connect to each other and it gives us a nice overview of our site. Additionally, the layout in **Plan** mode determines the automatic layout of menus.

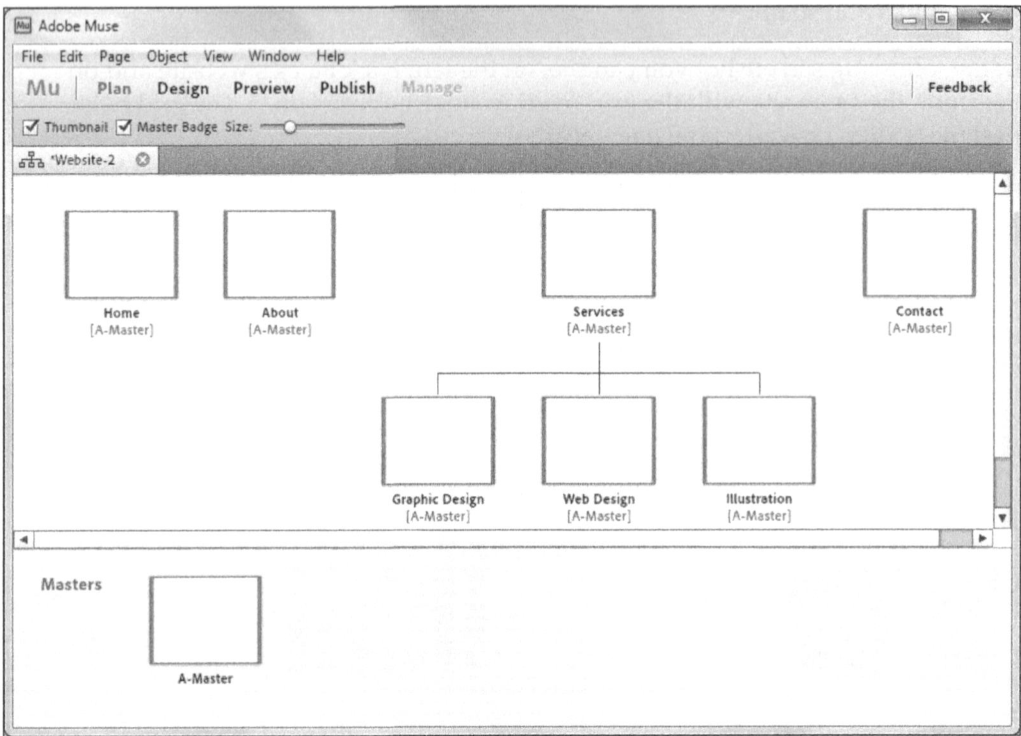

Design your site

After all your research, exploration, and planning, we've now reached the really fun part of the process: designing! With "traditional" website design, we'd write out HTML code, which holds the structure of our page. We would then style it using Cascading Style Sheets (CSS).

To use the analogy of a house, we could think of HTML as being the floor, the walls, the roof, and the windows, while CSS could be the carpets, the wallpaper, and the paint on the ceilings.

However, rather than writing the code and stylesheets ourselves, this is where Muse steps in and shields us from the dark underbelly of coding.

To get to the Design view, simply double-click on any of the thumbnails in the preview. Your page will open and you'll see the toolbar, panels, and the document window. We can add text, images, and lots of very cool functionality by dragging-and-dropping them onto the page.

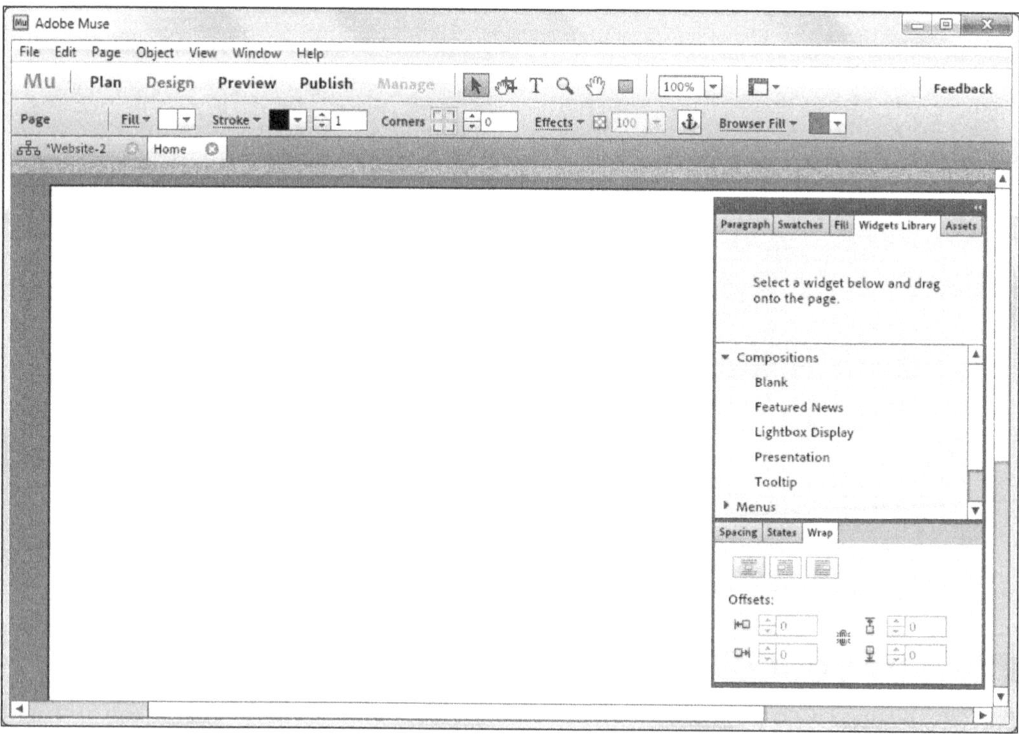

If you've used Adobe's Dreamweaver software, you'll know that even though it attempts to be designer-friendly with a visual approach to web design, you cannot drag-and-drop your design elements precisely onto the document in the same way you can in Muse. This has been a source of frustration for people who are used to Photoshop, Illustrator, or InDesign.

The ease with which you can place images and format text makes this program a joy to use. Muse is well integrated with Photoshop and Fireworks, making it simple to copy and paste graphics from those programs into your web page. Slideshows and lightboxes can all be added effortlessly; design elements which just a few years ago would have required extensive programming skills to implement.

The following screenshot shows a vertical menu system created by dragging out from the widgets panel. The options for the panel allow us to customize it to our heart's content, changing text and background colors, sizes, and positions.

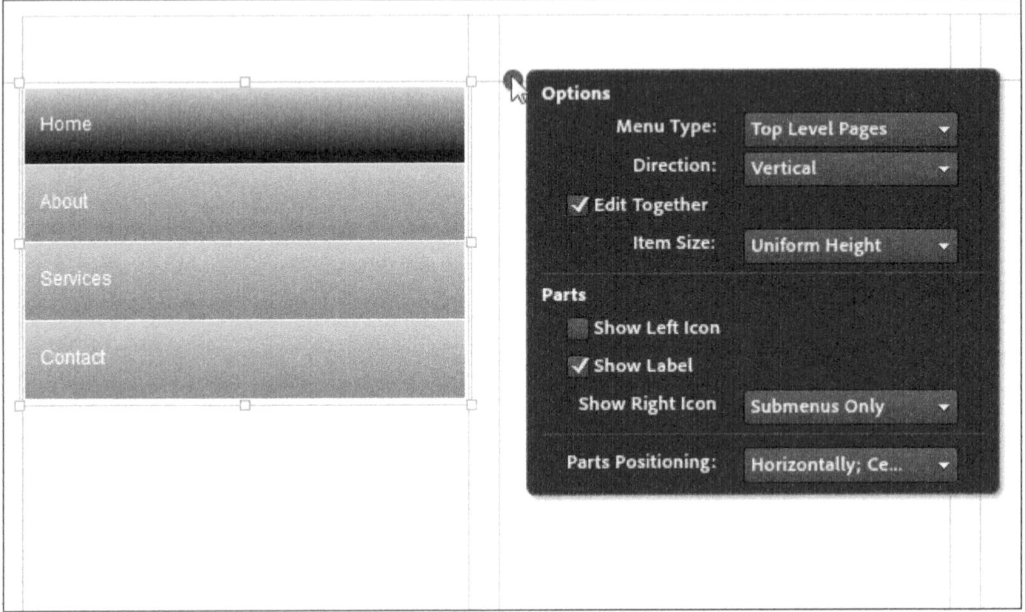

Preview your site

As part of the design process, we need to check regularly to see how our website will look in the browser. We can do a check from within Muse by clicking on the **Preview** link at the top of the screen.

Preview uses WebKit as its rendering engine. This is the same engine that powers the Apple Safari browser, the Google Chrome browser, and most mobile phone browsers, so it gives us a fairly accurate representation of how our design will look in *most* browsers.

To preview a page in Muse:

1. Open the page that you want to preview in **Design** view.
2. Click on the **Preview** link on the upper-left corner of the Muse interface.

While this gives us a handy "in-program" preview, it's very important to test your pages in the real thing, that is, in as many browsers as possible. This can be a laborious process but it is worthwhile to ensure there are no surprises when your page loads up.

Get the browsers

In order to test in the browser, you need to make sure you have the latest versions installed on your computer so you can test your website. You can do so by using the following links:

- Firefox: `http://www.getfirefox.com`
- Opera: `http://www.opera.com`
- Safari: `http://www.apple.com/safari/download/`
- Google Chrome: `http://www.google.com/chrome/`
- Internet Explorer (IE) v7: `http://www.microsoft.com/download/en/details.aspx?id=2`
- Internet Explorer (IE) v8: `http://www.microsoft.com/download/en/details.aspx?id=43`
- Internet Explorer (IE) v9: `http://www.beautyoftheweb.com/`

To preview a page in a browser, use the following steps:

1. Open the page that you want to preview in the **Design** view.
2. Choose **File** | **Preview Page in Browser**.

We'll start to build a new site in earnest in the next chapter, but for now, let's move on to the next step in the Muse Workflow.

Publish your site

So when all the hard work is done, it's time to put your wonderful design work online for the whole world to see, but wait! There is a substep we need to consider before hitting the **Publish** button.

Reviewing and testing a website

It could well be argued that reviewing and testing is something that should happen right from the start of the design and development process. As we've already seen, Muse offers a Preview view, which gives us a pretty good indication of how the site will look in the browser, but there are a number of questions you can ask yourself as you work through your web project:

- Who is my target audience for this site?
- Am I giving them what they want?
- Is the page layout consistent? We'll see in a later chapter how Muse's master pages can help us with consistency.

- Is there a sense of balance and order? Is it easy to get around the site?
- Are all links working?
- Does the website function and display properly in all of the main (and older) browsers?
- Has the website been spell-checked? Incorrect spelling and bad grammar have proved to be major turn-offs for visitors on e-commerce sites. Don't lose visitors because of bad spellings.
- If your site includes multimedia, does it work properly?
- Are your contact details easy to find?

These questions are just some of the issues you need to consider on your web design journey.

Use individuals and groups to test your site. As the designer, you are too close to the site and everything from the design to the functionality will seem obvious to you. But is it obvious to a new visitor? It's amazing what a fresh pair of eyes can pick out. Get as much feedback as possible.

When you're happy with your design and have tweaked it and tested it to a finely-tuned machine, you're ready to unleash it and share it with the world. To do that, you need to publish the site to a host.

Publishing a website means making it available to your visitors. This requires that you upload the website and all its assets to a server. Once you upload to a server, all your pages should be retested, just in case a file did not upload properly.

There are two options available when publishing with Muse. You can have your site hosted by Adobe using Business Catalyst or you can export the HTML files and use any host of your choice.

Adobe Business Catalyst

Business Catalyst is Adobe's hosted application for building and managing online businesses. It is tightly integrated with Muse and could be considered the easiest option for getting your website online. Prices for basic hostings with Business Catalyst start at $5.99 per month. You can find a full pricing list at `http://www.adobe.com/products/muse/buying-guide.html`. It should be noted that in the future Muse may include Content Management System (CMS) features that will not be available by exporting HTML and will require the use of Business Catalyst.

You can also publish your Muse-built website temporarily to Adobe Business Catalyst at no charge for a 30-day trial period. This allows you to send a live URL to your client for review. All sites in trial mode on Business Catalyst will include the Business Catalyst domain, for example, `http://mysite.businesscatalyst.com`. If you decide at a later stage to take the site "live" by paying for the monthly hosting, you can transfer it to your own domain and remove the `.businesscatalyst.com` subdomain.

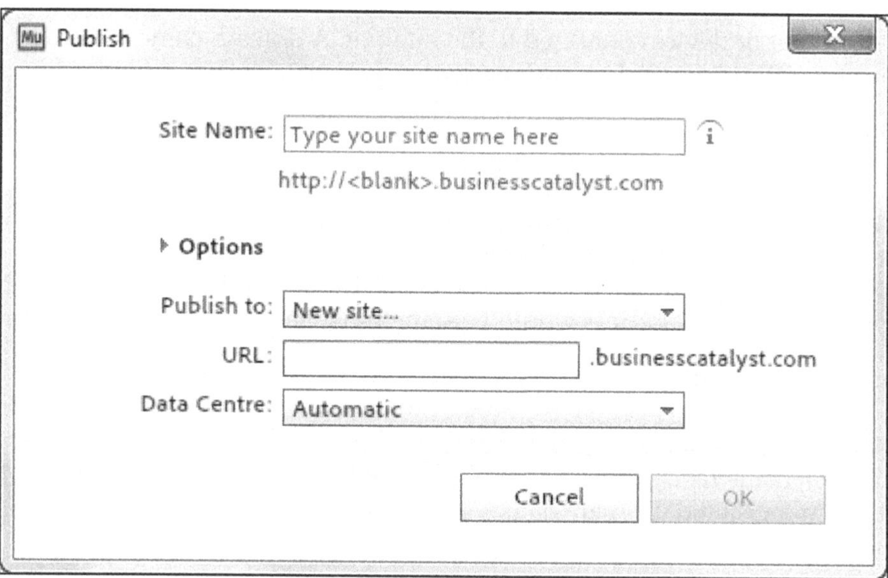

The alternative to Business Catalyst is to export your files and use an FTP program to upload the site files to a host. It's very easy to output your site as HTML from Muse, but this method requires using extra software such as FileZilla to transfer your files to the host's server. You would also need to arrange hosting and buy a domain name.

A brief overview of publishing

If you decide to go along the route of arranging your own hosting, there are some concepts you'll need to familiarize yourself with. Your site will only become available for others to view online when you acquire server space, get a domain name, and upload the site.

Domain names

In order for visitors to find your site, you need to get a domain name. Your domain name is a bit like your postal address. It may be possible to find your house without the postal address but it's much, much easier to find it with the address to hand. Visitors access websites by an IP address or a domain name.

An **IP address (Internet Protocol address)** is a unique number, which identifies every computer or device connected to the Internet. A domain name is the text version of an IP address and is much easier for us humans to remember.

The **Domain Name System (DNS)** is an Internet service, which translates domain names into their corresponding IP addresses.

The **Uniform Resource Locator (URL)** is also a web address and it tells the browser on which server your web page is located. It does this using a communications protocol, such as **Hypertext Transfer Protocol (HTTP)** plus the domain name. For example, a typical web address would be something like `http://www.nytimes.com`.

Domain names are unique. That's why there is only one `amazon.com`, one `microsoft.com`, and one `facebook.com`. Domain names must be registered. Most hosting service providers will provide a domain registration service so it's easy to get a domain name registered. The hard part is to find a domain you want that hasn't already been registered. Domain names are cheap too. You should expect to pay between $5 and $30 for a domain name for one year.

Acquire server space

An Internet Service Provider (ISP) hosts your website. Their business is to offer a connection to a host where you can keep your web pages and all the files that are part of your site.

Many ISPs provide web space for free or for a fee. Some people find that free web space is useful while learning the ropes and it's somewhere to upload your files while testing. However, many providers that provide free space put advertisements and pop-up windows on your site, which are intensely annoying and look very unprofessional. One of the advantages of using Muse is that you have access to Business Catalyst for publishing for free for 30 days.

If you want to look professional and get good service, it is worth paying for a domain name and some decent hosting. It's also worth doing some research to see which providers other developers recommend and which ISPs they would steer clear of.

Uploading your site

Once you've arranged your hosting and domain name, it's time to upload those web files you've worked so hard designing. Some ISPs provide an uploading or file management system to get your files up onto their server. The most efficient way to get your files onto the host's server is to use File Transfer Protocol or FTP. Using FTP software such as FileZilla (`http://filezilla-project.org/`) or Smart FTP (`http://www.smartftp.com/`) you can quickly set up a link between your computer, where you create your web pages, and the host or remote computer, where visitors can see your site. Both of these applications are free to download.

Summary

In this chapter we discussed some of the challenges faced by designers creating web pages. These include making your design look good when viewed on multiple browsers at a variety of resolutions, and making it fast-loading. We also looked at the Muse Workflow and the steps involved in taking a website from an idea to a published site.

In the next chapter, we'll use Muse's wonderful wireframing tools to create a sitemap and a working prototype of a website.

3

Planning Your Site

A site is a collection of web pages containing assets such as images or Flash. In this chapter, we'll look at how to plan a new site and use Muse's excellent wireframing tools to put together a mock up of our website.

Fail To Plan, Plan To Fail

Yes, that may be an old cliché, but like many clichés, this one is certainly true when it comes to our websites. If you spend some time planning your website upfront, you'll prevent a lot of headaches later in the process.

In the previous chapter we looked at the Muse workflow and how planning is an integral part of the development of the site. Now we'll take a look at some of the basics of web page layout that are useful to know while planning our sites.

Page layouts

The layout of your website can be a deciding factor on whether your visitors will stay on your website or leave with an impatient click. You could think of the layout as a map. If it's easy for the visitors to "read" the map, they are more likely to stick around and find the content you're providing. Let's take a look at some of the typical layouts we see on the Web today.

Bread and butter layouts

When we're designing a layout for a web page, there are a number of sections that we need to include. These sections can be broken into the following:

- **Consistent content**: This does not change throughout the site. Examples of this type of content are logos, navigation bars, and footers.
- **Changing content**: This is the part of the page that changes throughout the site, usually the main content. In some situations, the content of the sidebar may also change.

A web designer's job is to create a layout that keeps the visitor focused on the content while keeping it nice and easy to navigate around the site. Some examples of conventional or bread and butter site layouts are shown in the following figure:

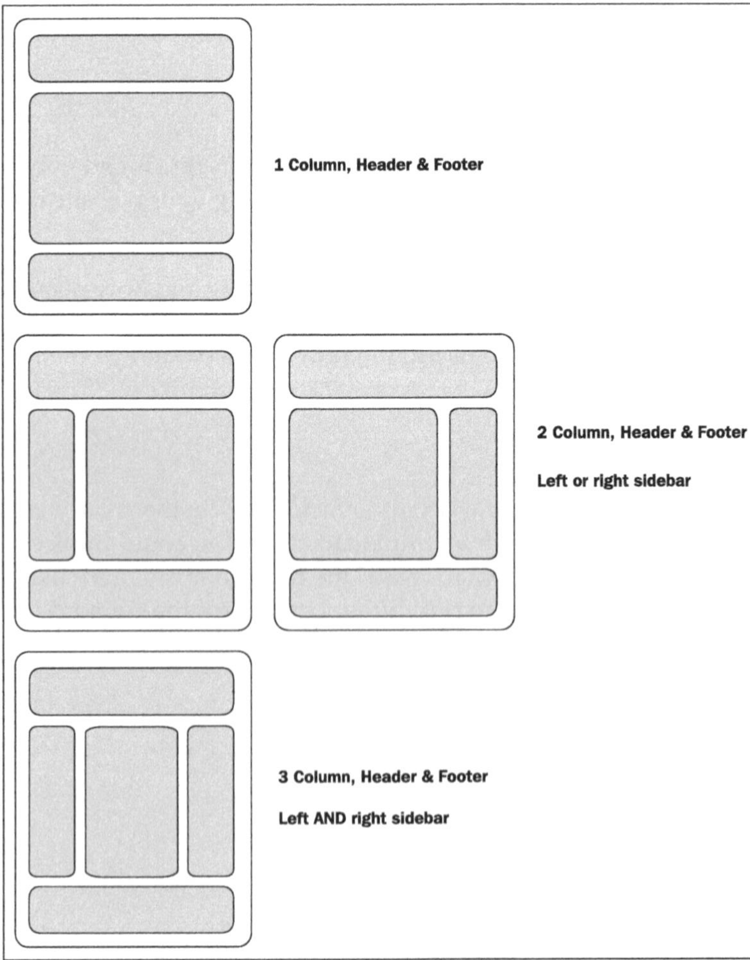

You have a very short amount of time to capture a visitor's attention. So by choosing one of these basic layouts, you're using a tried and tested setup, which many web users will feel at home with. Don't worry that these layouts look "boxy". You can use images, colors, and typefaces, which complement the purpose of your site to completely disguise the fact that every web page is essentially made up of boxes.

The bread and butter layouts featured previously are well-tested guides; however, there is absolutely no obligation for you to use one of these.

What appears on a typical web page?

So we've seen some basic layouts. Now we'll look at some of the elements that appear on (nearly) every web page.

Logo

The logo is the part of a company's overall branding and identity, and appears at the top of each page on the site along with the company name and tagline, just as it would on printed forms of marketing, such as business cards, brochures, and letterheads. This identity block increases brand recognition and ensures users know that the pages they're viewing are part of a single site. Frequently, the logo is also a link back to the home page of the site.

Navigation bar

The navigation for your site should be easy to use and easy to find. Just like the logo, it should appear near the top of the page. You may decide to use a horizontal menu across the top of the page, a vertical menu in a sidebar, or a combination of the two. Either way, your main navigation should be visible "above the fold", that is, any area of a web page that can be viewed without visitors having to scroll.

Content

Content is the King. This is what your visitors have come for. If the visitors can't find what they're looking for, they will move on very quickly. The main content is an important focal point in your design; don't waste time filling it with unnecessary "stuff".

Footer

Sitting at the bottom of the page, the footer usually holds copyright information, contact links information, and legalities of the site. Some designers have become very imaginative with footers and use this area to hold additional links, tweets, and "about me" information.

The footer clearly separates the main content from the end of the page and indicates to users that they're at the bottom of the page.

In the following screenshot, you can see a page from the Apple website, which is highly regarded for its aesthetic design. Each section is clearly delineated.

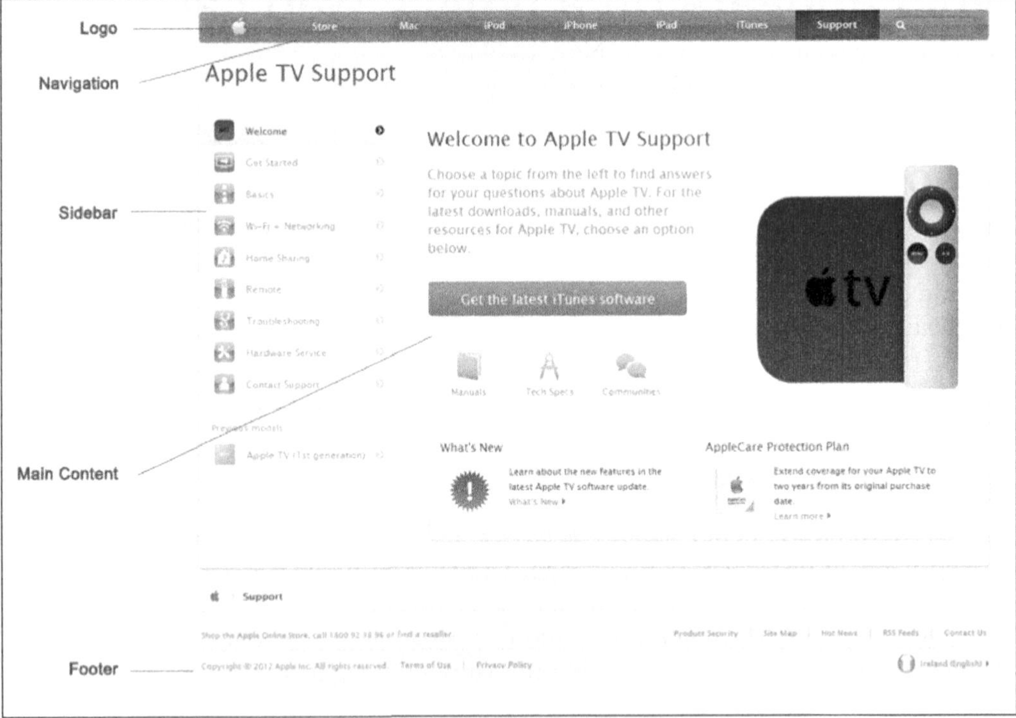

If you keep in mind the idea of your site's layout as a map, then you can determine where you want to lead your visitors on the site.

Wireframes

Wireframing is an important part of the design process for both simple and complex projects. If you're creating a website for a client, a wireframe is a great tool for communicating your ideas visually at an early stage rather than just having a verbal description.

If you're creating a website for yourself, the wireframe helps to clarify what is required on each page of your website. It can be considered an overlap between the planning process and the design process.

Creating a simple wireframe ensures that your page designs take into account all of the elements you'll add to your pages and where they will be positioned. Wireframes are cost-effective because the time spent in the initial stages potentially saves you from losing much more time revising the design at a later stage.

Wireframes can be created in several ways, including pen and paper and computer-based tools.

In the previous chapter, we mentioned the use of pen and paper in the planning process. This is a quick and inexpensive method for producing wireframes. Many designers use graph paper with feint ruled squares, acting as a ready-made grid. The grid lines help to create elements in proportion to each other.

When it comes to computer-based applications for wireframing, there are many options available. Some designers use Photoshop, Illustrator, or even InDesign to put together their wireframes. Specific wireframing software packages that are popular with web designers include Balsamiq and OmniGraffle.

Wireframes and Mockups and Prototypes. Oh my!

You may hear web designers refer to wireframes, mockups, and prototypes. Although these terms are sometimes used interchangeably, it's important to understand that they are three different things.

A wireframe is a basic illustration showing the structure and components of a web page.

A mockup is an image file focusing on the design elements in the site. It contains the graphics and other page elements that make up the web page but may contain dummy text and images.

A prototype is an almost-complete or semi-functional web page, constructed with HTML and CSS. Prototypes give the client (or yourself) the ability to click around and check out how the final site will work.

What to include in a wireframe?

Think about which design elements will appear on each page of your website. As mentioned already, most websites will have elements such as logos, navigation, search bars, and footers in consistent positions throughout the site.

Next, think about any extra elements that may be specific to individual pages. These include graphics and dynamic widgets. Once you know what's required, you can start to create your wireframe based on these elements.

Some designers like to create their wireframes with the "big picture" in mind. Once the basic layout is in place, they get feedback from the client and revise the wireframe if necessary.

Others like to create a very detailed wireframe for each page on the site, including every single design element on the list before showing it to the client.

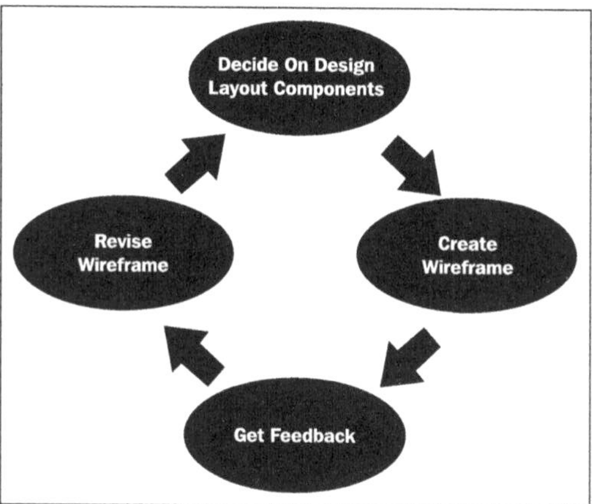

Wireframes let us try out several different ideas before settling on our favorite design, which can then be brought forward to the mockup stage.

Obviously our focus in this book is on using Muse, but I would urge you not to rule out using paper sketches. It's a great way to quickly get ideas out of your head and into a tangible, visible layout.

Web.without.words (`www.webwithoutwords.com`) is an interesting website dedicated to showing popular and well-known sites as wireframes. The text and images on each site are blocked out and it's a nice way to look at web pages and see how they can be broken down into simple boxes without getting caught up in the content.

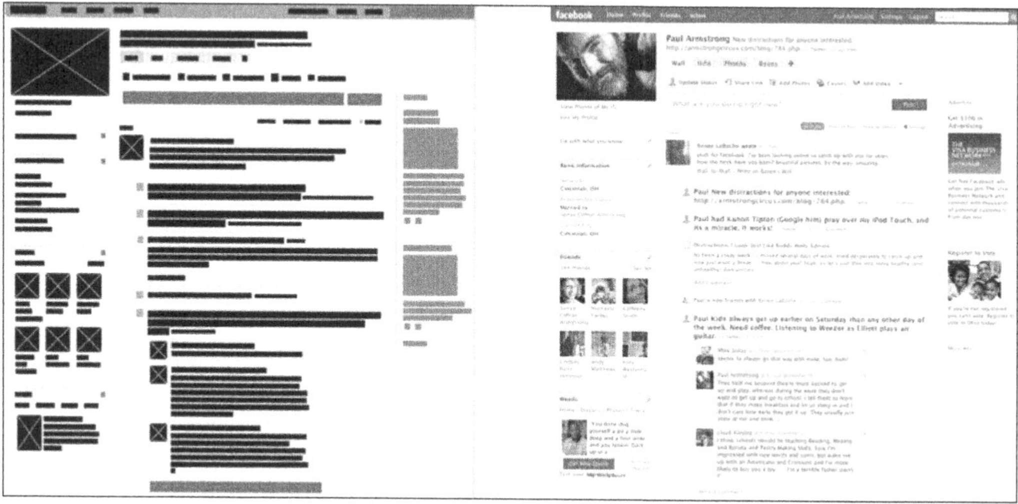

Wireframes with Muse

So what are the advantages of using Muse to create our wireframes? Well, Muse not only lets you create wireframes, but it also allows you to quickly create prototypes using those wireframes. This means you can show clients the functionality of the website with the basic layout. The prototype produced by Muse can be reviewed on any web browser giving the client a good idea of how the site will appear. This kind of early testing can help alleviate time-consuming problems further down the line of the design process.

We're going to prepare a site and wireframe now for a fictitious website about windsurfing. First, we'll create a new site, and then add pages in the **Plan** view.

Site structure with Plan view

Let's start by creating a new site.

1. Open Muse. Choose **File | New Site**. In the **New Site** dialog box, set **Page Width** to **960** and **Min Height** to **800** pixels. Set **Margins** to **0** all around and **Padding Top** and **Bottom** to **10** pixels each. Set the number of **Columns** to **16**. The columns appear as guidelines on the page and we use them to help us align the design elements on our layout. Note that **Gutter** is set to **20** by default, leave this as it is. The **Column Width** is calculated by Muse and you should see a value of **41** appear automatically in that field. Remember that all of these values can be changed later if necessary.

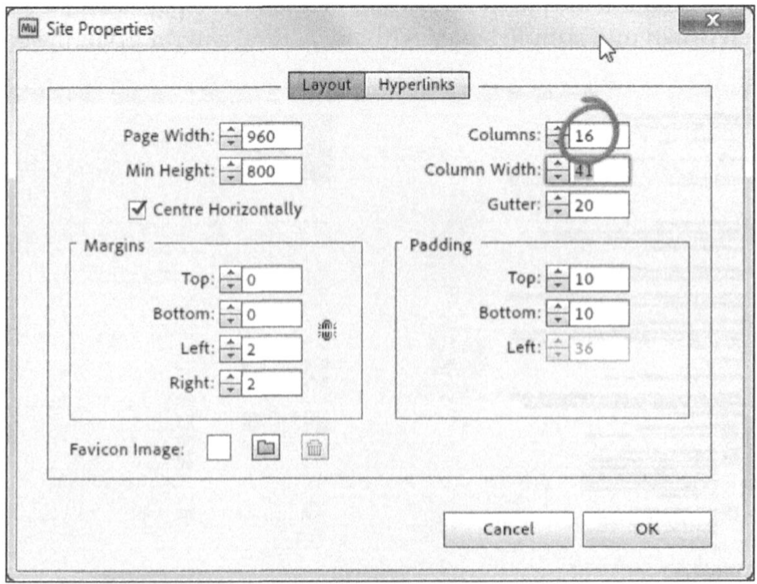

2. Click on **OK**. The **Plan** view opens and you'll see a thumbnail representing the Home page at the top left, and a thumbnail representing the A-Master page on the bottom pane.
3. Save your site right away by selecting **File | Save Site**. Give it a descriptive name you'll recognize, such as `Windsurf.muse`.
4. To create new pages, click on the plus (+) sign to the right of or below the existing pages, and then click on the page's name field to type its name.

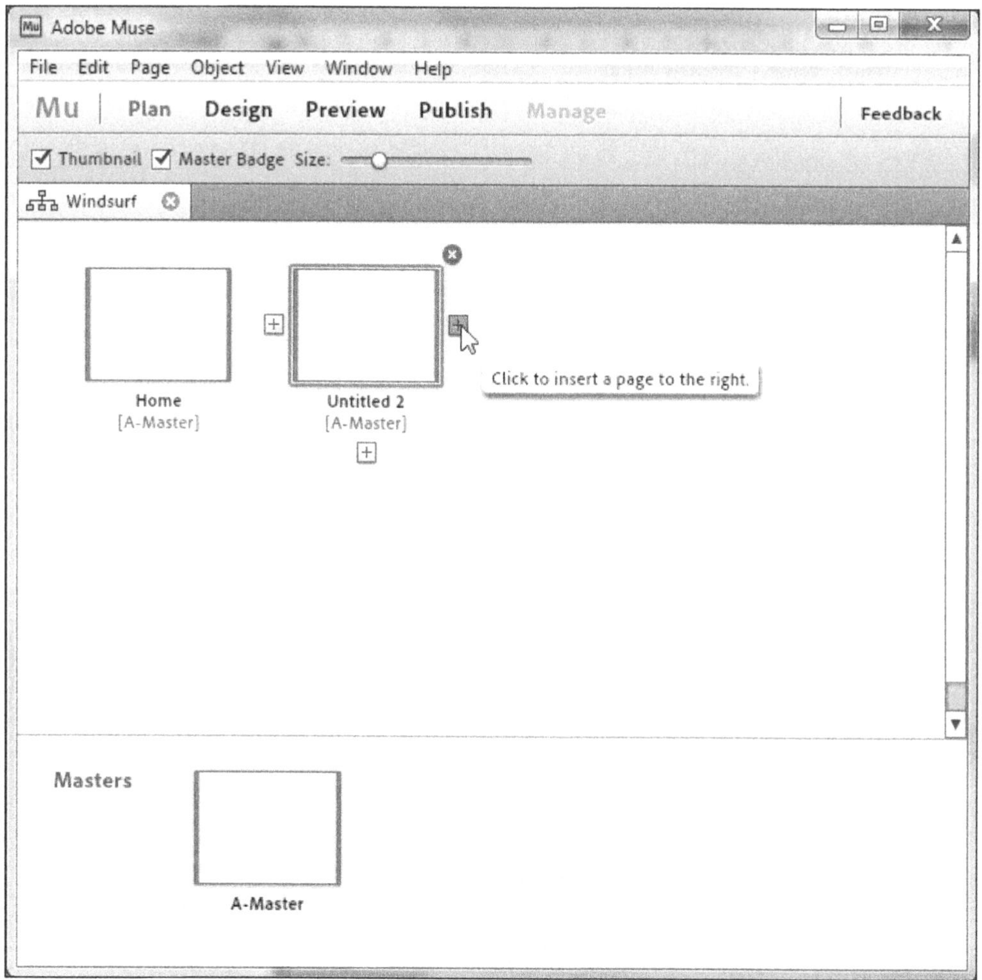

5. Click on the plus sign to the right of the **Home** page and name the new page `Gear`. Click on the plus sign below the `Gear` page to add a subpage and name that page `Sails`. Click on the plus sign to the right of the Sails page and name the new page `Boards`.

6. `Sails` and `Boards` are now on the same level and are subpages of the Gear page.
7. Click on the plus sign to the right of the `Gear` page and name the new page `Learning`.
8. Click on the plus sign to the right of `Learning` and add one more page called `Contact`. Your **Plan** view should now look like the following screenshot:

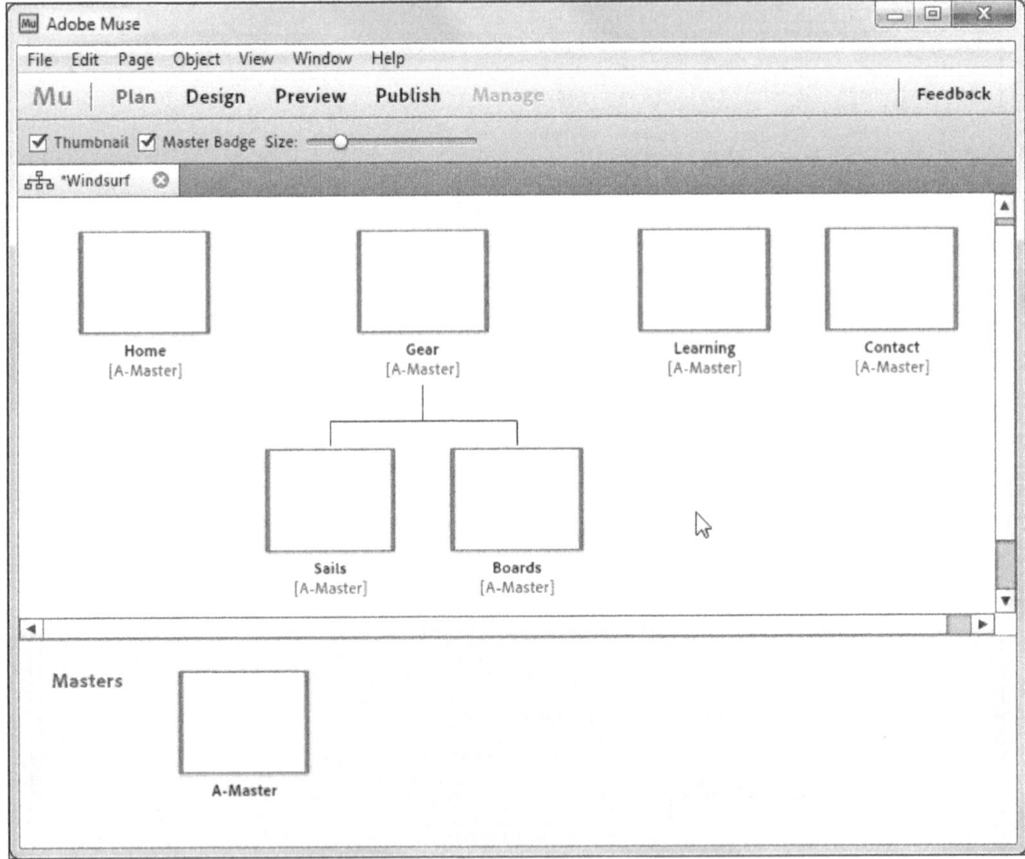

Working with thumbnails in the Plan view

It's easy to add, delete, reposition, or duplicate pages when working in the **Plan** view. Right-click (Win) or *Ctrl* + click (Mac) on a thumbnail to see a contextual menu. This menu provides every option for managing your pages.

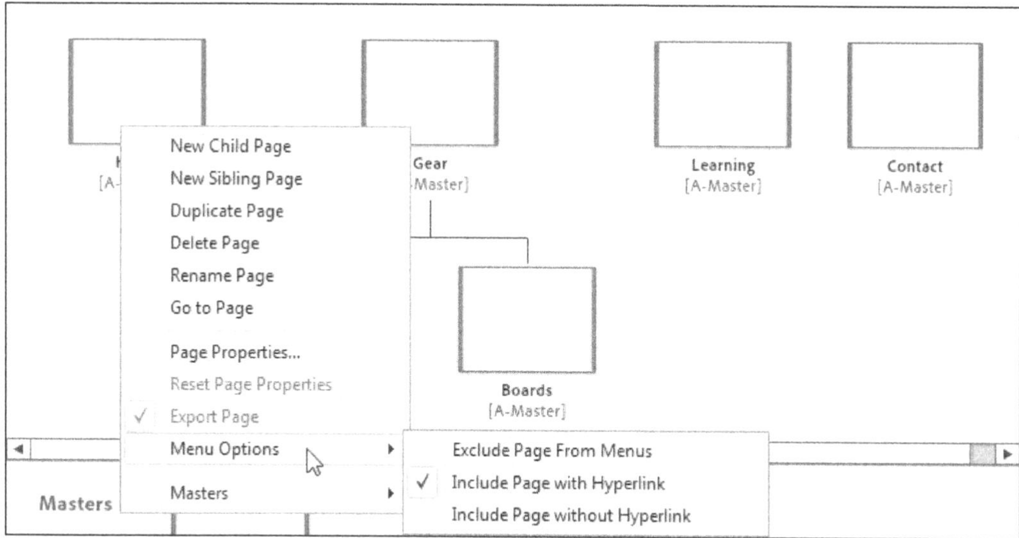

In the previous screenshot, you can see the menu that appears when you right-click/*Ctrl* + click.

- **New Child Page**: This option creates a new blank page at a lower level as the current thumbnail.
- **New Sibling Page**: This option creates a new blank page at the same level as the current thumbnail.
- **Duplicate Page**: This option makes an exact copy of the current page. This is most useful when you have added content and applied some formatting.
- **Delete Page**: This option gets rid of the page.
- **Rename Page**: This option allows us to change the name of the page.
- **Go to Page**: This option opens up the current page in the **Design** view.
- **Page Properties**: This option opens the **Page Properties** dialog box allowing you to set properties for the current page only.
- **Reset Page Properties**: This option reverts to the original settings for the page.

- **Export Page**: This option allows you to export your page as HTML and CSS.
- **Menu Options**: This option allows you to choose how the page will be included (or not included) in the automatically-created menu.
- **Masters**: This option lets you choose which Master design will be applied to the page.

The context menu is not the only way to get to these options, for example the most common tasks in the **Plan** view can be completed as follows:

- You can rename a page by double-clicking on the page name
- You can delete a page by hovering your mouse over the thumbnail and then clicking on the x icon that appears in the top-right corner

To reposition a page in your site map hierarchy, you can drag-and-drop a thumbnail on the same level or on a sublevel.

Spend a couple of minutes adding, deleting, and repositioning pages so that you get a feel of creating the site structure. You'll find the **Plan** view to be intuitive to use and extremely fast for creating site maps. You can choose **Edit | Undo** to undo any of the steps you've taken.

Muse tracks all the page names, and later in the design process it allows us to create menus quickly using menu widgets. All links created in the **Plan** view are maintained and are updated automatically if we make a change to the site structure. You can come back to the **Plan** view at any point during your web design process.

Working with wireframes

Now that we've set up the site structure and can see how the site flows, our next step is to use Muse's tools to draw a simple wireframe.

Muse provides several features to allow us to create wireframes. These include:

- A rectangle tool to create graphics and text placeholders
- Column grid for alignment of layout elements in the **Design** view
- The Assets panel, which includes features to update placeholder images

For the windsurfing site, we're going to use a one-column layout with a header at the top, a main content area in the middle, and a footer at the bottom of the page. The header will include the site name with a tagline, links to Facebook, Twitter, and YouTube, and a navigation bar containing links to the pages on the top-level of our hierarchy.

The main content area is the part of the page that will change throughout the site.

The footer at the bottom of the page will hold copyright information.

Let's start by adding one more page to our site. This will be our wireframe prototype page. Follow the given steps:

1. Add a new thumbnail to the right of the `Contact` page by clicking on the plus (+) icon. Name the page `Prototype`. This won't be part of our final site, but it allows us to set aside a page where we can try out different layouts and produces a working wireframe.
2. Double-click the `Prototype` page thumbnail in the **Plan** view. The `Prototype` page opens in the **Design** view. You'll see a blank white page with a number of vertical guidelines. The vertical guidelines represent the number of columns we set earlier in the **Site Properties** dialog box. They are used only to help us with alignment and do not appear on the final web page.
3. We're going to make those columns even more obvious now by right-clicking/*Ctrl* + clicking anywhere on the page. From the pop-up menu, choose **Show Grid Overlay**. The pink areas are the columns and the white bars in between are the gutters. Your page should now look like the following screenshot:

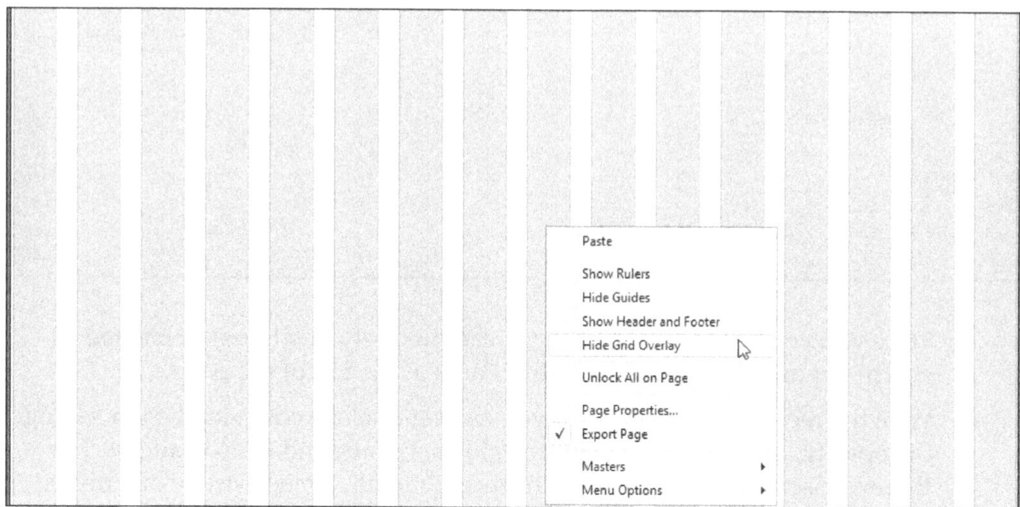

If you find the pink overlay too distracting you can turn if off again by right-clicking/*Ctrl* + clicking and choosing **Hide Grid Overlay**.

4. Select the Rectangle tool and draw out a large rectangle from the left-hand side of the first white bar to the right-hand side of the last white bar. Make the height approximately 150 pixels. As you drag out the rectangle, a tool tip will tell you the width and height of the shape. The dimensions and X and Y location of the rectangle will also appear on the bar at the top of the page, as shown in the following screenshot:

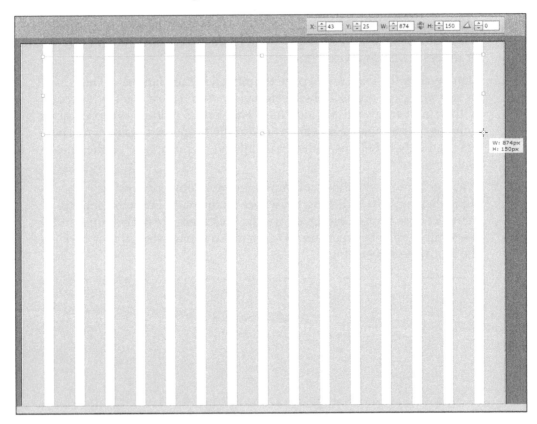

5. Once you've drawn a rectangle, you can precisely position it or change its size by typing values in the Control Panel at the top of the page.
6. With the rectangle still selected, you can set a stroke color, a fill color, change the opacity, and add effects such as glows, bevels, and drop shadows. For this exercise, set the rectangle to have a white fill, a black stroke of 2 pixels, and no effects applied, as shown in the following screenshot:

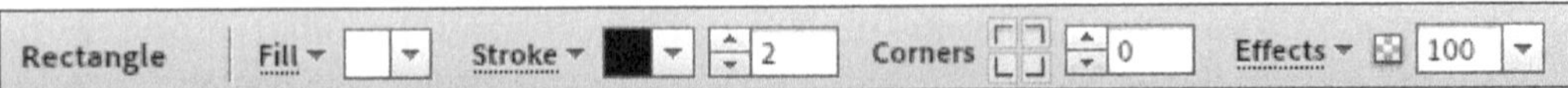

This is the simple style, which is handy for use in wireframing. In Muse, we can save the settings for our rectangle as a graphic style, which we can then reuse for drawing our wireframes.

Saving the graphic style

If you've used InDesign before, you will be familiar with the concept of reusable styles for characters and paragraphs. We use graphic styles to quickly format objects and maintain a consistent look in our wireframes and designs. It's then really easy to update a set of site assets quickly if a client requests changes.

1. While the rectangle is selected, click on the **Create new style from the attributes applied** icon at the bottom of the **Graphic Styles** panel. If you can't see the **Graphic Styles** panel, choose **Window | Graphic Styles** to open it. The style is saved in the panel and is based on the formatting of the selected rectangle.
2. Double-click the new graphic style to name it with a good descriptive name, such as `Wireframe Rectangle` in the **Style Options** dialog box. Click on **OK**.

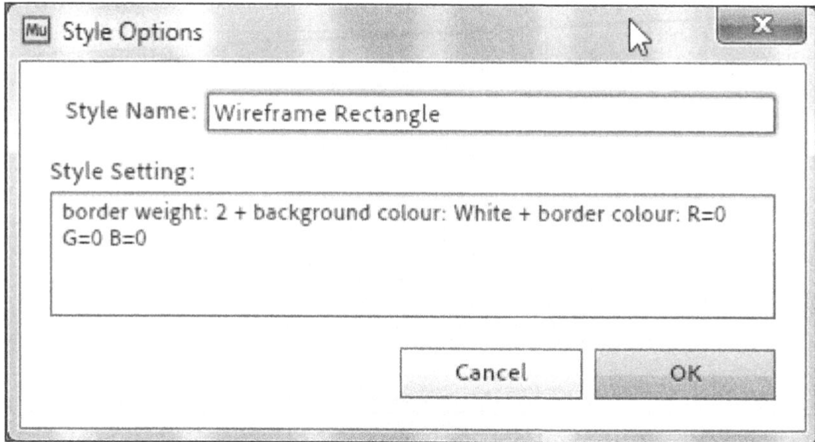

   To apply this style to any other shapes you draw later, select the shape and then click on the style's name.

3. Now, to continue with the header section of our wireframe, select the Type tool and drag out a rectangle approximately 245 x 45 pixels on the left-hand side inside the first rectangle.

4. When you let go of the mouse, the cursor will be flashing inside the rectangle. Type the word `Logo`. To increase the size of the type, using the **Type** tool, click and drag over the word **Logo** so it is highlighted in blue (indicating it is currently selected). On the Control Panel at the top of the page or in the **Text** panel, choose a font size of **36** from the drop-down menu and set the text style to **Bold** by clicking on the heavy **T** icon beside the **Size** drop-down box, as shown in the following screenshot:

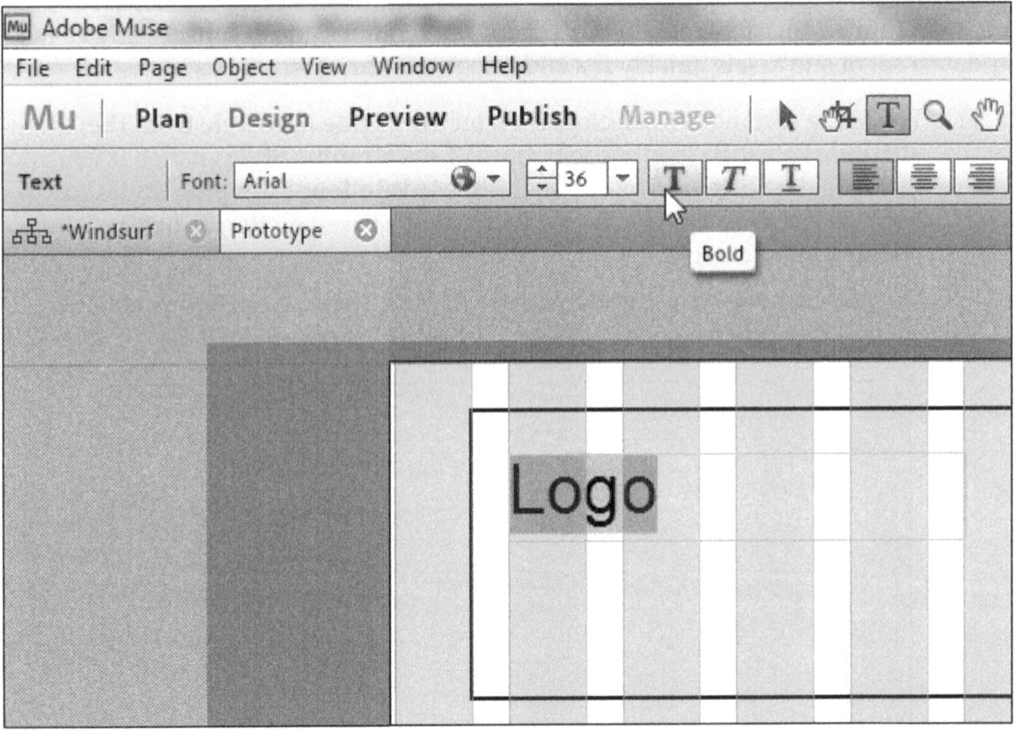

5. Again using the Type tool, draw out a second rectangle of the same size and place it underneath the **Logo** rectangle. Add the words `Tagline goes here` in this rectangle.

6. Pick the selection tool (black arrow) from the toolbar, then *Shift* + click the two text rectangles you've drawn to select them. In the **Graphic Styles** panel, click on the **Round Rectangle** style we created earlier. This makes all our rectangles look consistent.

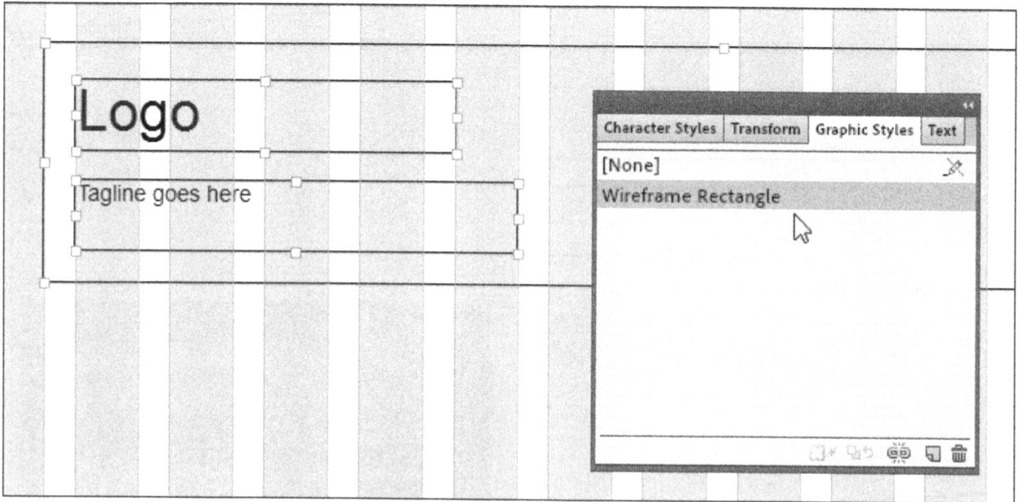

7. We're going to add a link to the **Logo** rectangle. Make sure nothing is selected on the page by choosing **Edit | Deselect All** or if the selection tool is active, click outside the page area. Using the selection tool, click on the **Logo** rectangle, and then click on the drop-down menu beside the hyperlink on the Control Panel. Choose **Home** from the drop-down menu on the Control Panel. This applies a link to the home page from the **Logo** rectangle.
8. The next step is to add our navigation bar. This is where Muse does much of the heavy lifting for us. Click on the **Widgets Library** tab to activate that panel. If you can't see the panel on your screen, choose **Window | Widgets Library**. Under **Menus**, choose **Horizontal**. Click-and-drag from the panel out onto the page. A widget appears with the names of the top-level pages we created in our site structure.

9. To extend the menu across the page under our header, click on the white arrow in the blue circle, which appears to the right of the menu. On the **Item Size** drop-down menu, choose **Uniform Width**. Then hover the cursor over the bottom-right handle on the menu widget's bounding box so that it changes to a double arrow, then drag out to increase the width of the box.

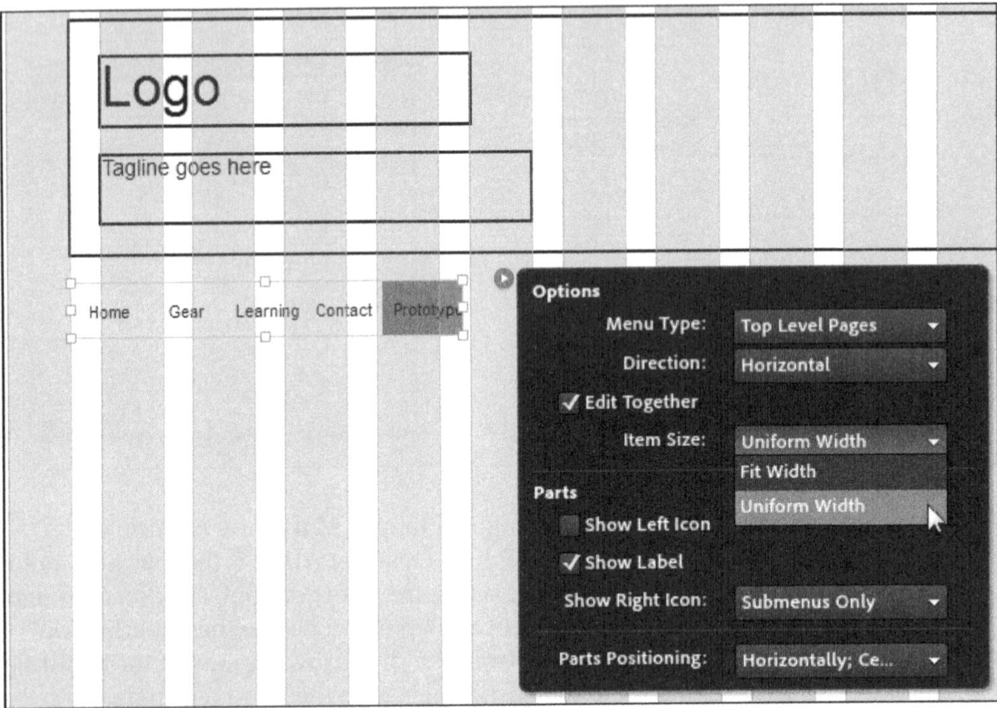

10. Once again, with the menu rectangle selected, click on the **Graphic Style** panel and choose the **Rounded Rectangle** graphic style we created earlier.
11. Your wireframe should now look similar to the following screenshot:

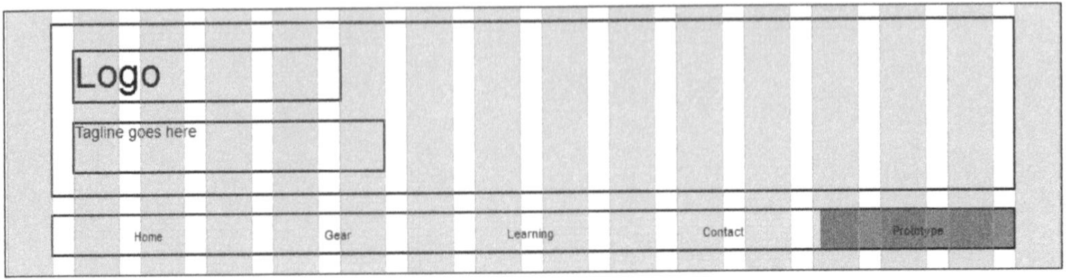

Using the grid overlay makes it really easy to align the various elements in our layout.

12. Go ahead and create a full-width rectangle to represent the main content and a full-width text rectangle under that to represent the footer area. Add the words `Copyright` followed by your name to the footer section.
13. Select both rectangles by *Shift* + clicking with the selection tool. Apply the **Rounded Rectangle** graphic style. When you've done that, your Prototype page should look similar to the following screenshot:

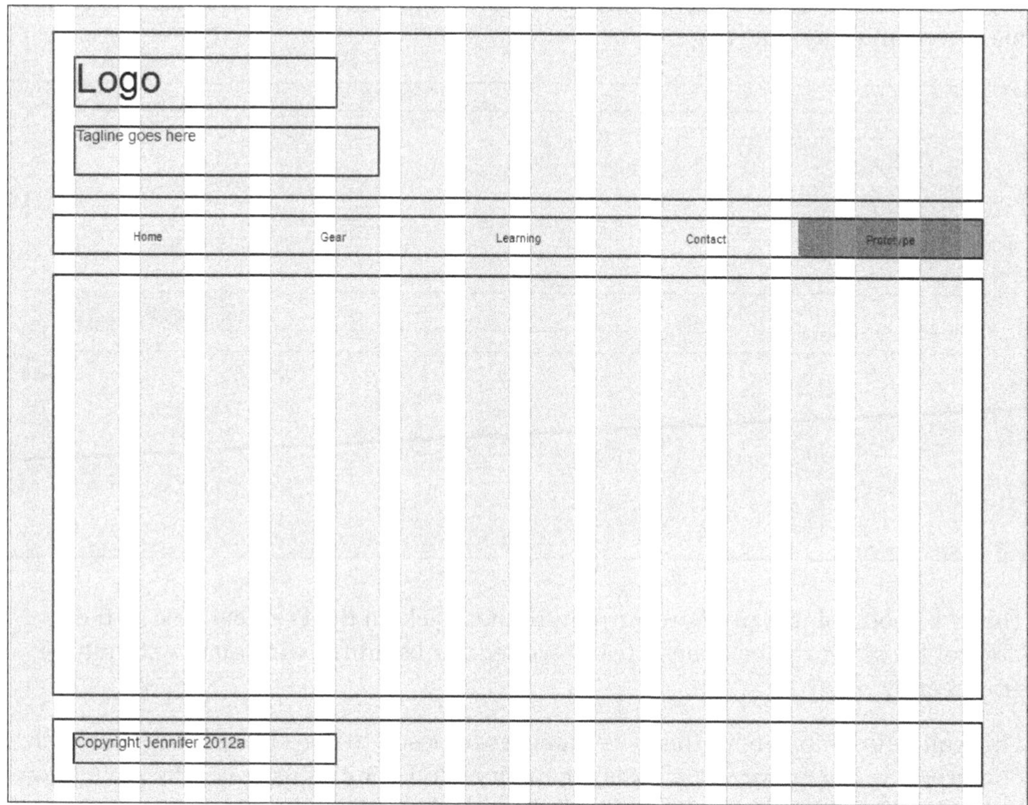

Using placeholder images

While you're planning your site and creating your wireframe, you probably won't have the final images for use on your website, but you can place a placeholder image on your wireframe.

Let's say that on your home page you knew you were going to have a photograph of a famous windsurfing champion, but at this early stage you're not quite sure which one. You could make a blank image in Photoshop or Fireworks and save it with an appropriate name: `WindsurfingChamp.jpg` for example.

For this example and layout, the image file is 300 x 170 pixels and saved in the `Windsurfing website` folder. It's important to keep all your assets for your site together.

To add the temporary placeholder image to the page, choose **File | Place** and browse to find the image. When the image is selected, it is loaded into the "gun". This simply means that you move your cursor to the position on the page where you want to place the image and then click to drop it on the page. Drop it on the right side of the main content area of the page.

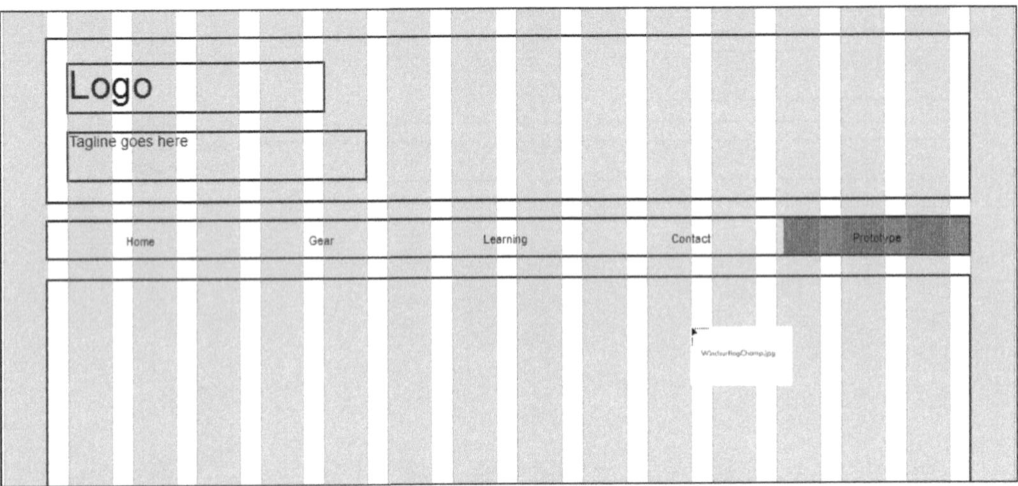

This is a good point to preview our wireframe. Click on the **Preview** link on the Control Panel. Our page opens up and we see our beautiful wireframe without the grid overlay.

The really nice thing about this wireframe, as opposed to one created on paper or in Photoshop or Illustrator, is that it is interactive. Roll your mouse over the navigation bar and notice the rollover states. The link on the **Logo** text is also active. When you click on the **Logo** link, it will take you to the **Home** page which is currently blank. This is something we could share with a client to get their feedback on how things are going so far. It's much easier to fix the functionality at this stage than when we've built the entire website.

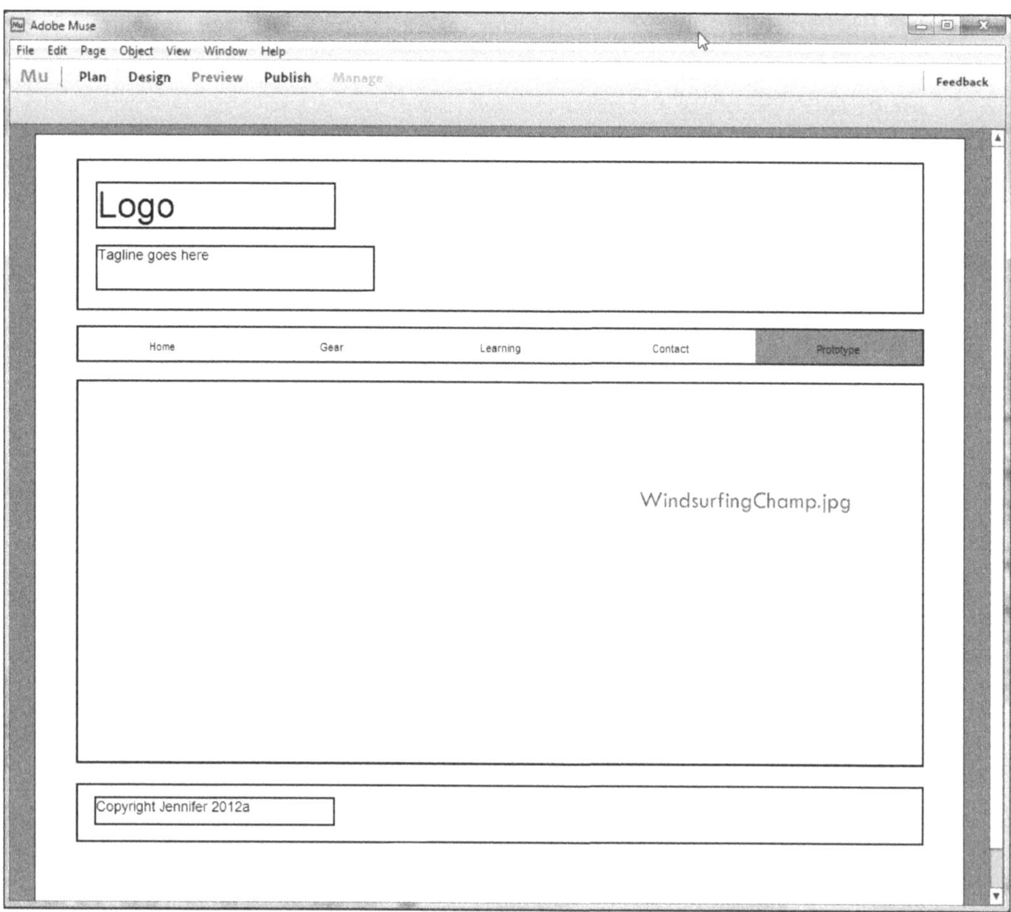

When you have finished previewing your page, click on the Design view to go back to editing the page.

Updating placeholder images with final site graphics

Let's pretend that our client has approved the wireframe for this page and is so impressed that he has rushed over the correct photograph of our windsurfing champ. Because we used an image placeholder, it's now easy for us to quickly update the site to use the actual image files:

1. Open the original image in Photoshop or Fireworks and paste the photograph on top and, if necessary, resize so it fits into our original image. Save the file, replacing the original.

2. In Muse, select the image placeholder on the page.
3. Open the **Assets** panel to locate the selected page element; in this case it's the image called `WindsurfingChamp.jpg`.
4. Right-click on the page element. In the menu that appears, choose Relink Asset. Instantly your image will be updated on your web page.

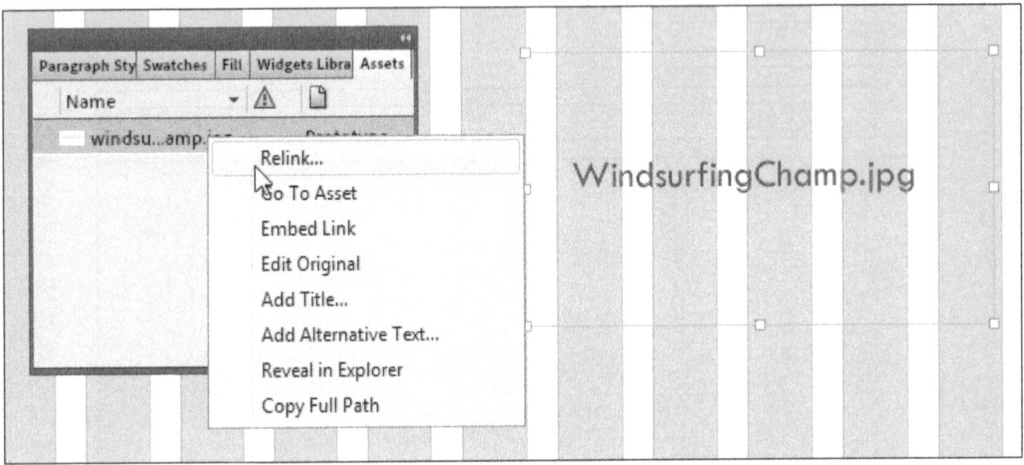

Adding dummy text and paragraph styles

As you build out a wireframe site, you can use the Text tool to create text frames and add placeholders or dummy text, which can easily be replaced later. After creating text elements, you can use the Text panel or the Control Panel to apply formatting to the text. Text headers and paragraph styles help you create structured pages and change text formatting easily.

What Is Lorem Ipsum?

Lorem Ipsum is simply dummy text used by the printing and typesetting industry. Lorem Ipsum has been the industry's standard dummy text ever since the 1500s. It is a long established fact that a reader will be distracted by the readable content of a page when looking at its layout. The point of using Lorem Ipsum is that it has a more-or-less normal distribution of letters, as opposed to using "Content here, content here", making it look like readable English. Today Lorem Ipsum is used by web designers for the same reason.

Some paragraphs of Lorem Ipsum text have been supplied in a `.txt` file.

Using paragraph styles, you can define header text and paragraph tags to structure the text content of the page and maintain consistency. Let's add some text to our `Prototype` page:

1. Open the `Loremipsum.txt` file in the text editor on your computer. Select all of the text in the file and copy it by choosing **Edit | Copy**.
2. In the **Design** view in Muse, select the **Text** tool and drag out a rectangular text frame onto the left side of the main content area of the page. Make sure the left side of the rectangle lines up with the left side of the **Logo** and **Tagline** textboxes in the header.
3. You can either type or paste text into a text frame to populate it, but in our case, we're going to paste in the Lorem Ipsum text by choosing **Edit | Paste**.
4. With the text added, click after the words **Lorem ipsum dolor**. You'll see the cursor flashing. Press *Enter/Return* on the keyboard to push the rest of the text onto a new line and create a new paragraph. We're going to use **Lorem ipsum dolor** as our main heading.
5. Select all the text except **Lorem ipsum dolor** by clicking and dragging, then use the **Text** panel or the options in the Control Panel at the top of the **Design** view workspace to set the formatting options. You can choose the typeface, size, color, and other type-related properties.

   Set the **Font** to **Arial**, size **12**, dark gray color, left-aligned with a line height of **100%**. Line height is the space between the lines. Increasing line height can make blocks of text easier to read depending on the font face and size.

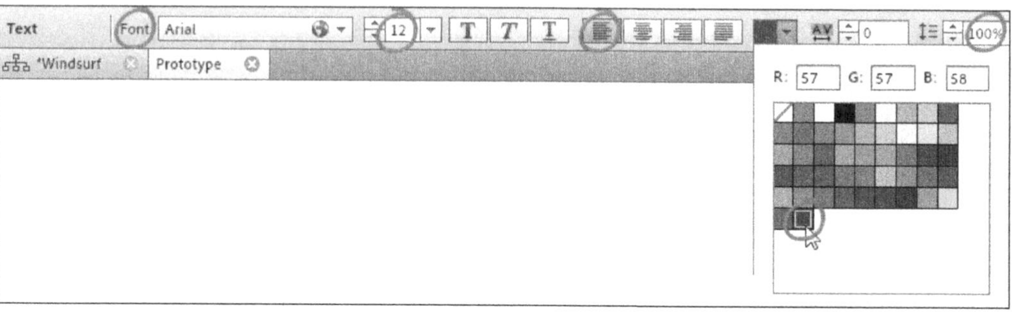

6. Click on **Create a new style from the attributes applied** at the bottom of the **Paragraph Styles** panel to create a new paragraph style. If you can't see the **Paragraph Styles** panel, choose **Windows | Paragraph Styles** to open it. Double-click on the name of the new style to give it a descriptive name. For this example let's call it `Body Paragraph`.

7. We use the **Paragraph Tag** menu to set the paragraph style to target a specific HTML tag, such as P, H1, H2, or H3. In this case we want **Default (p)**:

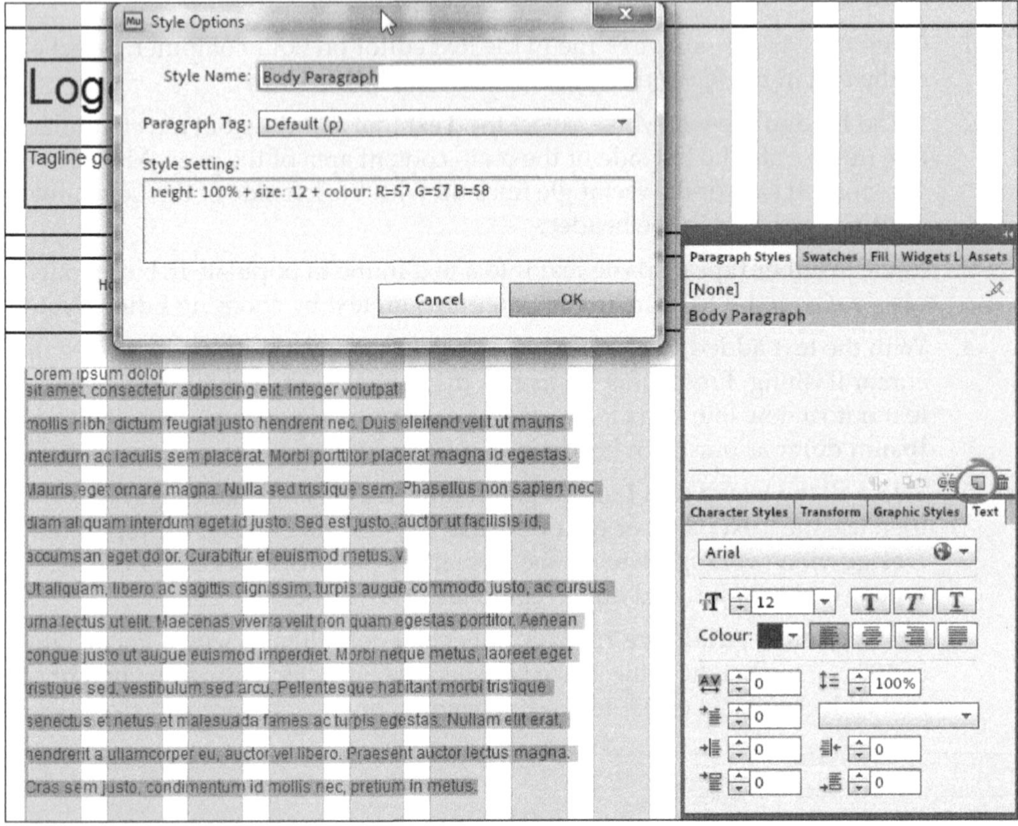

8. Now select the words **Lorem ipsum dolor**, which we'll set up as a heading. On the **Text Panel**, choose properties for this font. Set the font to **Georgia**, size **24** and **Bold**, and **Space After** to **10**. Space After is the icon on the bottom right of the panel and it sets the amount of space, which will be applied underneath the text you are formatting.

9. Click on **Create a new style from the attributes applied** at the bottom of the **Paragraph Styles** panel again to create a new paragraph style for our heading. Double-click on the name of the new style to give it a descriptive name. Call it `Heading H1` and set the **Paragraph Tag** menu to target **Heading (h1)** as shown in the following screenshot:

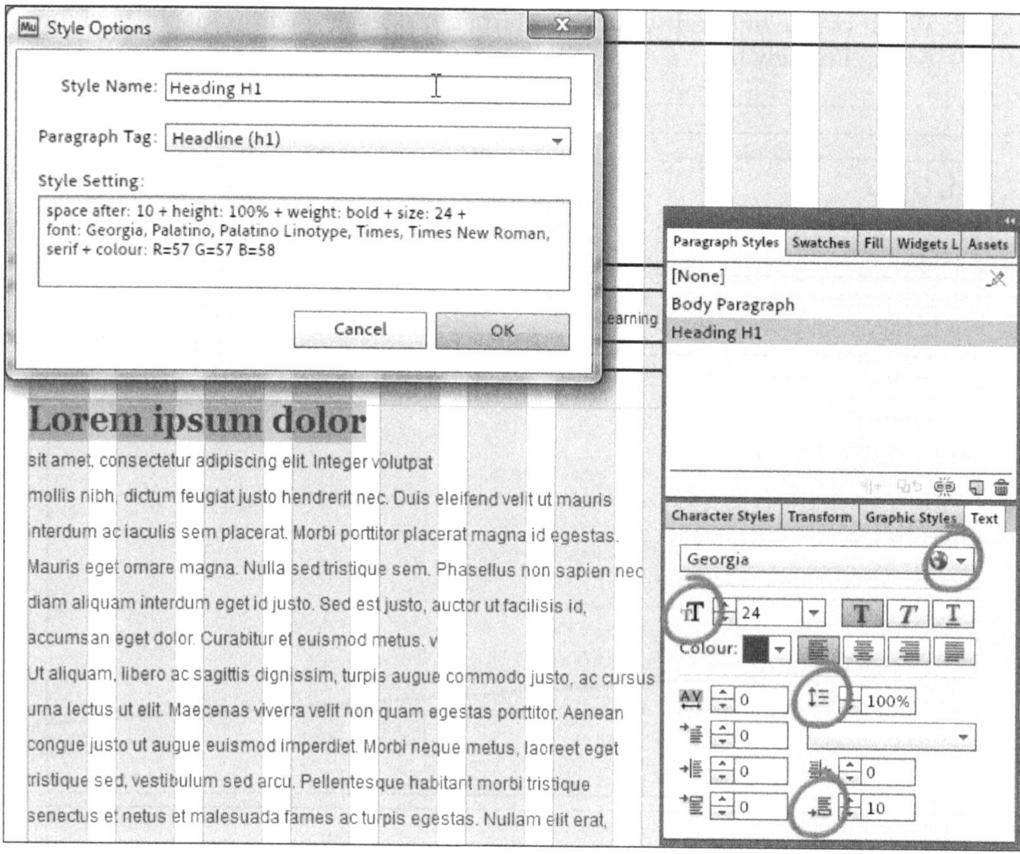

10. By setting up paragraph styles in this way, you ensure consistency in styles across your pages. This is very similar to how graphic designers set up their print stylesheets.
11. You may wish to set up styles for the **Tagline** section of the header and for the **Copyright** section of the footer. Repeat steps 8 - 10, choosing your own font sizes, styles and colors for the Tagline, and the Footer text.

12. When you've finished setting up your styles, test the wireframe by clicking on the **Preview** tab.

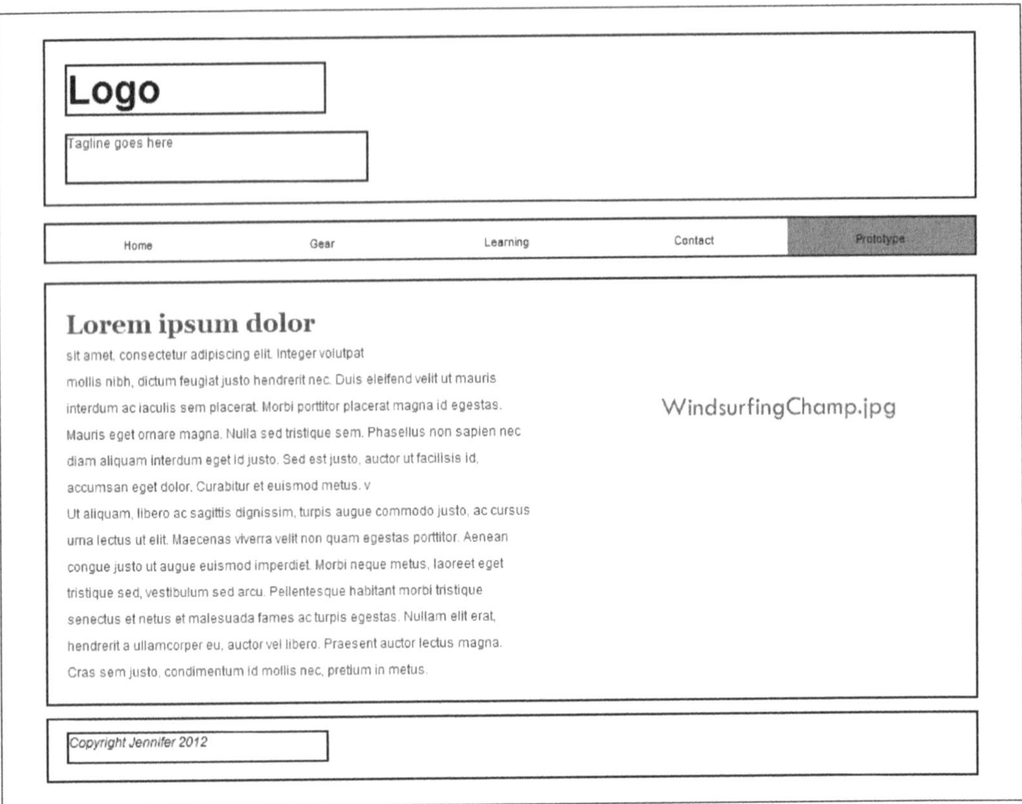

The great thing about this process is that we've not only created an interactive wireframe, we've also got a working prototype; basic but working. We've also created a number of styles, which can be reused across our entire website.

Where are the files generated by Muse?

When you are finished with creating your wireframes and you're ready to share them with a client, you can publish them directly using Adobe Business Catalyst by clicking on the **Publish** link. To do this, you will need an Adobe ID, which you should have created when you first installed Muse. This is an easy way to get your web pages online.

The alternative to Business Catalyst is to publish your Muse site to your own host server, which you may have already set up. To get the files for your website, you need to export the entire site. Muse will generate the HTML, CSS, and folder of images required for the site to function.

1. Choose **File | Export As HTML**. The **Export to HTML** dialog box appears.
2. Select the location on your computer to which you want to export the site files, and then click on **OK** as shown in the following screenshot:

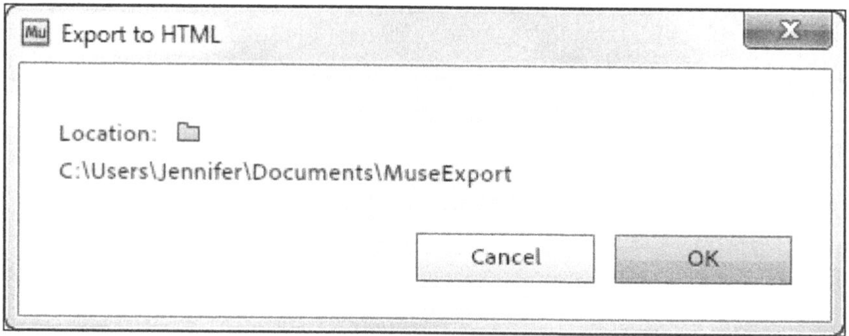

After completing this operation, Muse exports the files and saves them in the local folder you specified. Navigate to the folder and open the image folder to access the optimized image files. You can repurpose these image files to create newsletters, mobile apps, social networking pages, and other related projects.

Exercise

Now that we've created a new site and a wireframe to go with it, it's a good idea for you to practice mocking up a site in Muse.

Create a wireframe and site map for a fictitious website about your favorite movie. The site should include a home page, a cast page, a gallery page, a links page, and a contact page. A navigation bar should allow you to go to any part of the site with just one click.

Create a simple wireframe of your design on paper and then recreate the wireframe in Muse. Preview your wireframe.

Downloading the example text and images

You can download the example text and images files for this book you have purchased from your account at `http://www.packtpub.com`. If you purchased this book elsewhere, you can visit `http://www.packtpub.com/support` and register to have the files e-mailed directly to you.

Summary

In this chapter we discussed some of the basic layouts used in web design. We looked at the idea of wireframing using pen and paper and also how to set up a site structure and wireframe in Muse.

In the next chapter, we'll look at individual and master pages.

4

Powerful Pages

Within Muse, we have two different kinds of pages—Master pages and web pages. In this chapter we'll work with both types. We'll also look at tools to help us layout and align the content on our pages and how to add links.

By the end of this chapter you will know how to:

- Create web pages and Master pages
- Add content to the pages
- Use rulers, guides, and the grid overlay to align the content
- Zoom into and fit pages
- Add links

Pages

The vast majority of websites are made up of at least two pages, which are linked together. Again, in most of these websites there will be shared or consistent attributes across the pages that make up the site. As we saw in the previous chapter, Muse lets us easily create a site structure where we can organize and maintain our pages.

When creating our websites, it's a good practice to follow a style or standard format throughout all the pages in the site. While the content, which is the information you provide, will change from page to page, some elements such as the logo or navigation bar will remain the same, having the same size and position on the pages.

In this chapter, we'll continue building using the site structure we set up for the Windsurfing site and make changes to the master page, so that those design elements will appear on each page of our site. The following screenshot shows the sitemap as seen in the Muse's **Plan** view:

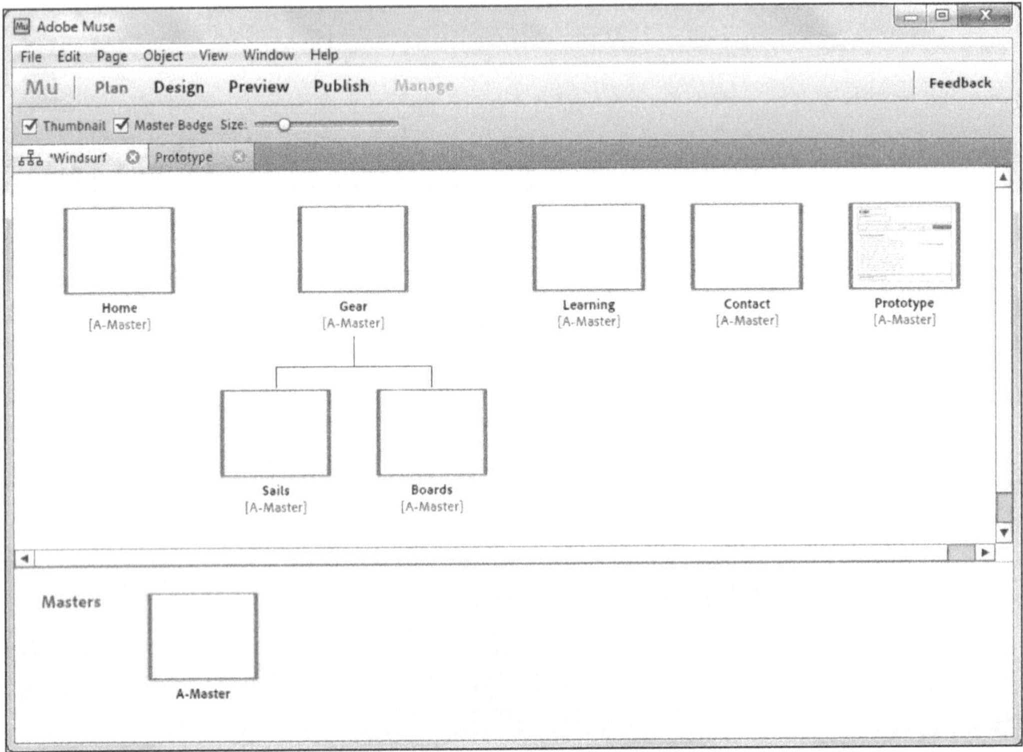

Notice that the **Prototype** thumbnail shows us the content of that page. We can use the **Size** slider in the **Plan** view to zoom in and out. Our home page, often referred to as the Index page, contains links to the Gear page, Learning page, and a Contact page. The Gear page contains links to two other pages—Sails and Boards. This site structure lets us present the information to the users in a logical order, making it easy to always return to the home page from any point within the website.

Note that under each thumbnail we can see **[A-Master]** in blue. This tells us that the A-Master page (or first Master page) has been applied to each of our web pages.

Master pages

Let's look at the Master pages and how they help us create consistency across our website. If you've used Adobe InDesign or QuarkXpress before, you will be familiar with the concept. Page consistency is critical for multiple-page printed documents too. Even if you haven't used these sort of programs before, you have undoubtedly seen magazines where repeating elements such as page numbers, article titles, or the name of the magazine appear on the corner of each page.

With print layout programs, items placed on Master pages appear in the exact same location on every document page. Changes made to a master page will ripple through the entire document which saves time and reduces the margin of error. This is exactly the same with your websites you create in Muse.

As we saw in the previous chapter, Muse creates a blank home page and a blank Master Page by default, every time you create a new site. Whether you are making a one-page or multiple-page website, this initial setup is the starting point for any website and provides a useful overview or sitemap for your site.

There are two ways to use the Master pages:

- Plan out your sitemap by using blank pages (as we did in the previous chapter) and then apply the masters later
- Apply the master to your home page at the start and then create new pages based on that design

Working with pages within your site

In the previous chapter, we created a new site, a sitemap, and a working wireframe prototype using Muse's Plan view. We quickly created six pages for our site. Now we'll take a look at how to add, duplicate, delete, and rename pages quickly using the Plan view.

There are two types of basic pages:

- **Sibling pages**: These are pages that share the same parent page; in the case of our Windsurfing site, all top-level pages (Home, Gear, Learning, and Contact) are siblings.
- **Child pages**: These pages appear below a particular page on a level of the site's organization. In our example, **Sails** and **Boards** are child pages of **Gear**. Any page on any level of your site can have sibling pages or child pages.

Adding a sibling page

To add an extra sibling page to any level in your website, do either of the following:

- In the Plan view, hover your cursor over the page thumbnail you are interested in. You'll see the plus signs appear at the left or right side of the page.
- Right-click (*Ctrl* + click) on a thumbnail of a page and choose **New Sibling Page** from the context menu that appears. Click on either the plus button to the right or left of the page. Type a title for the new page and press *Enter* (Windows) or *Return* (Mac OS).

Adding a child page

To add a child page underneath any of your existing pages in your site, perform either of the following:

- In Plan view, hover over any page's thumbnail until you see a plus sign appear at the bottom of the page.
- Right-click (*Ctrl* + click) on a thumbnail of a page and choose **New Child Page** from the context menu that appears. Click on the plus button at the bottom of the page. Type a title for the new page and press *Enter* (Windows) or *Return* (Mac OS).

Creating a duplicate page

If you've already added some content to your page, or perhaps you have styled the page in a certain way that you want to re-use, you can easily make a duplicate page by performing the following step:

- In the Plan view, either *Alt* + drag (Windows) or *Option* + drag (Mac) an existing page's thumbnail

Deleting a page

Sometimes you'll find that you just don't need a page you created and you want to get rid of it.

In the Plan view, hover over the page you want to delete until the delete icon (**X**) appears in the upper-right corner of the page.

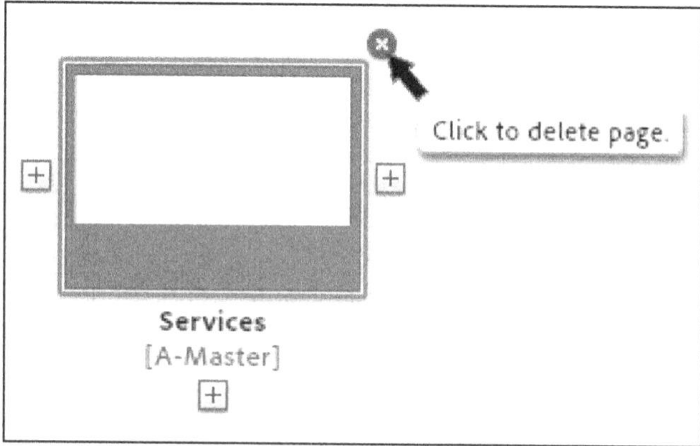

Click on the delete icon and your page is gone.

Renaming a page

Accidentally named one of your pages "Portfolio" but would prefer to call it "Gallery"? Muse easily takes care of any page name changes without breaking any links. To rename a page in the Plan view, double-click on the page title (beneath the page), and type the new page title.

Rearranging pages

In the Plan view, drag a page to a different place in the site plan (for example, to the right of another page). When you see the blue drop zone, release the mouse.

To get the full range of options we've discussed, just by a single click you can move your cursor over a page's thumbnail, then right-click (*Ctrl* + click) and choose the option from the context menu that appears, as shown in the following screenshot:

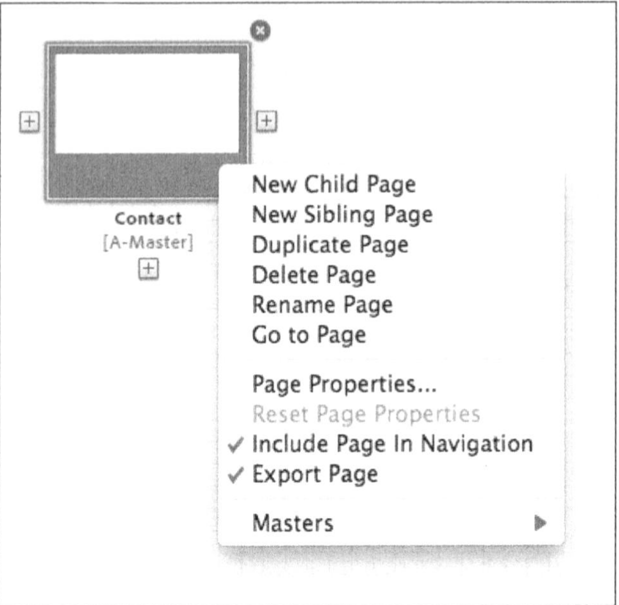

Editing page properties

You'll remember from *Chapter 2, The Muse Workflow* that when you first create your site, you fill in the **Site Properties** dialog box. This allows us to set up measurements for the page height, gutter, the number of columns, and margins. These values are not set in stone and you can come back to any individual page and make changes to those properties in the Plan view.

First though, let's ensure we understand the relationship between the page properties specified under **Site Properties**, properties of Master pages, and our normal web pages:

1. The Master pages inherit their properties from the settings in the **Site Properties**—those we set up right at the start when creating our site.
2. Web pages inherit their properties from the Master page that is applied. If a regular page has a `None` master applied, it inherits its properties from the **Site Properties** settings.

To change the page properties for all pages and masters in your site, choose **File | Site Properties**.

If you want to customize a page so that it is different from the settings in its applied Master page, choose **Page** | **Page Properties**. This lets you apply settings just to this individual page.

For example, the **Prototype** page we made in the previous chapter should not be included in the navigation menu on each page. We'll change the properties of that particular page by performing the following steps:

1. In the **Plan** view, double-click on the **Prototype** page. This opens that page in **Design** view.
2. Choose **Page** | **Page Properties**. The **Page Properties** dialog box opens up.
3. On the **Menu Options** drop-down box, choose **Exclude page from menus** and click on **OK**.

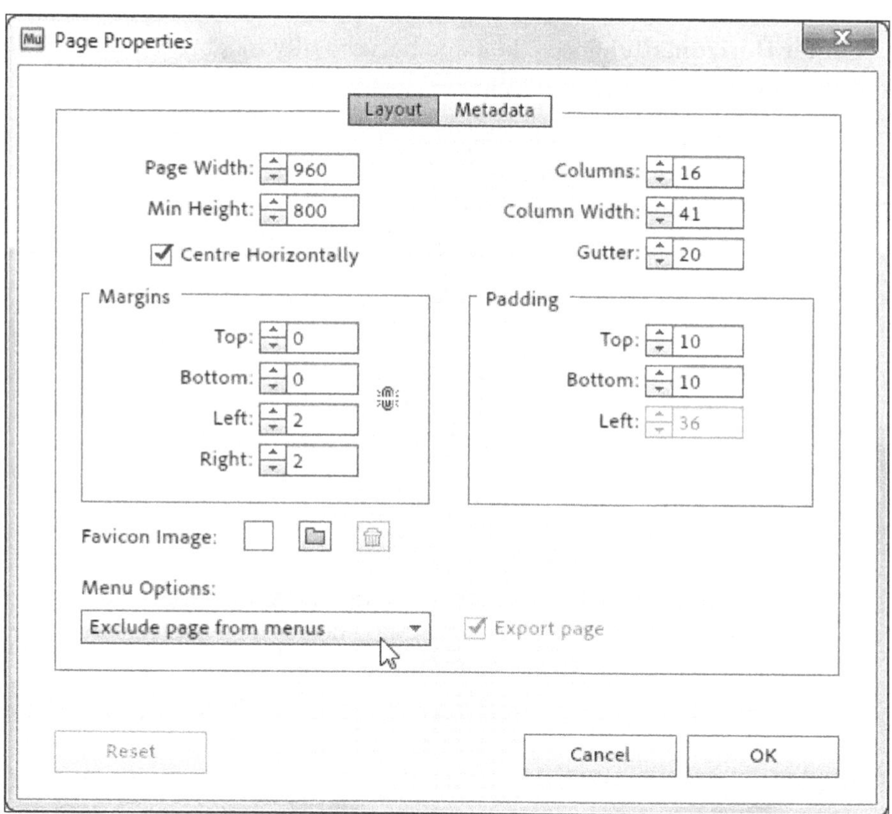

4. Although they are very similar, we can notice some slight differences between the **Site Properties** and the **Page Properties** dialog boxes. One of the main differences is that there are two categories in the **Page Properties** dialog box: **Layout** and **Metadata**.

5. In the **Layout** category, let's change the number of columns from `16` to `2`. We can see that once you make that change, the column width changes to `468` automatically.
6. Click on **OK** to apply the changes.

The following list provides a brief explanation of each of the other fields in the **Layout** category of the **Page Properties** dialog. We'll look at the **Metadata** category in the next chapter. Remember all the units are measured in pixels.

- **Page Width** sets the width of the page.
- **Minimum Height** sets the height of the page. This is not an absolute value because Muse supports dynamic page height based on page content. In plain English, that means the more content you add to your page, the longer the page will become.
- **Center Horizontally** places the page horizontally in a browser. If this option is not enabled, the page is aligned to the left in the browser.
    - **Columns** sets the number of vertical columns on your page. Designers love columns! They let us create a grid, which then makes it easy to layout our text, images, and other content.
    - **Column width** sets the width of each column.
    - **Gutter** sets the space between the columns.
    - **Margins** specify a safe area of the page to place our page content. Margins, columns, and gutters in Muse are just like margins and columns as used in InDesign. You can hide margin and column guides by choosing **View | Hide Guides** or **Ctrl+:** (Win) or **Cmd+:** (Mac).
    - **Padding** controls the space (in pixels) between the edges of the browser window, and the edges of your web page.
    - **Favicon image** lets us pick an image, which is displayed as a tiny icon in the browser's address bar. The Favicon can be considered part of our overall site branding.
    - **Include Page in Navigation** ensures the Include page is added in any menu widgets that you add to the page.

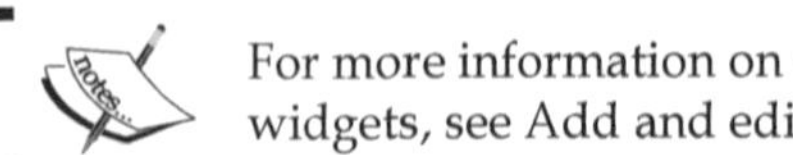

For more information on working with widgets, see Add and edit widgets.

    - **Export page** includes the page when you publish or export your site as HTML.

Page sizes

Pages in Muse have a fixed width but are dynamic in height. Let's say you have a header which takes up to 150 pixels and a footer which takes up to 200 pixels. These values are set using the page guides. Now let's say that you set the minimum height to 600 pixels. If the length of your content is only 150 pixels, we get 150 + 150 + 200 = 500 pixels. Our page is rendered as 600 pixels because that is the minimum height specified.

If, however, we had content which takes up 500 pixels and add that to our values for the header and footer, our page will expand to display the content added to each page. The minimum height ensures a small level of consistency on pages which may not have much content.

Opening, saving, and closing a page

To open any page in your site for editing, simply double-click the page in the **Plan** view. The page will spring open in the **Design** view. You can open as many pages as you want at one time. Each page appears as a tab along the top of the interface. The tab for the currently open page is highlighted, as shown in the following screenshot:

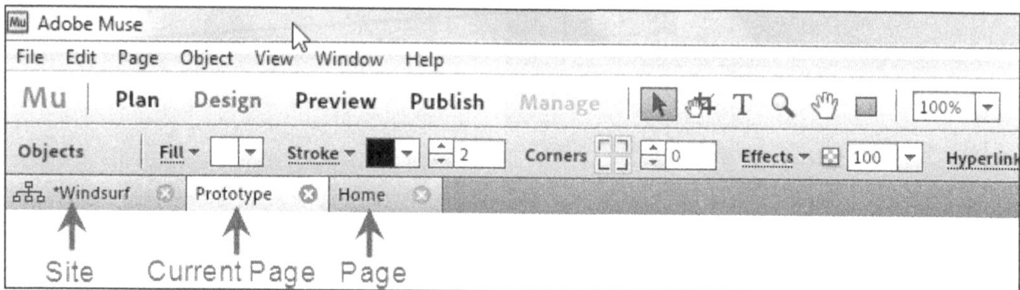

When you've made any changes to your pages, you can save them by choosing **File** | **Save Site**. This saves the changes to all your pages and your site plan in one go. It's a good idea to be cautious and save your work regularly, just in case of a computer crash.

When you've finished working on a page, you can close it by clicking on the Close icon (**X**) on the page's tab.

An asterisk in a site's **Plan** tab indicates that the Muse site (`.muse` file) contains unsaved changes. You can see an example of this in the previous screenshot where the site name `Windsurf` has an asterisk beside it.

Working with Master pages

We're going to open up our Master Page now and add a few simple design elements which will be applied to each page, by performing the following steps. Remember, in our plan view we could see that each page in our website had the A-Master page applied.

1. Open the **A-Master** page, by double-clicking on its thumbnail in the **Plan** view.
2. In the **Design** view, click on the swatch beside the **Fill** drop-down box in the options bar. Choose a mid blue color, with hexadecimal value `# 29ABE2` and press *Enter*/*Return* on the keyboard.

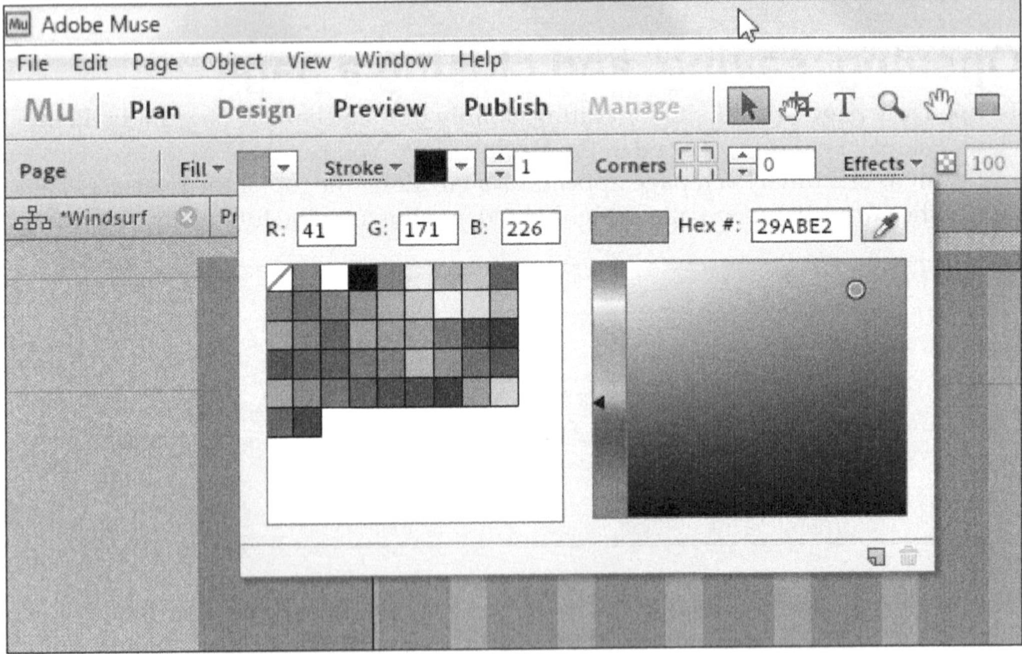

   Instantly, you'll see that blue color is applied to the entire background of your page. The area outside the page remains dark grey.

3. Now to add some type to the top of the page, select the **Text** tool and drag out a rectangle just above the **Header** guideline. The **Header** guideline is the second blue horizontal line.
4. You'll see your cursor flashing inside the text bounding box. Type the words `Windsurf Wild`. Then click on the **Select** tool on the toolbar to commit your text to the page. Your default text is probably small and black, and won't stand out on the page, so we'll edit it and choose a different typeface and color.

5. Choose the **Text** tool again and click anywhere between the text you just added. Your cursor will flash on and off between two letters. Double-click here to select both words or hit *Esc* on the keyboard, then click on **T** to select the entire text box to apply formatting.
6. For the typeface choose **Web Safe Fonts | Century Gothic** from the Font drop-down box, set the Size to `48`, and set the Color to **white** by clicking on the swatch drop-down box. Click on the bold icon (the first **T** to the right of the Size field).

7. Click on the **Select** tool to commit your type changes. To precisely position the text, use the **Control Panel** and set **X** to `42`, **Y** to `20`. This will place the bottom of each letter on the Header guideline.
8. Let's go back to the **Plan** view and take a look at how the changes in our Master Page have affected all of the pages in our site. Click on the **Plan** button at the top of the screen. Lo and behold, you should see all of the thumbnails appearing in blue with the Windsurf Wild heading appearing at the top of each page.

Creating a new Master page

Now, let's say we want some of our pages to have a blue background and some to have a red one. We could do this easily by creating a new Master Page with a red background and we'll do it by duplicating our existing A-Master.

1. In the Plan view, duplicate the Master Page by right-clicking (or *Ctrl* + clicking) on the A-Master page thumbnail. From the menu choose **Duplicate** page.
2. A duplicate page appears with the words **A-Master copy** highlighted in blue appearing underneath.

3. Type a title for the new page; name it `Red Background` and press *Enter* (Windows) or *Return* (Mac OS).
4. Double-click on the **Red Background** master page and change the background of the page to red using the steps outlined previously.
5. Return to the **Plan** view. Your two Master pages' thumbnails should now look different—one red and one blue.

Applying a Master page to a web page

To try out our new Master page, drag the **Red Background** master page from the **Masters** area to the **Sails** page in the **Document** window. You'll see the title of the **Master** page applied to the **Sails** page.

Repeat the process and change the Master page applied to the **Boards** page. Your Plan view should now look similar to the following screenshot:

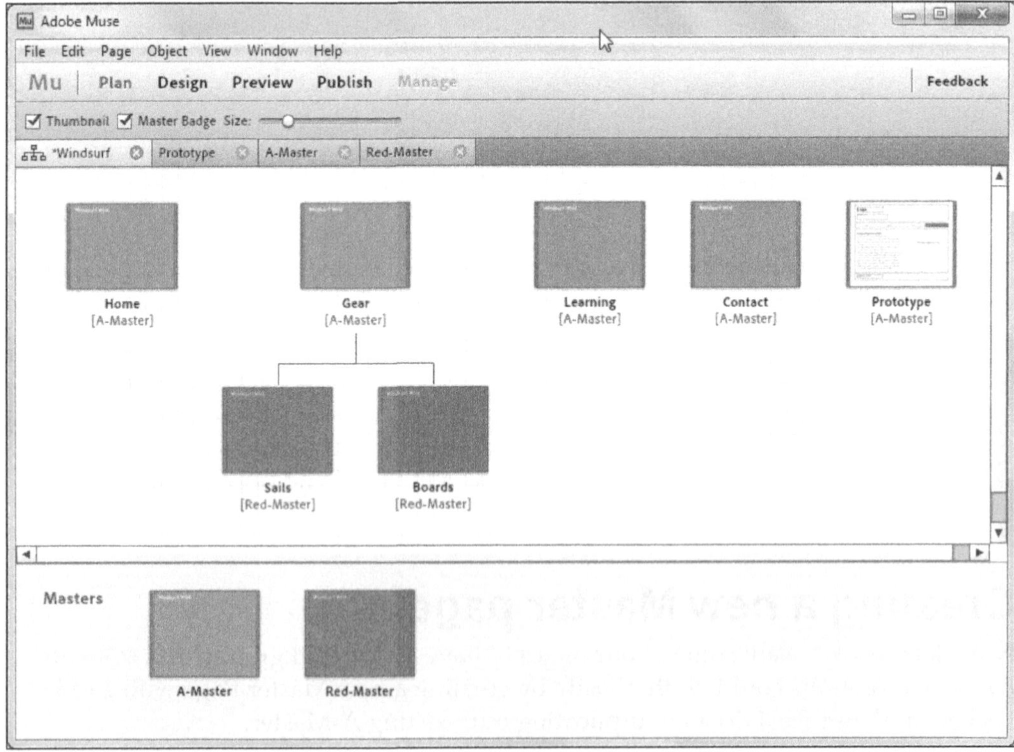

As you can see, it's very easy to make changes to one Master and then apply it quickly to several pages.

If you don't want any Master page applied, that is, you just want to keep your original site settings on a particular page, right-click on the thumbnail of the page, and choose **Masters** | **No Master** from the drop-down menu.

Header and footer guides

Muse provides an option to display a ruler along the top and along the left side of the workspace. The units on the ruler are in pixels and it is a useful layout tool. As for the rulers, Muse can display five page guides, which we'll now take a look at.

As you hover over these guidelines on the left-hand side of the page, you'll see a tool tip which describes the functionality of each guide.

The first, fourth, and fifth guides give us our overall page size. Dragging the first guide upwards increases the amount of padding between the top of the page and the browser. Dragging the fourth guide down extends the size of the page. Dragging the fifth guide extends the amount of padding beneath the bottom of the page.

The second guide defines the bottom of the header. As you drag this one down, you are increasing the height of the header.

The third guide defines the top of the footer. If you'd like a smaller footer, drag this guide downwards. If you'd like a bigger or taller footer, drag this guide upwards.

The header and footer guides can only be moved on Master pages. On normal pages, you'll find that you can't drag them to a new location and they are displayed for visual reference only.

To show or hide header and footer guides, choose **View** | **Show/Hide Header and Footer,** *Ctrl* + *Shift*+*:* (Win), or *Cmd* + *Shift*+*:* (Mac OS).

To show or hide rulers, choose **View** | **Show/Hide Rulers**, *Ctrl* + *r* (Win), or *Cmd* + *r* (Mac OS).

To show or hide the grid overlay, choose **View | Show/Hide Grid Overlay**, *Ctrl* + ' (Win), or *Cmd* + ' (Mac OS).

To show or hide page guides, choose **View** | **Show/Hide Guides** or *Ctrl* + *;* (Win), or *Cmd* + *;* (Mac OS).

Adding text to a page

In the next chapter, we'll devote a lot of time to text and typography on the web, but for now let's get a bit of practice with adding some text to one of our pages:

1. Open the **Learning** page by double-clicking on the thumbnail in the **Plan** view.
2. Turn on the grid overlay if it is not already visible by choosing **View** | **Show Grid Overlay**, *Ctrl* + ' (Win), or *Cmd* + ' (Mac OS).
3. Turn on the rulers by choosing **View** | **Show/Hide Rulers**, *Ctrl* + *r* (Win), or *Cmd* + *r* (Mac OS).
4. Open the text file provided by `Learning.txt` in a text editor of your choice. Select all the text and copy it.
5. Return to the **Learning** page and choose the **Text** tool.
6. Drag out a rectangle from the left-hand side, underneath and in line with the column where our title **Windsurf Wild** appears. As you drag, a tool tip provides information on the width of your text box. Drag out a box of width `631` pixels. While dragging across, start to drag down the page until your rectangle meets the footer guideline. As you drag, you will feel the edge of the rectangle snap onto the grid and the footer guideline.
7. When you release the mouse, the cursor flashes in the top-left corner of the rectangle. Paste the text you copied by choosing **Edit** | **Paste**. Your text will now appear in the box. To precisely position the textbox when you've added it to the page, select it then use the **Control Panel** and set **X** to `42`, **Y** to `105`.

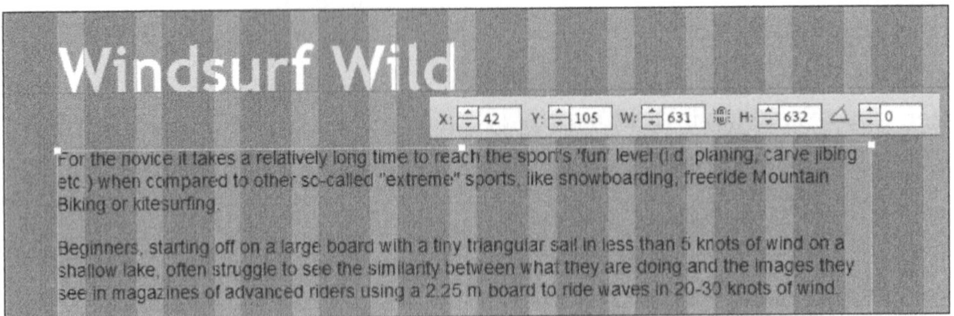

8. Use the steps described previously to change the color of the newly-added text back to white. Set your text to `Arial`, color as `White`, and size as `12`.
9. Turn off the grid overlay by choosing **View | Hide Grid Overlay**, *Ctrl* + ' (Win), or *Cmd* + ' (Mac OS).
10. Leave the **Learning** page open.

Creating links

Without links the Web would simply not be a "web" but rather a huge collection of isolated individual pages. To connect the pages within a website, we create links. A link, also known as a hyperlink, is the path to another document, to another part of the same document, or to other media such as an image or a movie.

Links are usually displayed as colored and/or underlined text that looks different from the main body of text. As well as linking from text, you can link from an image or another object.

Clicking on a link opens up the corresponding document or web page in the browser window. Links can also open up documents such as PDF documents or they can perform a jump to another place within the same document.

When you hover your cursor over a link, the cursor changes to a pointed finger and the web address of the link appears in the status bar at the bottom of the browser window.

Creating a link to a page in our site

We'll now add a couple of links to our **Learning** page, by performing the following steps:

1. Select the word **board** in the second paragraph of text we recently added to the **Learning** page.
2. In the Control Panel click on the **Hyperlink** pop-up menu and select the destination page from the list, in this case choose **Gear:Boards**.

Note that as well as setting up where this link will take the visitor, you can use the **Hyperlink** drop-down menu to set the defined hyperlink to open a new browser window if required. In this case, do not check the **Open the link in a new window or tab** checkbox.

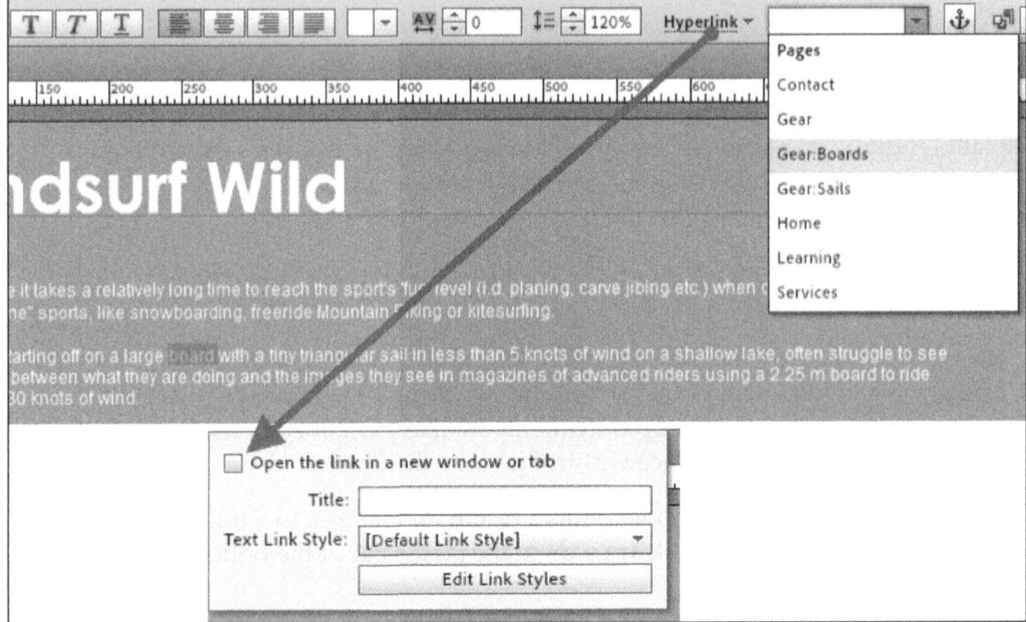

3. Repeat steps 1 and 2 and highlight the word **sail** in the same paragraph and add a link to the sails page. You now have two text links from this page to two other pages within your site.

Creating a link to an external web page

It's just as easy to add a link to another website. The following steps show how we do it:

1. Select the word **Kitesurfing** in the first paragraph on the **Learning** page.
2. In the Control panel, click inside the **Hyperlink** text box—the same one in which we chose the boards and sails links earlier. In here, we type the address of the page we are linking to.
3. Type `http://www.internationalkiteboarding.org/` and press *Enter* (Windows) or *Return* (Mac OS).
4. You'll see that a third link has now been added to our **Learning** page.

Creating a link anchor

When you add a link to another page or another website as we did in the previous exercises, the link opens up at the top of the page. Sometimes you may want to link to a specific part of a page. You've probably been on a long web page that contains a lot of text where the designer has provided a link back to the top at several points down the page.

Another example where link anchors are often used is on **Frequently Asked Questions** (**FAQ**) pages where there are a number of questions at the top of the page. When a visitor clicks on a question, the page jumps or scrolls smoothly to the corresponding answer further down the page.

You can also create links from one page to a link anchor on another page; links to other pages jump directly and don't use the smooth scrolling behavior. The following steps show how to add a link anchor to a page:

1. With your page open in the **Design** view, click on the **Link** anchor button in the **Control** panel. When you click on this button, it loads the *gun* with an anchor name.
2. Move your cursor to the top left of the content where you want the user to view, then click to place the anchor.

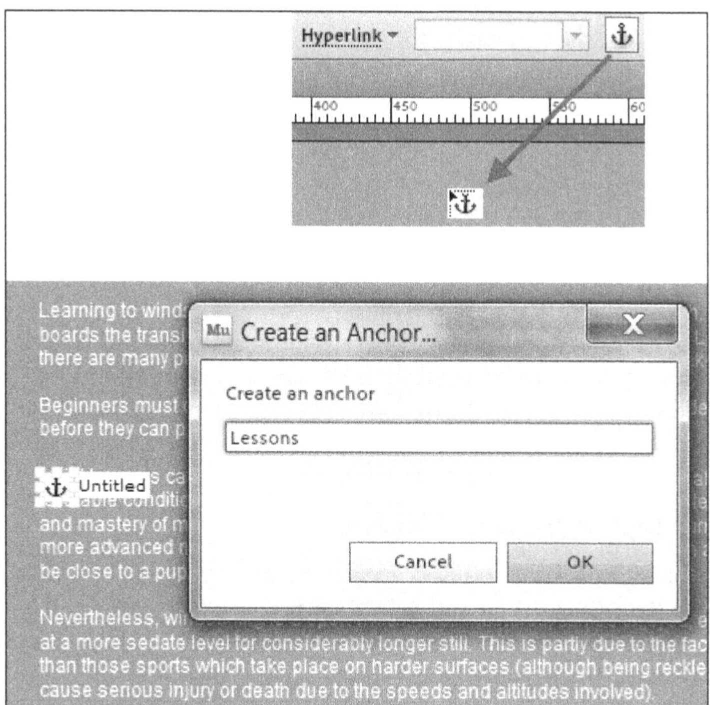

3. Enter a name for the link anchor in the **Create an Anchor** dialog box.
4. To link to the link anchor, select any piece of text or an image that you want to link, and then select the correct link's anchor name from the **Hyperlink** option in the Control panel, just as we did when we linked to the other pages in our site. If you find the small anchor icon annoying or off-putting, you can hide it by choosing **View | Hide Anchors**.

Creating an e-mail link

An e-mail link is simply a link that, when clicked, will open the user's e-mail program and populate the *To* field automatically with the e-mail address in the link. The following steps show how to add an e-mail link:

1. Select some text or an image that you want to link.
2. In the **Control** panel, click inside the **Hyperlink** text box.
3. Type the e-mail address in the format `myemail@email.com`. Muse recognizes the @ symbol and knows it is an e-mail link rather than a regular link.

Understanding two different types of links

In the exercises we've just completed, we dealt with two different types of link paths:

- Absolute
- Relative

An absolute link provides the complete URL of the document you're linking to. This type of link is also referred to as an external link. Absolute links generally contain a protocol (such as http://) and primarily are used to link to documents on other servers. In our example, we linked to the external site of the International Kiteboarding Association using the absolute address `http://www.internationalkiteboarding.org/`.

A relative link is used for local links. This type of link is referred to as a document-relative link, or an internal link. We created relative links to the sail's page and the board's page. Muse takes care of the code for us, we just tell the program where we want to go when the link is clicked.

Changing the color of links

The default color for a link is blue and a visited link is purple. You can easily make changes to these default settings and select colors that complement the background and other colors you are using on your web pages by performing the following steps.

1. Choose **File** | **Site Properties** after clicking on the **Hyperlinks** button or clicking on the **Hyperlink** drop-down menu. Then click on **Edit Link Styles**.

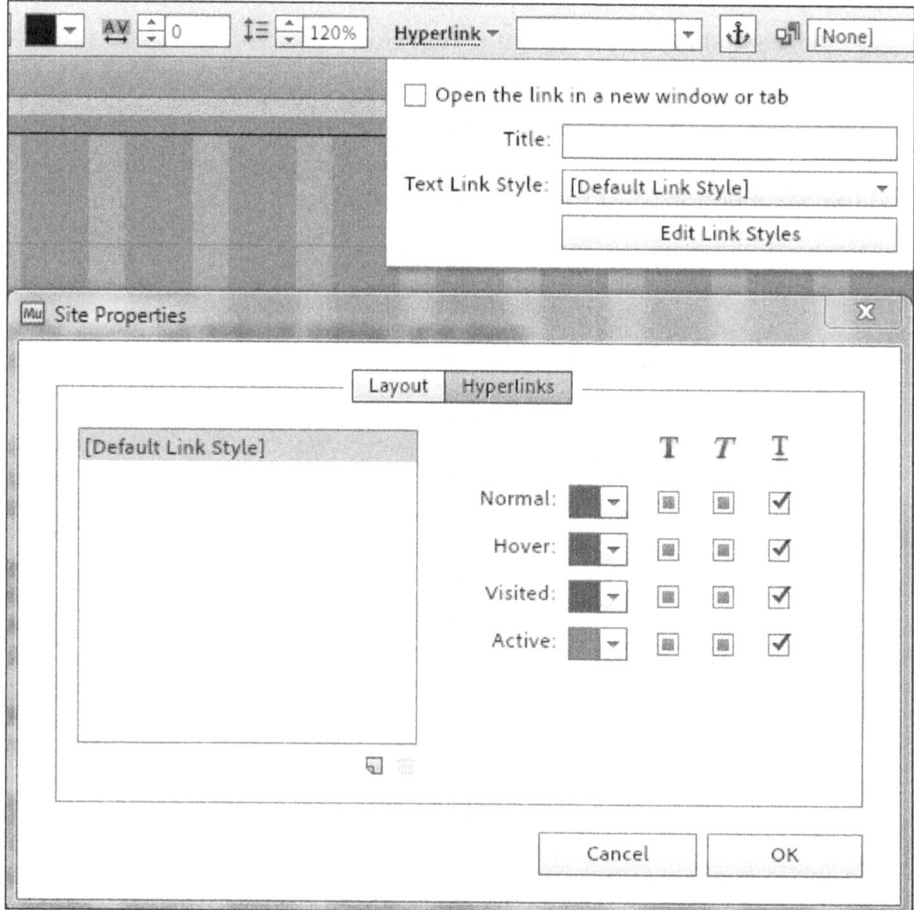

2. The first time you set link styles, there will be one default link style listed called **Link Style**.
3. Notice there are four color swatch boxes. These represent the color and text style options for each link:
    - **Normal** defines the style for normal unvisited links.
    - **Hover** defines the style for hovered links. A link is hovered when the mouse moves over it.
    - **Visited** defines the style for visited links.
    - **Active** defines the style for active links. A link becomes active once you click on it.

4. Starting with the **Normal** link, click on the color swatch and set the link color to white and leave the underlined checkbox ticked.
5. Set the **Hover** link to light blue with no underline.
6. Set the **Visited** link to dark blue with an underline.
7. Set the **Active** link to navy with an underline
8. When you have finished making changes to your link colors, you can save the set as a link style. To add a new link style to the list, click on the **New Link Style** button (next to the trash can icon).

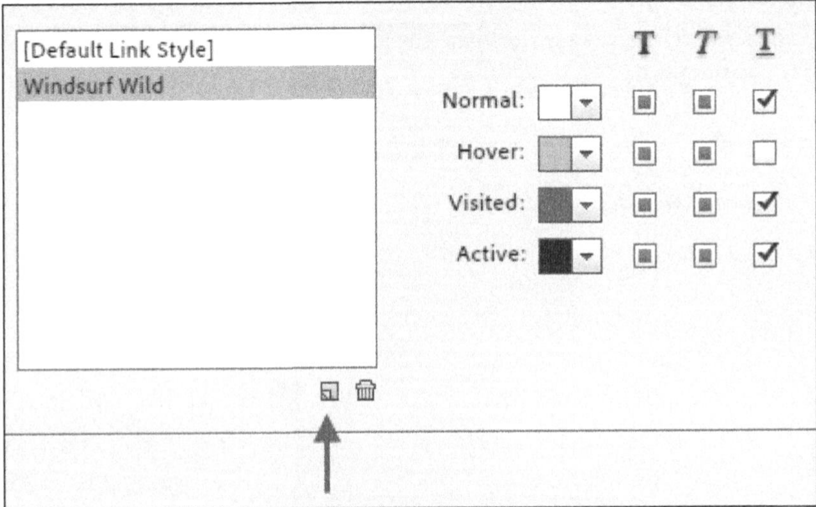

9. To rename a style, double-click on it to make it editable.
10. To delete a link style, select it and click on the trash can icon.
11. Your changes will be saved when you click on **OK** and close the dialog box. You will be able to apply the custom style to any link on any page, just as you would apply any character style to text.
12. Click on the **Preview** tab to see your new link colors in action on your **Learning** page.

Editing and deleting links

Web development is a constantly changing process. There are times when you'll want to edit or delete a link. A URL to an external website may change, an e-mail address may change or you might find a link that contains an error.

To edit a link

Select the link, then simply re-type the correct URL or e-mail address into the Hyperlink field on the Options bar.

To delete a link

Select the link, then highlight the URL, internal page link, or e-mail address in the Hyperlink field and press *Delete/Backspace* on the keyboard.

Creating a navigation bar

Most websites include a navigation bar along the top of the page. For consistency, the navigation should be in the same place on every page. This avoids any confusion for the visitor and lets them move freely and easily through your website.

In a traditional web design, we would manually need to link each page we wanted in the navigation bar by writing code and then adding the navigation bar to the top of each page.

With Muse, however, we can very quickly add smart and robust site navigation that automatically reflects our sitemap layout.

Let's go back to our A-Master and use a menu widget that will automatically pick up the site structure and page names in our sitemap. We'll add the menu to the page header. In the previous chapter, we set up a menu for our wireframe **Prototype** page. In this situation we are adding the menu to our Master page using the following steps, so it is repeated through every page which has that Master applied to it:

1. Open your A-Master page in the **Design** view.
2. We'll increase the header height by dragging the header guideline down to the 100 pixel mark on the vertical ruler.

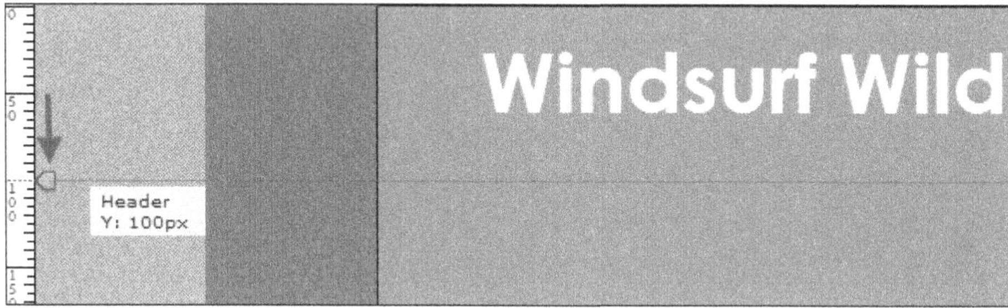

3. Go to the **Widgets Library** panel (on the right side of the screen) and click on **Menus**, or choose **Object** | **Insert Menu**. The **Menus** list expands and offers three different types of menu.

4. Choose the **Horizontal** widget and drag it to the header section of your page. You'll see that the menu items automatically show the names of the pages in your sitemap.
5. By using the **Selection** tool, align the horizontal menu under the **Windsurf Wild** text so that the menu text looks like it's sitting right on the **Header** guideline. Notice the smart guides which appear to help you align the menu text with the **Windsurf Wild** text.

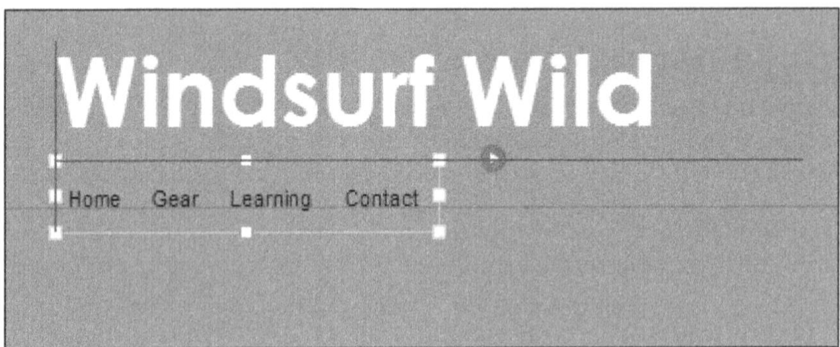

6. When the menu bar is correctly aligned and placed, click on the blue arrow to the right of the menu. This opens the **Options** panel for the horizontal menu.
7. Set **Menu Type** to **All Pages**. This ensures that our child or submenu pages appear in the navigation bar.
8. Set **Item Size** to **Uniform Width**. This will allow us to change the overall width of our menu while keeping the menu items evenly spread out.
9. Move your mouse over the center handle on the right-hand side of the menu and drag out until the menu width matches the width of the **Windsurf Wild** text above it. Use the smart guides to help line it up nicely.

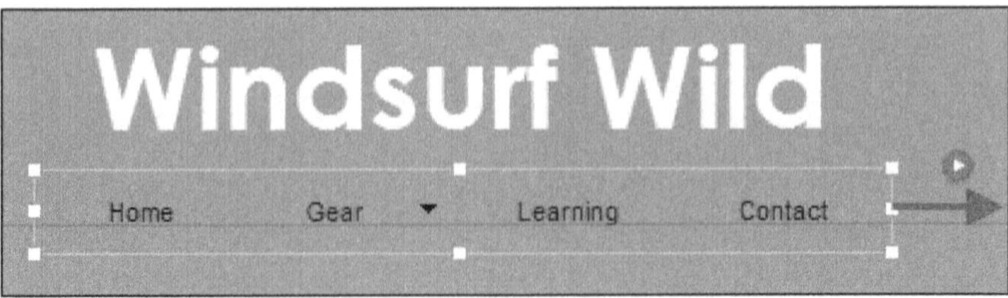

10. By using the **Selection** tool, select the menu, then click on the **Type** tool, or press **T**. By using the text options, set the menu typeface to **Century Gothic**, size **12**, **bold**, and using the color picker, set the text to light blue **#00FFFF**.

11. Click on the **Preview** link to test how your menu looks. You should find that in just a matter of a few clicks you have created a fully functioning menu with a drop-down submenu under **Gear**.

We'll come back to our menu in the next chapter to do some further formatting.

Tips for navigation links

Visitors to your website will use the links you provide to navigate around your site. Anyone who has been using the web for more than a week has come to expect the navigation to include the following:

- **Links to the home page**: Most websites are organized around a home page, so you should always include a link to the home page from every other page on your site.
- **Links to main topics**: For each web page that discusses a main topic, include links to other main-topic web pages.
- **Descriptive links**: The name and text link of your pages should make sense to the visitors. You will have spent a lot of time working on your site so it will all make sense to you. Make sure it makes sense to someone who has been to your site earlier too. Use simple but descriptive text in your links.
- **Link to a contact page**: If you're providing a service or selling something, people will want to get in contact to get more information. Make it easy for them by providing a link to a contact page.

Zooming in, out, and about

When you're working in the **Design** view, don't be afraid to zoom in closely so that you can clearly see where you are placing objects on your page. When you're finished making changes, zoom out to get the full picture. The following sections show how you can change the magnification of your web pages in the Design view.

Zooming in

It's important to get in really close, when aligning or placing objects on your page, so that we zoom in. Click on the **Zoom** tool in the **Toolbox** and then click on the page to zoom in, or press *Ctrl* (Windows) or *Cmd* (Mac OS) + the equal/plus sign.

Zooming out

When you're finished zooming in, you'll need to zoom out again. Click on the Zoom tool in the toolbox. Press on *Alt* + click (Windows) or *Option* + click (Mac OS) on the page, or press *Ctrl* (Windows) or *Cmd* (Mac OS) + the minus sign.

Fit page to window

When you fit a page to a window, the page resizes to the dimensions of your workspace. Choose **View** | **Fit Page to Window**, or press *Ctrl* + zero (Windows) or *Cmd* + zero (Mac OS).

Making page to its actual size

If you've been zooming a lot, or changing the dimensions of your page in the workspace, you can always return the page to its actual size by choosing **View** | **Actual Size** or press *Ctrl + 1* (Windows) or *Cmd + 1* (Mac OS) on the keyboard.

Summary

In this chapter we've looked at the concept of Master pages and how we use them to apply a look and feel across many pages. We learned how to add simple text onto individual web pages and how to add links. We used some of Muse's layout tools, namely guidelines and the grid overlay to align our content.

Congratulations, you can now build a fully-functioning website! Yes, it's a basic site with just text and some links, but these are the fundamental building blocks of every web page.

In the next chapter we're going to look at another important building block in Muse - the rectangle.

5

The Joy of Rectangles

In the previous chapter we looked briefly at how to add some text to our pages and also, how to add links to allow us to jump from page to page in the browser. These are an essential part of website building. In this chapter, we're discussing another important fundamental building block of Muse websites – the rectangle.

A rectangle is exactly as it sounds, that is, a shape. When we draw a rectangle, we're creating a shape to layout objects in place on our pages. A rectangle can hold text or images, they can be filled with color and outlined with a stroke. And even though they are called rectangles, they can be square in shape and we can round their corners off to make them circular in shape.

In this chapter we'll learn how to do the following:

- Set up a background rectangle
- Create a rectangle
- Select or adjust a rectangle
- Cut/copy/paste rectangles
- Position and rotate rectangles
- Duplicate a rectangle

Working with rectangles

The main purpose of a rectangle in Muse is to act as a layout object on our page. They let us define sections on our page. Once a section or rectangle is created it can be filled with color and/or have a stroke applied around the edge. We can also fill a rectangle with a background image. Although every single web page is essentially made of boxes (whether you're using Adobe Muse or some other web design tool), imaginative use of background images allows us to take the *boxiness* off a site. We'll talk about images in much more detail in a future chapter.

Another way to take the boxiness off a web page is to make the corners of a rectangle round. We can actually round the corners of a square so completely that it becomes a circle.

In the following screenshot you can see that the rectangles on the left have straight corners while the rectangles on the right, which are exactly the same size, have round corners.

The Grid Overlay has been turned on by choosing **View** | **Grid Overlay** to help with the alignment of these rectangles.

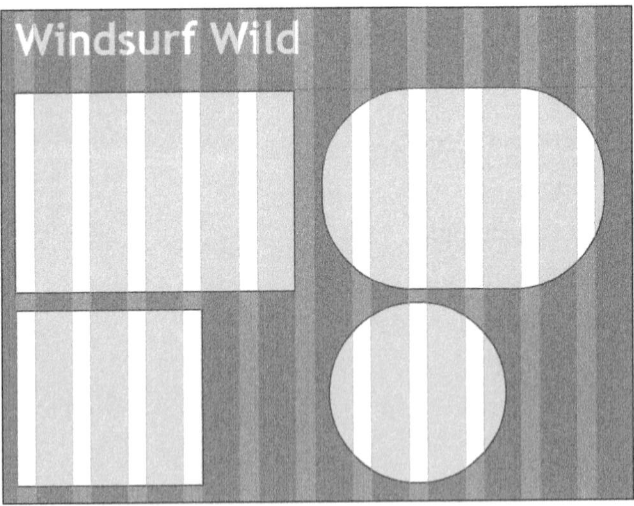

If you cast your mind back to *Chapter 3, Planning your Site*, you'll recall that we created a wireframe layout on our homepage using rectangles, which represented the different parts of our page using rounded rectangles. We used the rectangles to block off areas of the page which would represent the header, a navigation bar, the main content area, and the footer. In a traditional web design this sort of setup is created using the HTML `<DIV>` tags. Our prototype looked similar to the following screenshot:

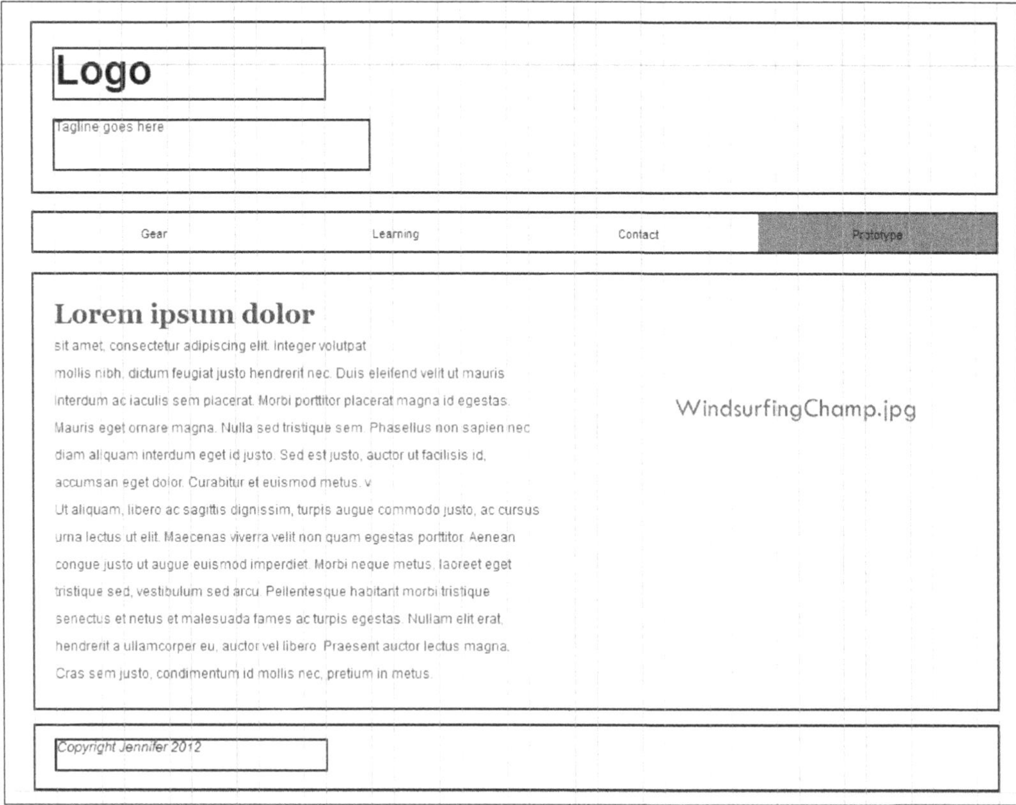

In the previous chapter, we added text to the page by selecting the text tool and then clicking-and-dragging a rectangular shape out. This created a text frame. Text frames and other objects such as widgets and images behave very much like rectangles in respect to their design. For example, if you want to add a bevel or a stroke to a text box, you would follow the same procedure for both.

> You can convert any rectangle into a text frame by double-clicking on it with the text tool.

So let's get started and create some rectangles on our pages. If you've been following along, open up the Windsurfing site in the Plan view so that you can see your site map.

Setting up a master background rectangle

A master background rectangle, is simply an area that we define on our master page. This area can hold an image or a block of color. The height of this rectangle is flexible and its height will vary with the amount of content which appears on each page. To set up a master background rectangle, perform the following steps:

1. Double-click on the **A-Master** page to open it in the **Design** view. Notice the main section of our page is blue and around it there is an area of dark grey. When we originally set up our site with the width and height values of 960 x 800 pixels, we created a container to hold our content. This container sits in the middle of the browser window—this is the blue area. When we first started working on our A-Master, we set our page color using the **Fill** option on the **Options** bar. The dark grey area around it is the space left on either side of our content in the browser. This is known as **Browser Fill** in Muse. Using **Browser Fill**, we can create the impression of a huge seamless background that runs the full width of a page on any screen, or we could create a background with distinct edges.
2. We're going to set the **Browser Fill** area to be the same color as our main content area. On the **Options** bar, click on the **Browser Fill** button. A drop-down menu appears. Set the color to `#29ABE2`. You can set the color by typing in the previous Hex value, or you can use the eyedropper tool to click on the blue in the main content area. This eliminates the possibility of a typing error and ensures we have picked up exactly the same color.

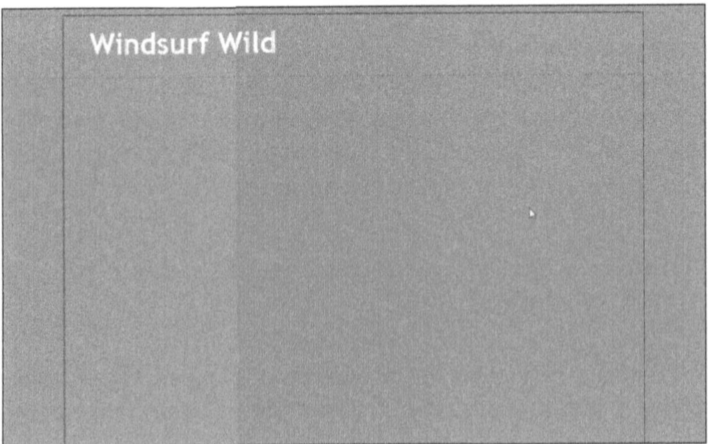

3. Now we're going to change the color of the **Fill** area and change the corner radius to create a rounded rectangle, which will act as the background for our container. Click on the **Fill** button on the Options bar. On the drop-down menu, set the **Color** to white and set the **Opacity** to `50`.

4. On the Options bar, set the **Stroke** value to `0`. This removes any stroke around the main container.
5. Again on the Options bar, set the **Corners** to `20`. You can either type in the number `20` or click on the up arrow on the Options bar repeatedly until it gets to `20`. When you've entered those values, your master page should look similar to the following screenshot:

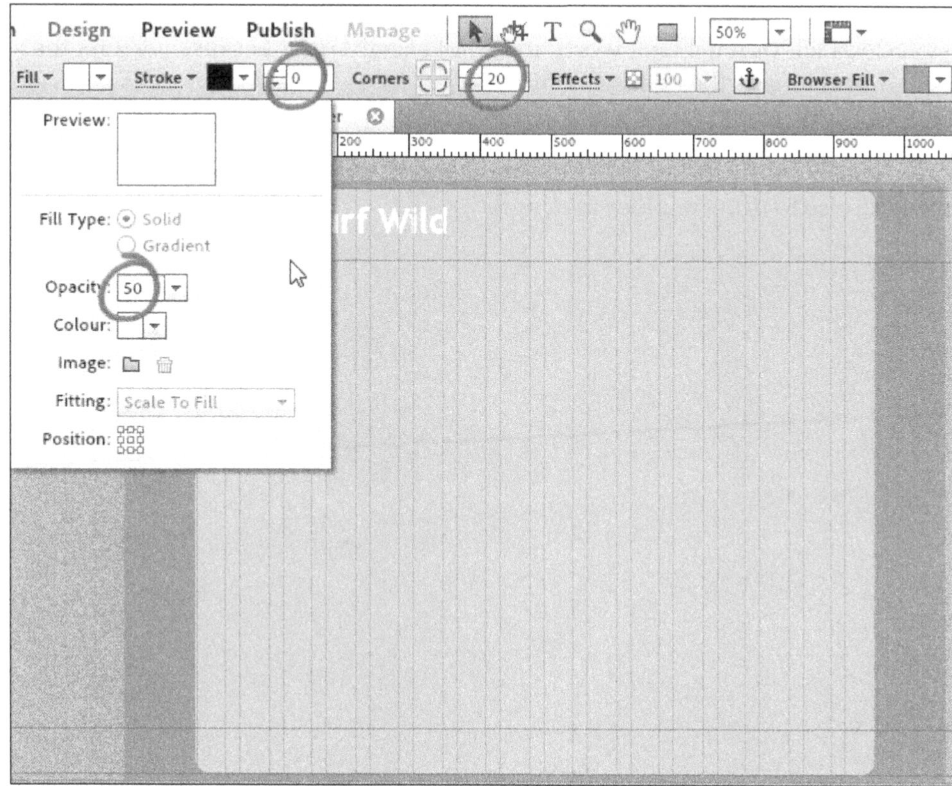

As we know from the earlier discussion on master pages, the changes we've just made will now affect any of the pages in our site which have this master page applied. In the Plan view, notice that all of our pages, except the Red master pages will appear the same.

6. Test how the changes affect the **Learning** page we created in the previous chapter by double-clicking on the **Learning** page in the Plan view. When the page opens in Design view, hit the **Preview** button to get a good idea of how the page will look in the browser.

The really great thing about setting up our background in this way is that the rounded rectangle we have created will stretch to accommodate all of our content.

Creating a rectangle on individual pages

Now let's take a look at how to add and manipulate rectangles to our other pages.

1. From the Plan view, double-click on the **Gear** page to open it in **Design**.
2. Click on the **Rectangle** tool in the toolbox at the top of the workspace.
3. On the right-hand side of the page, drag across to draw a new rectangle. Drag out so the rectangle measures *approximately* 300 pixels across and 320 pixels down. Don't worry if it's not exactly right because we'll fix the dimensions in the next section.

We can change the dimensions using the resize handles which appear on each side and each corner of the rectangle. The rectangle remains adjustable until you click somewhere else to draw another rectangle.

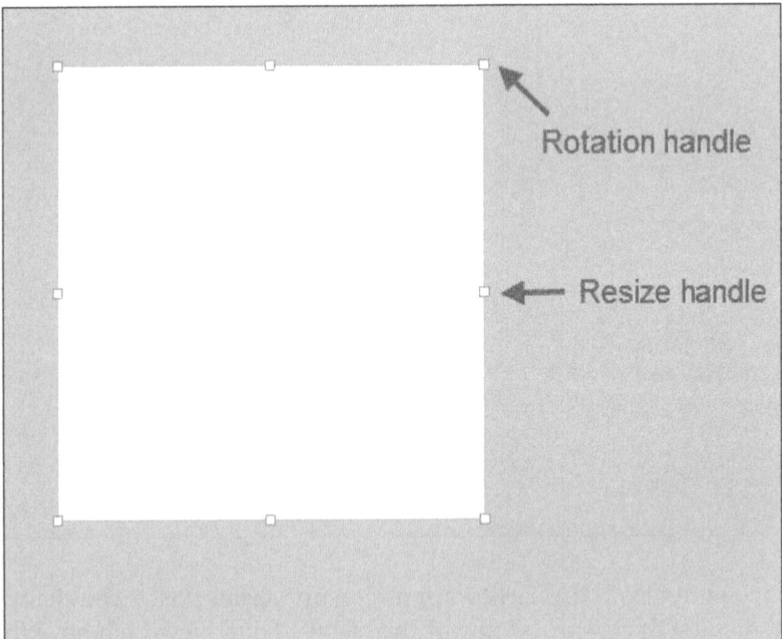

You can resize any rectangle by pressing *Ctrl* (Windows) or *Cmd* (Mac OS) - this switches to the **Selection** tool - then click on the rectangle and the resize handles reappear. Click and hold while dragging the handles to resize.

Deleting a rectangle

Let's say we've added a rectangle to our page and then decide we don't want it there anymore, it's easy to remove it. Simply select the rectangle by clicking on it using the **Selection** tool and press *Del* on the keyboard.

Adjusting a rectangle

Once a rectangle is added to a page, we can go back and modify it at any time, by performing the following steps:

1. In the Design view, click on the **Selection** tool in the toolbox at the top of the workspace.
2. Click on the rectangle you have just created. Once you select a rectangle, its dimensions become adjustable. To change the rectangle's dimensions, click and drag any of the resize handles on the selected rectangle.
3. To set the exact width and height of a selected rectangle, add the values in the Control Panel. Width is represented by **W** and height by **H**. Enter `300` for width and `320` for height.
4. You can also specify the precise location of the rectangle on the page by entering the **X** and **Y** location values. **X** is the distance in pixels from the left-hand side of the page. **Y** is the distance in pixels from the top of the page. Enter a value of `610` and `130` pixels for **X** and **Y** respectively, as shown in the following screenshot:

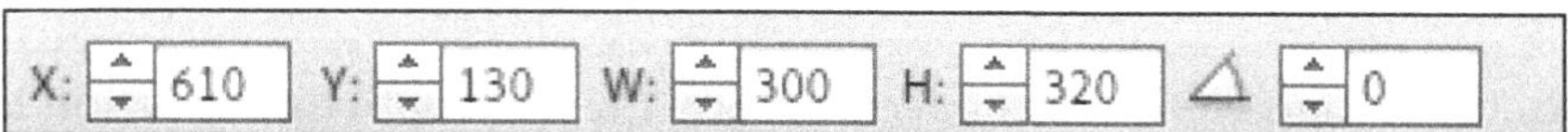

To create a perfect square instead of a rectangle when you are first drawing a rectangle, hold down the *Shift* key as you drag. Holding down *Shift* when you are resizing an existing rectangle constrains the proportions of the shape as you make the rectangle bigger or smaller.

Rotating a rectangle

We can create interesting design effects by rotating rectangles. An example of this is where a rectangle holds an image and we rotate it slightly to give a casual appearance of the image having fallen onto the page. Perform the following steps to rotate a rectangle:

1. In the Design view, select the rectangle you want to rotate.
2. Move your mouse over any of the corner handles which appear around the rectangle. The cursor will change to a rotation icon and now you can manually rotate the rectangle around its center point.

The previous steps can be performed or we can also increase or decrease the rotation angle in the Control Panel. The **Rotation Angle** option appears beside the X, Y coordinates and the Width and Height value field. It is the right most option in the Control Panel.

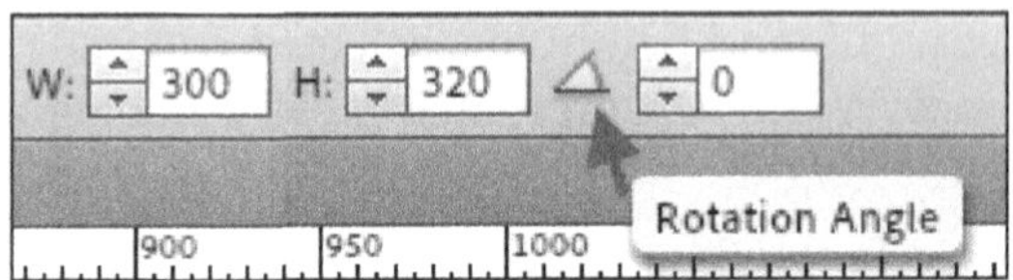

Cutting, copying, and pasting rectangles

So you've created a rectangle and now you'd like to re-use it somewhere else. The following steps show how to do it:

1. In the Design view, select a rectangle on the page with the **Selection** tool.
2. Copy the rectangle by choosing **Edit** | **Copy**, or press *Ctrl* + *C* (Windows), *Cmd* + *C* (Mac OS) to copy. Press *Ctrl* + *X* (Windows) *Cmd* + *X* (Mac OS) to cut.
3. Paste the rectangle by choosing **Edit** | **Paste** or press *Ctrl* + *V* (Windows), *Cmd* + *V* (Mac OS). The rectangle will appear on the page. Use **Edit** | **Paste** in places when you want to ensure the copied object is placed in the same exact location while moving it from one page to another.

What's the difference between Cut and Copy?

The Copy command makes a copy of the contents of the selection and when you paste it somewhere else, the original selection stays in place. The contents are now available in both the original location and the new location

The Cut command removes the contents of the selection and when you paste it somewhere else, the original contents are gone. It will appear in the new location only.

Duplicating a rectangle

An alternative to copying and pasting on the same page is to duplicate an existing rectangle. The following steps show us how to do it:

1. In the Design view, select the rectangle you want to duplicate.
2. Choose **Edit** | **Duplicate** or hold down *Alt* (Windows), *Option* (Mac OS) and drag to create a duplicate copy.
3. To create a duplicate that remains in alignment horizontally or vertically with the original rectangle, hold down *Alt* + *Shift* / *Option* + *Shift* while dragging.

Adding color – fills and strokes

Although we often use rectangles as "invisible" containers to hold our text or images, we can also apply color to them using fills and strokes.

Adding a stroke

Perform the following steps to add strokes:

1. In the Design view, select a rectangle.
2. With the rectangle still selected, add a stroke color by clicking on the **Stroke** color picker in the Control Panel, and then choosing a stroke color. We can use the eye-dropper tool to select a color from the color field, or from another area on the web page, or you can specify RGB values. For this exercise choose white as the stroke color.

Picking and Saving Colors

Anytime you use the color picker, whether it's for a stroke, a fill, or a browser fill, you can create a new color swatch in conjunction with the color picker. Click on the **New Swatch** icon next to the trash can icon in the lower-right corner of the color picker after specifying a new color and this will save the swatch for you.

Double-clicking on a swatch in the **Fill** color picker allows you to assign a friendly name to a color, such as Lime Green, rather than `#DBD820`. Once you've given it a more user-friendly name, that name is displayed as a tool tip when you hover your mouse over that color swatch.

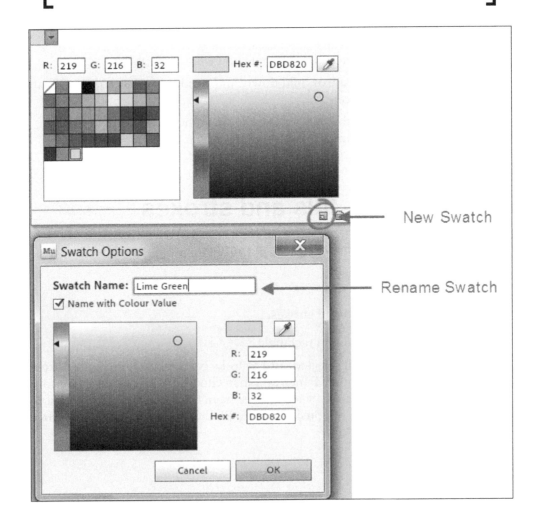

3. Change the stroke width by increasing or decreasing the number in the **Stroke** width box to the right of the color picker. Set the stroke width to `5` pixels.
4. To create round corners for this rectangle, set the **Corners** value to `15` pixels.
5. Optional: Click on the **Stroke** menu (the word **Stroke** in the Control Panel) to specify the additional options, as explained in the following sections

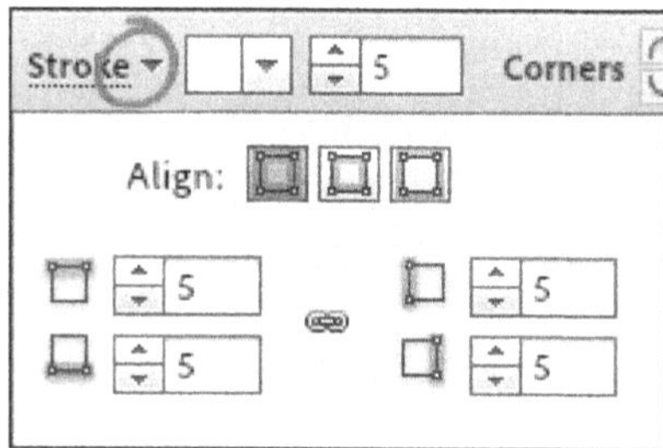

Stroke alignment

This option lets us choose exactly where the stroke appears on our rectangle. The choices are center, inside, or outside of the rectangle. Click on each one to see the effect it has on your rectangle stroke.

Stroke widths

This allows you to specify the width of the top, bottom, left, and right strokes individually. By default, these numbers are grouped so that when we increase or decrease the stroke width, all sides of the rectangle will change together. We can ungroup strokes by clicking on the link icon. When the link icon looks as if it is broken, the strokes are ungrouped. Now we can change the width or any side at a time.

Changing rectangle fill

Just as we can change the stroke color on a rectangle, we can change the fill color. The fill color covers the entire width and height of the rectangle. When you add text to a rectangle, the text appears in front of the fill color. The following steps show us how to do it:

1. In the Design view, make sure your rectangle is selected.
2. Change the fill of the selected rectangle by clicking on the **Fill** color picker in the Control Panel, and then selecting a fill color as described for choosing a stroke color. You can specify RGB values, a hexadecimal value, or select a color from the color field or from another area on the web page.

If you don't want any color fill in your rectangle, click on the **None** swatch. That's the first swatch with the red diagonal line through it.

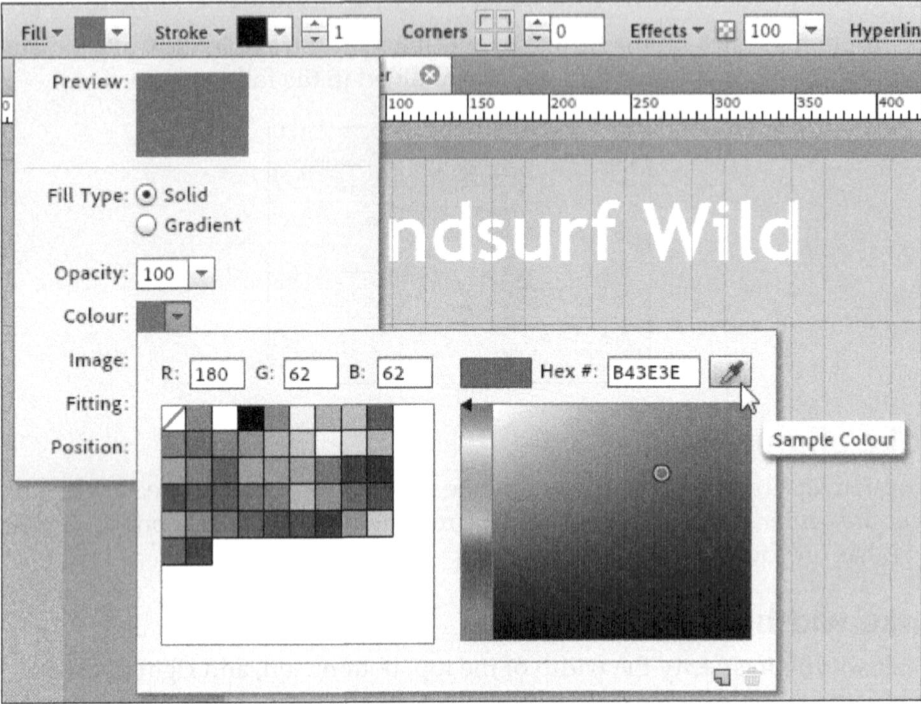

3. If you want to choose a color for your rectangle background, click on the **Fill** menu (the word **Fill** in the Control Panel) to specify the following options for solid fills:
    - **Opacity:** This option specifies the opacity (or how transparent the background color is).
    - **Color**: This option sets the fill color and brings up the same color picker as the one you can access from the Control Panel.
    - **Image:** This option lets you pick an image to use as a background in your rectangle.
    - **Fitting**: This option lets you fit the image within the rectangle according to a number of options, including **Scale to Fill**, **Scale to Fit**, and a number of tiling options. When you set the **Fitting** option to **Tile**, the tiled image is only downloaded once, reducing your page download time.
    - **Position**: This option specifies the position of the background image inside the rectangle relative to your selection.

Setting a gradient fill

Instead of using a solid color as a background to a rectangle, we have the option of using a gradient. The following steps show us how we do it:

1. Click on the **Fill** menu on the Control Panel.
2. Click on the **Gradient** radio button to reveal the gradient options.
3. Set your start color by clicking on the color picker on the left. Choose a light blue similar to the main page background.
4. Set your end color to a dark navy.
5. Set the direction to **Vertical** and leave the other options as they are. The changes to your rectangle fill will appear as you make changes.

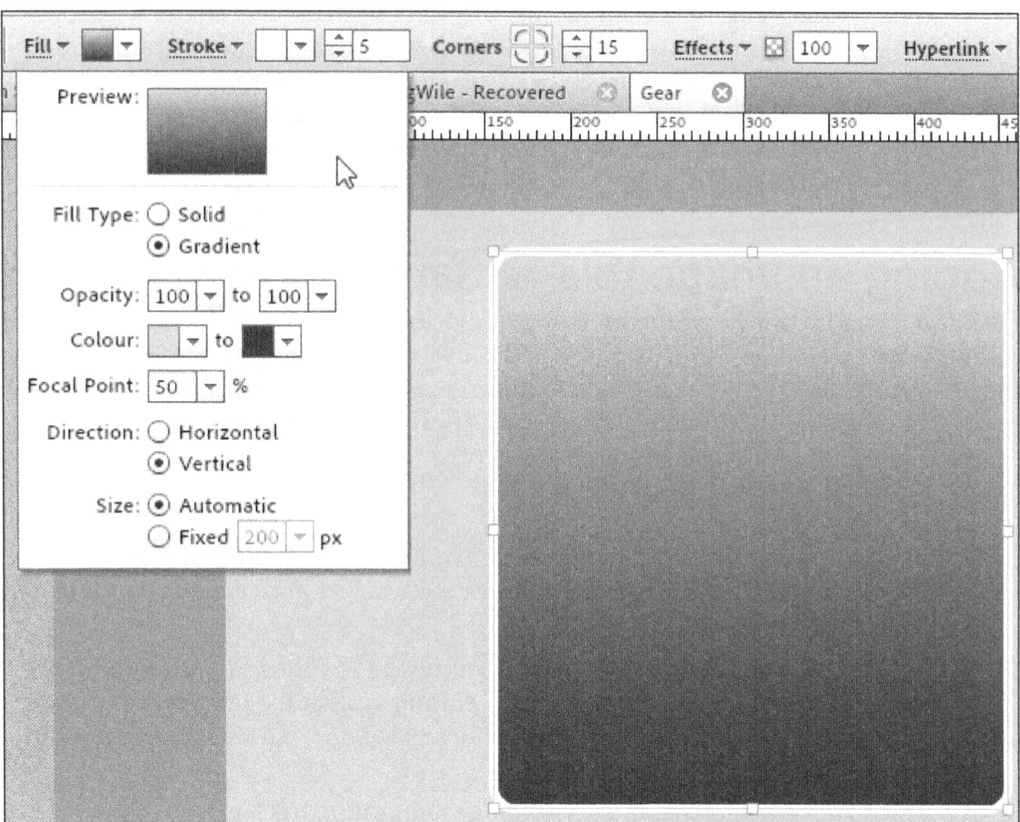

6. The options for **Gradient** fills are somewhat similar to the options when we choose a solid color, The following provides a brief explanation of each:

    - **Opacity**: This option allows us to specify the opacity at the start and end of the gradient. This is very useful for gradually blending a rectangle into the background of the main page
    - **Color**: This option lets us pick the two colors which will form our gradient.
    - **Focal Point:** This option specifies the point in the background color where the gradient begins. 50% or midway is the default.
    - **Direction**: This option lets us choose which way our gradient will run - either horizontally or vertically.
    - **Size:** This option allows us to specify how the two colors we choose will blend into each other. Setting **Automatic** creates a gradient that spans from the start color to the end color to fit the height or width of the object that the gradient is filling. The alternative is to enter a pixel value which causes the gradient to blend from the start to end color within that specified number of pixels.

Adding an image to a rectangle

Let's add a picture of two windsurfers to our existing rectangle. Remember that the rectangle we created has dimensions of 300 x 320 pixels. We're going to put an image into the rectangle which is about double this size and uses the options available to make it fit nicely. The following steps show us how to do it:

1. With the rectangle selected on the page, click on the **Fill** menu on the Control Panel.
2. We're replacing our gradient fill now, so click on the **Solid** radio button on the **Fill** menu. This gives us options for solid colors and images as outlined in the information box.
3. Click on the folder icon beside the word **Image** to choose a background image to go into the rectangle. The operating system file browser opens, so navigate to your images folder and choose the `Gear-Windsurf.jpg` file and choose **Open**.
4. The image appears inside the rectangle. Notice that the image appears cropped. We can change how the image fits inside the rectangle by clicking on the **Fitting** drop-down options. Choose **Scale To Fill**.

5. Now click on the **Position** icon to choose how the image is positioned. Depending on your image there may be a certain amount of trial and error when choosing your positioning. Click on each of the empty points on the icon to see how the position of the image within the rectangle changes. For this example, the center point seems to work quite nicely.

Adding effects to rectangles

In Muse, you can add effects such as drop shadows, bevels, and glows to a rectangle, an image, a text box, or any other object. The following sections show how we do it.

Adding a drop shadow

The drop shadow is certainly one of the most popular effects used by designers. It allows us to add some depth to our page and give the impression that the object is lifting slightly off the page. As with most design effects, moderation is the key. The following steps show us how to do it:

1. In the Design view, select the rectangle to which you want to add a drop shadow.
2. On the Control Panel, click on the **Effects** menu.
3. Click on the **Shadow** category and select **On**.
4. Set a **Color** for the shadow. Remember, not every drop shadow needs to be black. We can create a more subtle effect by choosing a color which is a darker shade of the main page's background color. Choose a dark navy color for this exercise.
5. Set the opacity of the **Shadow** to `60` as shown in the following screenshot:

6. Set the **Size** to `8`.
7. Set the **Distance** to `8` and leave the rest of the values at their default.
8. The following provides a brief explanation of the options available when choosing a Drop Shadow:
    - **Color:** Sets the drop shadow's color.
    - **Opacity**: Sets the drop shadow's opacity.
    - **Size**: Lets you set how thick the drop shadow appears.
    - **Angle**: Sets the location of the drop shadow in relation to the rectangle. The default is a 45-degree angle and this places the drop shadow to the right and the bottom edges of the rectangle. The higher the angle number, the drop shadow moves around the rectangle.
    - **Distance**: Specifies the distance between the drop shadow and the rectangle.
9. To remove the drop shadow, clear the **On** checkbox.

Adding a bevel effect

The bevel effect also adds depth to an object by adding light and dark edges. The following steps show us how to add the effect:

1. In the Design view, select the rectangle again. Note that it will be difficult to see the bevel in action when there is a stroke on the rectangle, so you may want to temporarily remove the stroke on the rectangle first.

2. In the Control Panel, click on the **Effects** menu to see a window as shown in the following screenshot:

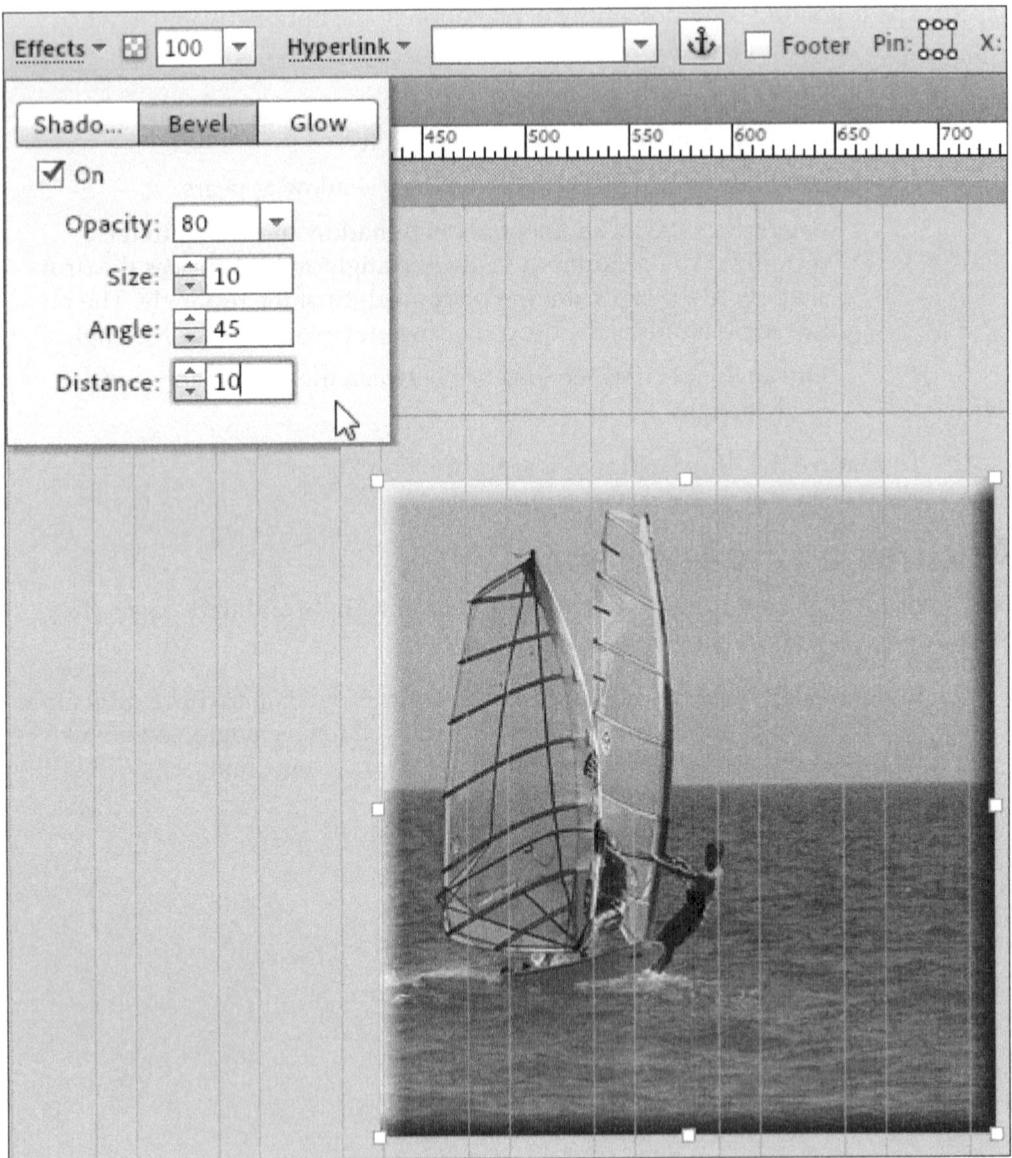

3. Click on the **Bevel** category and select **On** to activate the bevel options.
4. To remove the bevel, uncheck the **On** box.

Adding a glow

The third and final effect is the glow, which lets us apply a glowing edge to any rectangle. The following steps show us how to add a glow:

1. In the Design view, make sure you select the rectangle to which you want to add a glow.
2. In the Control Panel, click on the **Effects** menu to see a window similar to the following screenshot:

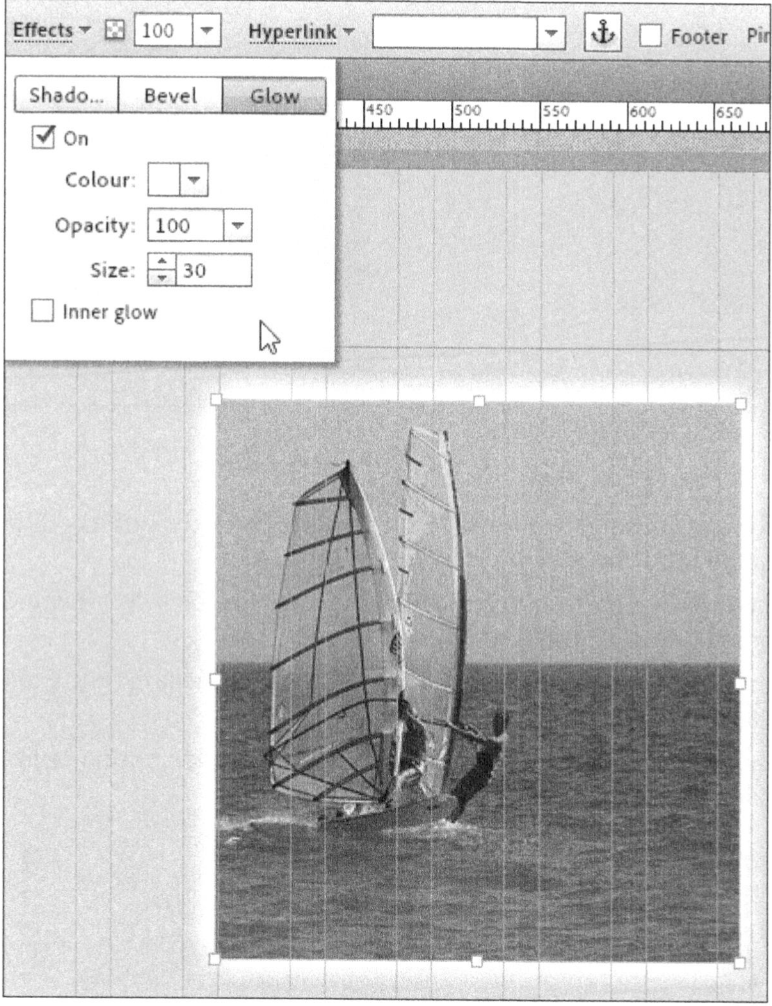

3. Click on the **Glow** category, select **On** to activate the options.
4. To remove the glow, uncheck the **On** box.

Change stacking order of rectangles

Frequently you'll find that you have more than one rectangle on a page. When you move a rectangle on top of another, you may get the unexpected result that the one you wanted on top is now underneath. This is because Muse creates what's known as a stacking order as it creates rectangles. Luckily, it's very easy to change the stacking order and this technique is applicable to other objects on the page too.

The rectangle on the right is brought forward in the stacking order

The following steps show us how to do it:

1. To bring a rectangle forward in the stacking order (or put it on top), select the rectangle and choose **Object | Bring Forward**.
2. To move a rectangle backward in the stacking order, select the rectangle and choose **Object | Send Backward**.
3. To bring a rectangle to the top-most level of the stacking order, select the rectangle and choose **Object | Bring to Front**.
4. To move a rectangle to the very bottom of the stacking order, select the rectangle and choose **Object | Send to Back**.

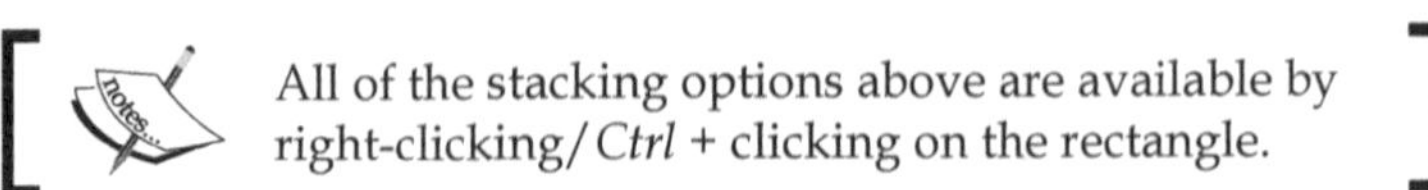

All of the stacking options above are available by right-clicking/*Ctrl* + clicking on the rectangle.

Creating a mixture of round and square corners

We can play around with the corner radius of individual corners on our rectangles to achieve some nice effects. Let's say we want to create a shape with 3 round corners and one straight corner at the top right. The following steps show us how to do it:

1. In the Design view, draw out a new rectangle or select an existing one on the page.
2. Select round corners for the top-left, bottom-right and bottom-left corners on the Control Panel. Click on the top right corner on the Control Panel so a straight corner icon appears.
3. Increase the rounding radius to `50` to get a dramatic rounding effect on the three round corners; this will make the straight corner stand out more.

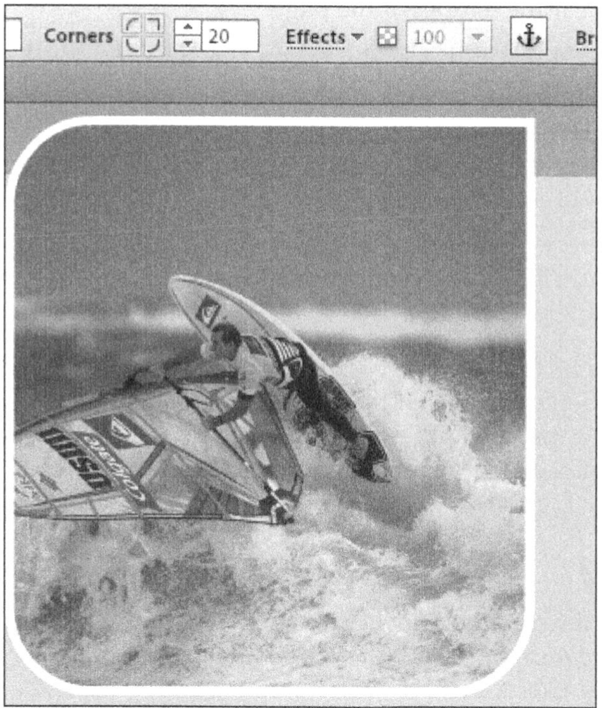

We can change back from round to straight on any of the four corners and the effect will be apparent immediately.

Creating full width rectangles

Most of the time, when we create rectangles with the **Rectangle** tool, we specify the size of the rectangle by entering values in the **Width** and **Height** fields of the Control Panel, or by dragging the transformation handles.

We can also set a rectangle to be displayed at the full width or 100 percent of the browser window. This means that the rectangle will resize itself to fill the page regardless of how wide the visitor has their browser window set.

A full width rectangle can be filled with a solid color, a gradient or an image background fill. If you set a tiled background image fill, the tiled image will tile seamlessly to expand as needed to fill the 100 percent width of the page.

The following steps show us how to set up a full width rectangle:

1. On the **Gear** page, in the Design view, use the **Rectangle** tool to draw a rectangle near the bottom of the page.
2. With the rectangle still selected, set up your **Fill** and **Stroke** options as described earlier.
3. Use the **Selection** tool to drag both the left and right sides of the rectangle to align them with the two left and right edges of the entire page width. The rectangle will span the entire horizontal width of the page.
4. You will notice a red highlight appear on the left and right edges of the page and you'll feel the rectangle snap into place as you align each side of the rectangle.

When using a tiled image, the image will repeat over and over to fill the rectangle. The advantage of doing this is that the browser only downloads the image once, reducing download speeds. With a clever choice of background image, a designer can create the illusion of a large image spanning the width of the page.

Summary

In this chapter we have learned how to set up a flexible background rectangle. We've added rectangles to our pages and manipulated their size, fill color, and stroke and learned how to add effects such as drop shadows.

In the next chapter we're taking an in-depth look at how to work with Type in Muse and how to deal with typography on the Web.

6

Typography, Muse, and the Web

In the previous chapter we looked at how rectangles are the building blocks of a Muse web page and how to use them both for content and as design elements. Yet another absolutely fundamental element of any web page is text. Websites are all about communication and naturally, text is a big part of that.

In this chapter we'll add text and learn how to edit it, apply styles, and use frames to control where it appears on your web page. We'll also discuss the role of typography in producing eye-catching and interesting designs, and why our choice of typeface for the Web is so important.

By the end of this chapter you'll know how to:

- Create text
- Edit text
- Create and edit character styles
- Create and edit paragraph styles
- Add headings
- Apply spacing and formatting to text
- Wrap text around an image
- Add metadata to your web pages
- Choose "web-safe" fonts

The power of text

When we talk about text and design, we're not just referring to the type of font we want to use. We need to present our text clearly and in an organized fashion so that our visitors can find the information they need quickly and easily.

Typography is a huge subject in itself and something to which some designers and typographers will devote years of study. Although we can't go into a huge amount of depth on the design of type, it's important to be familiar with the anatomy and categories of type so that we can make informed choices about the typefaces we use.

Anatomy of type

Type is a vital element in any design in which it appears. As well as being a piece of text to read, it can also be viewed as a shape or as a visual element. Before we start adding type to our designs, it's a good idea to understand a little bit about typography and some typographic terms. The following image shows a short visual glossary of some of the terms you will come across when working and learning about type:

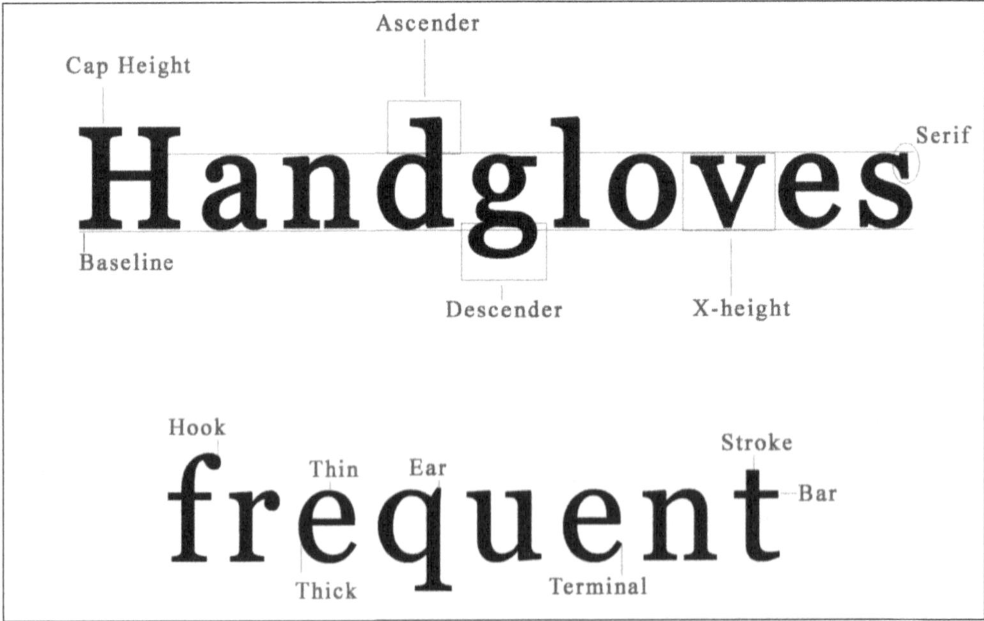

The following are the typographic terms along with an explanation:

- **The Baseline**: This is the imaginary line that the text sits on.

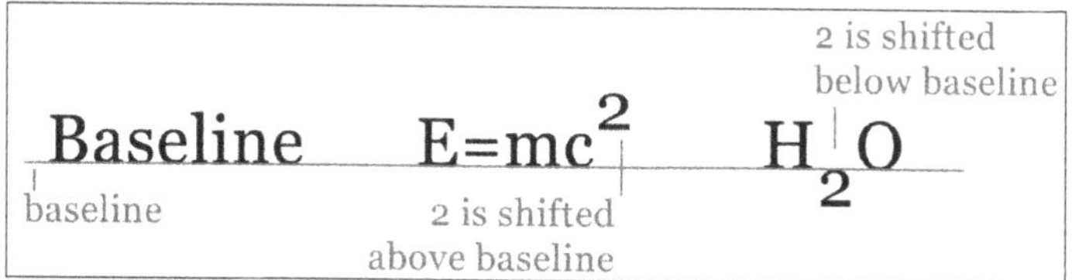

- **The x-height**: Based on traditional printing methods, the x-height is the height of the lowercase letter x. However, as a general rule, the x-height can be described as the height of lowercase letters in a font excluding the ascenders and descenders.

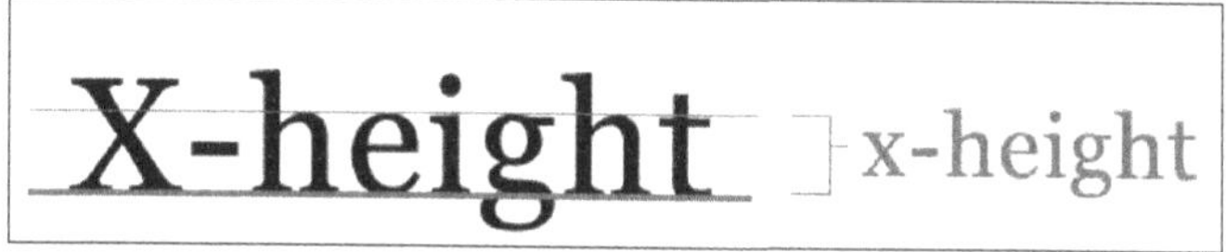

The x-height can vary quite a bit from font to font. The x-height gives the overall impression of the font's size. In the following illustration, all of the text is set to a point size of 21, but as you can see, each word looks quite different in height and weight.

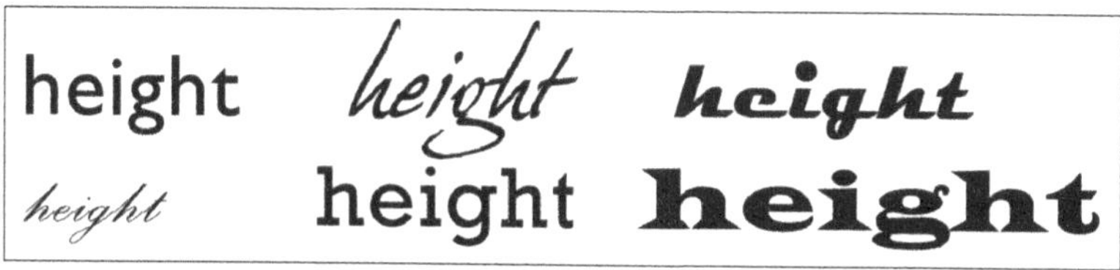

- **The Ascender**: This is the stem of lowercase letters (h, b, k for example) that rises above the x-height of the other lowercase letters in a typeface.

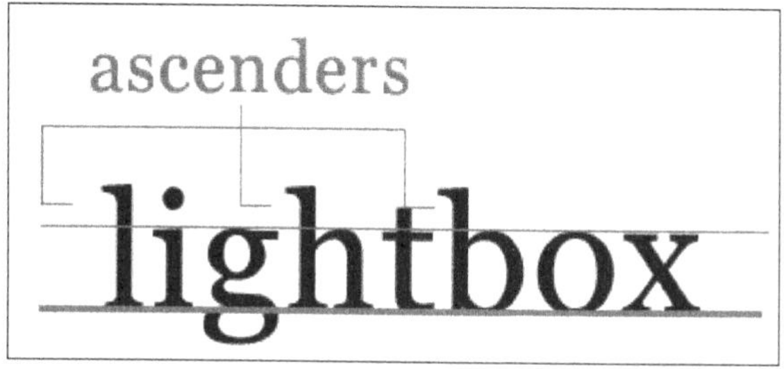

- **The Descender**: This is the part of a lowercase letter (g, q, y for example) that falls down below the baseline. Often the uppercase letters Q and J descend below the baseline.

- **Roman/Regular**: The upright style of a typeface.
- **Italic**: A slanting or script-like version of a typeface.
- **Boldface**: A typeface rendered in a heavier, thicker stroke, used to make text stand out.
- **Cap Height**: The height from the baseline to the top of the uppercase letters in a font. This is not always the same height as the ascenders.

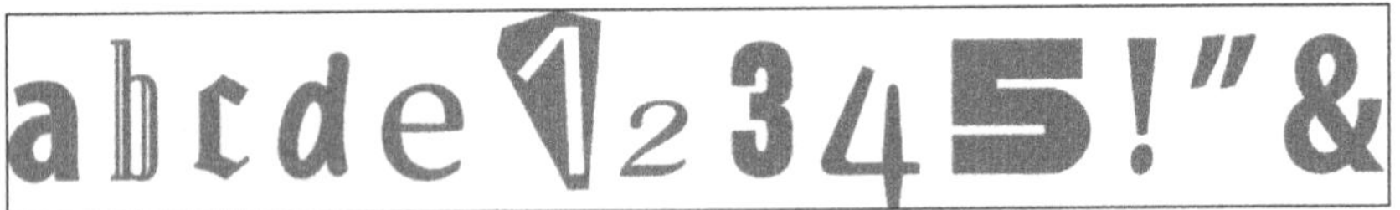

- **Character**: A single element such as a letter, a number, or a punctuation mark.

abcde 1 2 3 4 5 ! " &

- **Condensed Font**: This is a narrower version of a font. It is used to fit more characters into a given space.

Regular Light Condensed

Bold Condensed

- **Drop Cap**: This is a popular and effective design style in which the first letter (a capital letter) is set in a larger point size and aligned with the top of the first line. It is often used to indicate the start of a chapter or a new section of a document.

In a land, far, far away,
lived the beautiful princess ...

- **Raised Cap**: This is another design style where the first capital letter is set in a larger point size and aligned with the baseline of the first line of text.

In a land, far, far away,
lived the beautiful princess ...

- **Reversed Type**: This is the type that is printed or viewed on screen as white on black, or light-colored on a dark background.

Reversed Type

- **Left Align Text**: Text is aligned to the left, leaving the right edge of the paragraph ragged.
- **Centre Align Text**: Text is aligned to the center, leaving both edges of the paragraph ragged.
- **Right Align Text**: Text is aligned to the right, leaving the left edge of the paragraph ragged.

- **Justified**: Text is justified if it is flushed on both the left and right margins.

Left Aligned Text

John F. Kennedy's memorable inaugural address is famous for his use of the word "ask" five times in three sentences: "And so, my fellow Americans: ask not what your country can do for you, ask what you can do for your country.

Right Aligned Text

John F. Kennedy's memorable inaugural address is famous for his use of the word "ask" five times in three sentences: "And so, my fellow Americans: ask not what your country can do for you, ask what you can do for your country.

Center Text

John F. Kennedy's memorable inaugural address is famous for his use of the word "ask" five times in three sentences: "And so, my fellow Americans: ask not what your country can do for you, ask what you can do for your country.

Justified Text

John F. Kennedy's memorable inaugural address is famous for his use of the word "ask" five times in three sentences: "And so, my fellow Americans: ask not what your country can do for you, ask what you can do for your country. My

- **Kerning**: This is the adjustment of horizontal space between pairs of letters. It is used to create a perception of uniformity.

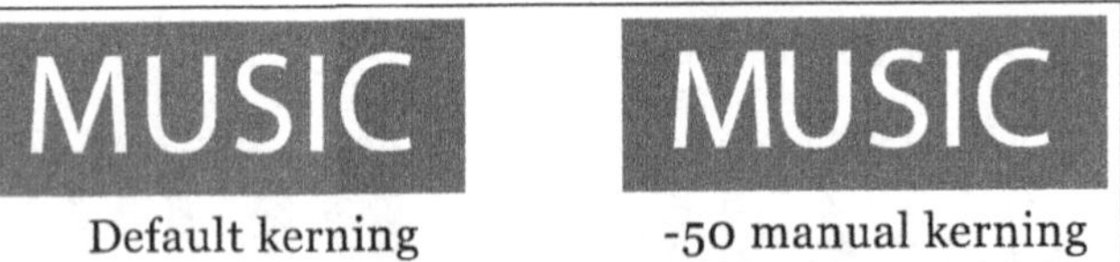

Default kerning

-50 manual kerning between M and U

- **Tracking/Letter spacing**: This is where an adjustment is applied to a whole block of text rather than just pairs of letters (kerning). It is used to improve legibility and to fit more or less text into a certain space. In the following illustration, the first line has tracking set to `0` (or normal), the second line has tracking set to `-100`, so all the letters are pulled tighter together, and the third line has tacking set to `+70` so there is more space between the letters.

Around the ragged rocks the ragged rascal ran

Around the ragged rocks the ragged rascal ran

Around the ragged rocks the ragged rascal ran

Creating text frames

In *Chapter 3, Planning your Site*, we had our first introduction to text boxes when we created a wireframe mock up and added a number of rectangles, including one text frame, to hold our dummy text.

In *Chapter 4, Powerful Pages*, we added the title of our website "Windsurf Wild" to our master pages and in *Chapter 5, The Joy of Rectangles*, we added some text content to our Learning page. We're going to continue adding text content to our windsurfing site now.

In Muse, if it's not already open, open your site by choosing **File | Open Site** from the menu or click on the name of your windsurfing site on the Muse Welcome page.

There is more than one way to add text to our pages. We can do any of the following:

- Draw a text frame and then type directly into the frame
- Draw a text frame and then copy the text from another source, for example, a word document or from an Internet site, and paste it into the text frame
- Place a `.txt` (basic text file) by choosing **File | Place** in the menu

We've already seen in *Chapter 4, Powerful Pages* and *Chapter 5, The Joy of Rectangles*, how we can add text by firstly drawing out a text frame, but for this exercise we're going to choose the third option, that is placing a text file to add some text to our **Gear** page:

1. In the Plan view, double-click on the **Gear** page to open it in the Design view. You'll recall that in the previous chapter, we added a rectangle to hold an image on this page and adjusted the corner radius to create a mixture of three rounded corners and one straight corner.
2. Choose **View | Show Guides** so that you can use the guides as an aid for aligning your images and text.
3. Choose **File | Place**, then browse to the `Chapter 6` folder and choose `Gear.txt`. You'll immediately notice that your cursor changes to show a loaded icon - it looks similar to a mini-page that is attached to your cursor.

4. Click just beneath the **Windsurf Wild** text and a new text frame is added containing the content of the `Gear.txt` document. Notice that the page stretches automatically to accommodate the text frame.

5. In the previous chapter we saw how we could select a rectangle, add a fill color, add a stroke color, resize it, add round corners, and add background colors to it. It just so happens that text frames behave in the same fashion. We can do all of these to a text frame.

If you create a text frame on top of a rectangle, the rectangle will resize for you as you add text to the text frame. This ensures that web pages created by Muse automatically stretch vertically to adapt to changes.

Clear, compelling, and correct content

Although this chapter is about typography, it's important to mention that the actual content is vitally important, no matter what your choice of font is. Many websites thrive despite a lack of design finesse and the reason is that their content is excellent. Perform the following steps to have a perfect content:

- Be clear, be correct and be compelling.
- Don't make silly spelling mistakes as Muse does not have a spell checker, don't make factual errors and don't ramble off the point.

Editing text

So now that we have some text in place on the **Gear** page, let's go back and edit it. The following steps show us how to do it:

1. While in the Design view, select the **Text** tool.
2. Select the text that you want to change.

3. We can edit the text using the Control Panel at the top of the screen (once our Text tool is selected) or in the Text panel, which we open by choosing **Window** | **Text**, as shown in the following screenshot, if it's not already visible:

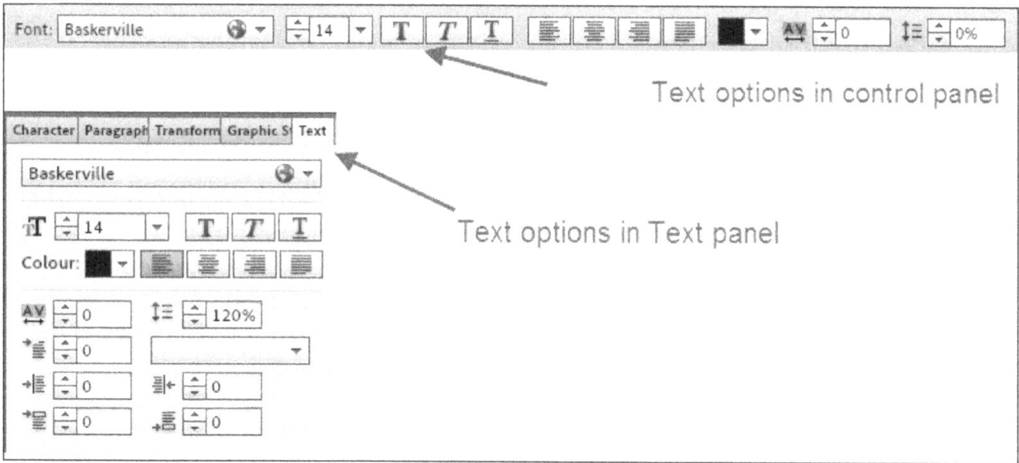

The following are the options available in both panels:

- **Font**: You can pick a font from a list of web-safe fonts (we'll talk about web-safe fonts in a bit more detail later), web fonts or from a list of system fonts. Muse exports system fonts that are not web-safe, as an image. Web-safe fonts and web fonts are listed with a small globe icon beside them. If you choose a font which needs to be exported, a small image icon appears beside the font on the list in the control or text panel and on the work area beside your text.

  If you want to hide the icon in your work area, choose **View** | **Hide Rasterized Text Frame Indicators**.

- **Font size**: The font size specifies the size of the font and is measured in pixels. There are a small number of pre-defined sizes which you can select from, or you can enter a specific font size by typing in a number.
- **Bold/Italic/Underline**: Makes the selected text bold, italicized or underlined.
- **Align**: Sets your text paragraph to left, center, right, and justify.

- **Color**: This lets you set the text color. To choose a text color , you can use the eyedropper tool, or you can select a color using the color swatches, or by typing in an RGB value or a hexadecimal value.
- **Letter Space**: Also referred to as tracking, letter space increases or decreases the spacing between letters of the selected text.
- **Leading**: This specifies the amount of space above and below a line of text. Leading is a paragraph attribute which means any changes you make here will affect every line in the selected paragraph. The leading field accepts either percentage values (a percentage of the font size) or pixel values.
- **Paragraph style**: This value lets you select a pre-defined paragraph style to apply to the text. By using paragraph styles, we can improve consistency across our site and speed up text formatting.

  Most of the time, we use Paragraph styles because we tend to work with lines of text. However, it is possible to create character styles which can be applied to individual text characters or small numbers of words.
- **Character style**: Lets you select a predefined character style to apply to the text.

The following options are available only in the Text panel:

- **Indent**: Lets you indent the first line of the selected text. It's possible to use positive and negative (minus) values in this field.
- **Links**: Lets you style text with a pre-defined link style.
- **Left/Right margin**: Put space in the left or right margins of the selected text (similar to padding).
- **Space before/after**: Specifies the amount of space before (above) or after (below) the selected paragraph.

It is not a good practice to export your body text as an image. Image files are not resizable or selectable in the same way HTML text is, and it is not search engine-friendly. Text exported as image files are not selectable or resizable when viewed in browsers.

Web Fonts provide hundreds of extra fonts on top of the web-safe fonts. Web fonts let you use fonts that aren't installed on the visitor's computer. This opens up a whole extra world of typography goodness for us as designers. When you choose to use a web font, the **Add Web Fonts** dialog box opens, as in the following screenshot, which gives a visual overview of all the fonts available. The web fonts are supplied by the Typekit service.

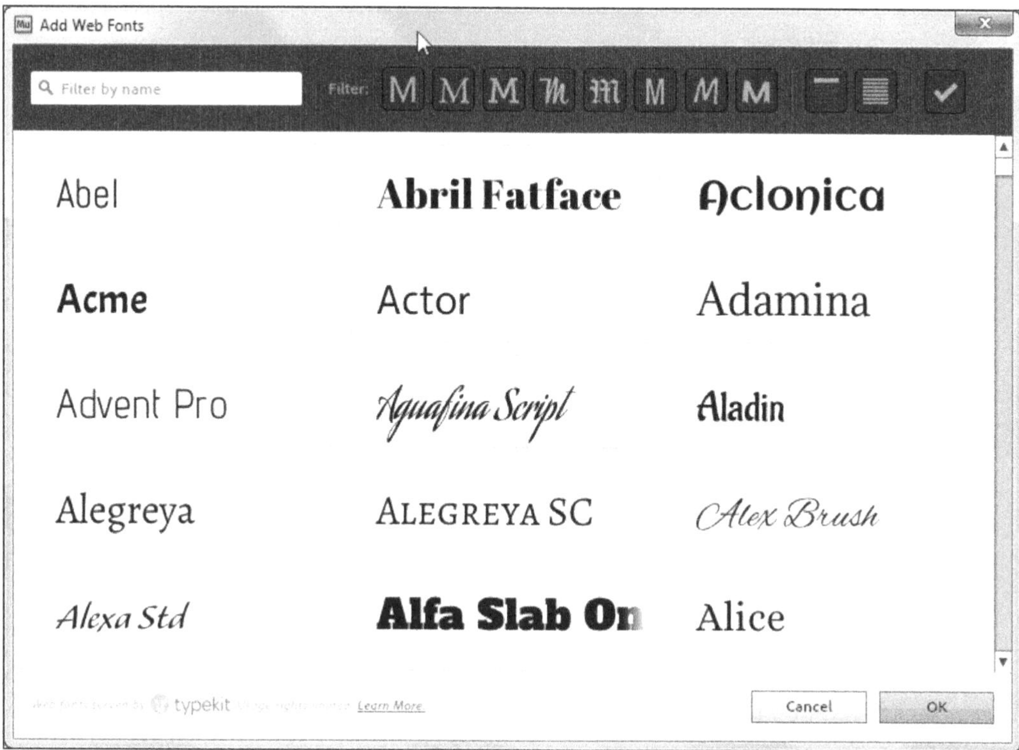

Creating and applying paragraph styles

Using paragraph styles allows us to save a set of definitions or rules for larger blocks of text, which we can quickly apply to any block of text we choose.

Let's say for example, that you wanted your block quotes to always look the same way, set in Georgia, Italic, and size 12 with a color of red. You would select some text, apply the formatting then save it as a paragraph style. You can then reuse that paragraph style by applying it to other block quotes on your pages.

Any paragraph or character styles that you create are available to use throughout your site, not just on the page on which you created the style. Let's make a paragraph style now, which will define how our main body text will look:

1. In the Design view, highlight a block of text – say one line within a paragraph – then set the following values in the **Text** panel:
    - **Font**: `Arial`
    - **Size**: `12`
    - Left Alignment
    - **Colour**: Dark Navy or Hex `000090`
    - **Line Spacing**: `140%`

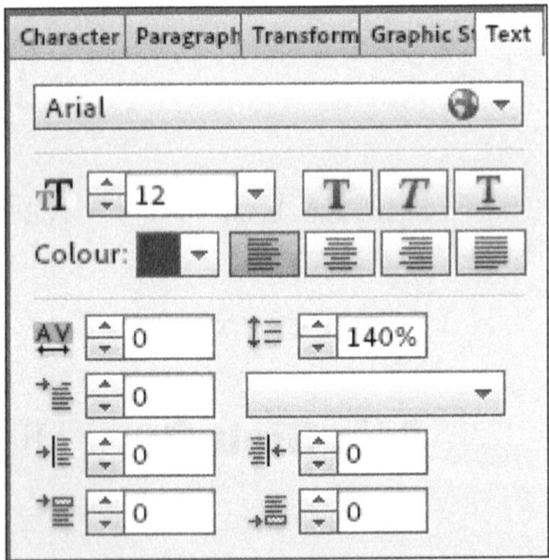

2. In the **Paragraph Styles** panel (choose **Window | Paragraph Styles** if you can't see it on your set of panels), click on the **Create New Styles** button in the lower-right corner.
3. Rename the new style by double-clicking on it and entering a descriptive name in the text box. In this case call it `Body Copy`.

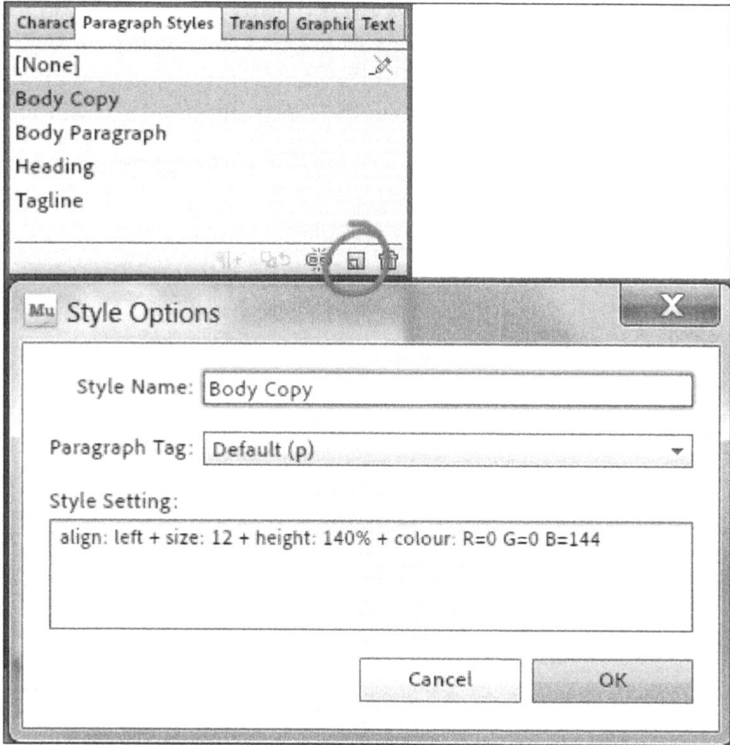

You'll notice that there are already some paragraph styles listed. These are styles we created in *Chapter 3, Planning your Site*, when we created our wireframe mockup. You can create as many styles as you want.

4. To apply the paragraph style to all of the text you placed on the **Gear** page, click once anywhere on the text frame with the text tool so that your cursor appears flashing in the text. Then click rapidly three times to select all of the text in the text frame.

> Click once on a text frame to place your cursor anywhere within that text frame. Click twice to select a word, click thrice to select the full line of text, and click four times to select all of the text in the text frame.

5. Now let's apply the new Body Copy Paragraph style to the text we added to our Learning page in the previous chapter. Go to the **Plan** view, then double-click on the Learning page to open it in the Design view.
6. On the Learning page, using the Select tool, simply click once to select the text frame on the page.

7. With the text frame selected, click on the **Body Copy** style you just created and you will see an instant change in the text formatting on the Learning page. The text should appear with the same formatting you applied on the **Gear** page. Notice that the links on the Learning page are still white.

8. To edit a paragraph style, select the style in the **Paragraphs Styles** panel, make your edits, and click the **Redefine Selected Styles** button in the lower right corner of the panel.

   Try this out by changing the color of the text within the body copy to bright yellow. Notice how the text changes color on the Learning page and on the Gear page. Try changing the text size, line spacing, and font face. When you've finished experimenting, set the body copy back to its original settings and don't forget to click the **Redefine Selected Styles** button at the bottom of the **Paragraph Styles** panel.

9. If you want to remove a particular style from a block of text, you can select a piece of text where the style has been applied and then choose **None** from the **Paragraph Styles** panel.

Creating and applying character styles

As we've seen, paragraph styles work great with several lines or blocks of text, but what happens if we want to create a style and only apply it to *certain* words? Well that's where character styles come in. Using character styles allows us to save a set of definitions or rules for a very specific group of characters or words.

Let's say, for example, that you wanted to highlight certain words on your page, this is how we do it:

1. In the Design view, on the Learning page, highlight the word **novice** in the first line. Then set the following values in the Text panel:
    - **Font**: `Arial`
    - **Size**: `12`
    - Bold and Italic
    - **Color**: Bright Yellow
2. In the **Character Styles** panel (**Window | Character Styles**), click on the **Create New Styles** button in the lower-right corner.
3. Rename the new style by double-clicking on it and entering a descriptive name in the textbox. Call it `Bold Yellow`.
4. Now that you've created a character style, you can apply it to any other text on your pages. On the Learning page, find the word **Beginner** or **Beginners**. Highlight each instance of the word and apply the new style by clicking on its name in the **Character Styles panel**.

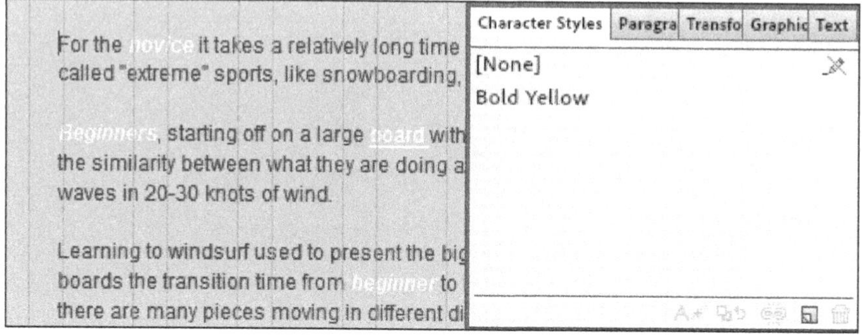

5. To edit a character style, select the style in the **Character Styles** panel, make your changes, then click on the **Redefine Selected Styles** button in the lower-right corner of the panel.
6. If you want to unlink a particular character style from a piece of text, click on the **Unlink Style** button in the lower-right corner of the **Character Styles** panel.

Using the Context menu in the Character and Paragraph Styles panels

When you're working with the Styles panels, you can find extra options by right-clicking or *Ctrl* + clicking on any style. You'll see the following options:

- **New Paragraph Style**
- **Duplicate Style**
- **Delete Style**
- **Unlink Style**
- **Clear Overrides**
- **Redefine Style**
- **Rename Style**
- **Style Options**
- **Delete Unused Styles**

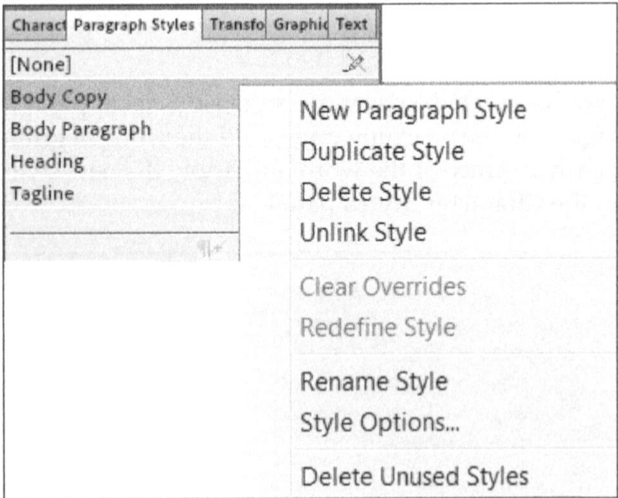

Headings

In web design, we use headings for several reasons, some of which may not be entirely obvious if you're new to the field. Headings let us organize our content, convey a logical hierarchy on each page, help with accessibility, and work as an aid to **Search Engine Optimization** (**SEO**). Let's take a look at each of these.

Content organization and hierarchy

HTML heading tags were created to provide a structure for web pages. H1 or Heading 1 is the most important heading. It is often the largest and boldest piece of text on the page. Headings run from H1 to H6 and get progressively smaller as we move from H1 to H6. It is important to always start with H1 and move through each level one at a time. You may find that we don't need to go past H3, but we may need this in order to create an organized web page. This is the specific purpose that HTML heading tags are used for—to structure your documents. You should always start with an H1 element and move through the other levels one at a time. For example:

- H1
- H2
- H2
- H3
- H4
- H5
- H6
- H6
- H5
- H4
- H3
- H2

It's important to use H1 or Heading 1 on each of your pages. If you consider that each page in your website should be focused on just one topic, then the name or title of that topic will be the most important heading at the top level on your page. There should really only be one H1 per page.

Headings and accessibility

Making our web pages accessible means making our site usable by people with disabilities. This may include:

- Visually impaired people using screen readers
- Hearing impaired people using browsers with no sound
- Physically impaired people
- Color blind people

By using headings correctly, we can make pages easier to read for people using assistive devices. Because headings indicate the start of important text within a document, screen readers use headings as anchors. Pages become easier to read because the relevant content can be accessed without having to read every word on the page.

Headings and SEO

This is an often-overlooked benefit of using headings correctly. Search engines place an extra emphasis or importance on the text within headings. The higher the heading tag, the more important that text is considered to be. An H1 heading has more weight in the search engine results than an H6 heading.

Creating headings

As mentioned, we use headings to provide structure to the page and we can use Paragraph or Character styles to define how those headings look. That's what we'll do now:

1. If it's not already open, open the Learning page in the Design view.
2. Select the Text tool and drag out a text frame under the **Windsurf Wild** text logo.
3. Type in the words `Learn How to Windsurf`.
4. Highlight the words you've just typed, then apply the following formatting either through the Control Panel or the **Text** panel:
5. **Font**: `Arial`
6. **Size**: `36`
7. Bold
8. **Color**: Navy (`#000090`).
9. In the **Paragraph Styles** panel, click on the **Create New Style** button.
10. Double-click on the new paragraph style and name it `Heading 1` in the **Style Options** dialog box. From the **Paragraph Tag** drop-down menu, choose `Headline (H1)`. This is how we tell Muse that this particular piece of text is the most important text on the page.

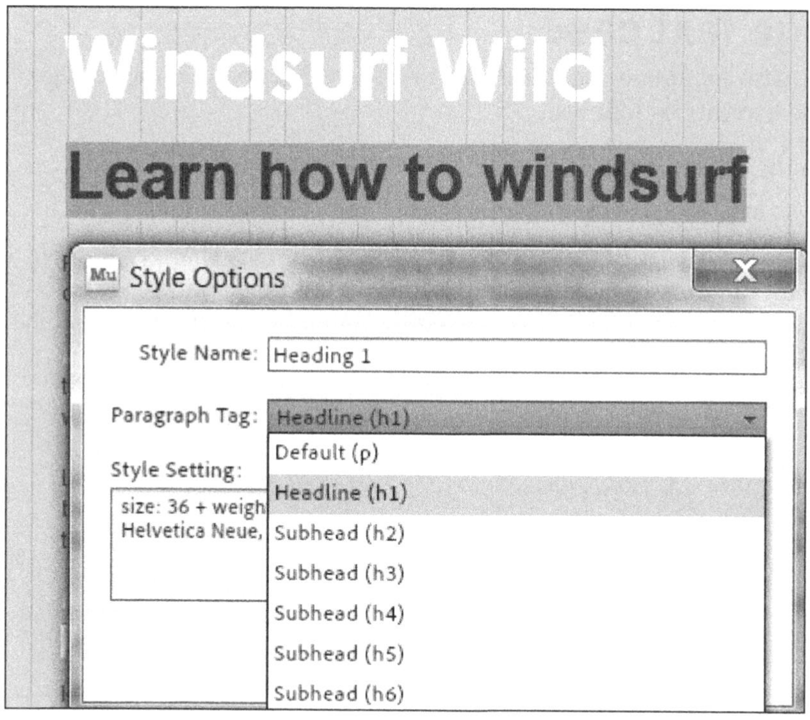

So that's our Heading 1 style created. Let's apply it on the **Gear** page:

1. Open the **Gear** page in the Design view.
2. Add a text frame under the Windsurf Wild text logo. Use your X and Y coordinates to ensure the new text frame is sitting in the same position as on the Learning page.

> You may need to move the body text down the page before adding the new text frame.

3. Type in the words `Windsurf Gear`.
4. Highlight the words (or any part of the words because we are applying a paragraph style), then click on the Heading 1 paragraph style you created.

Your text should now be formatted exactly as defined in the paragraph style.

Change text case

Let's say that we want our heading size 1 to be in all uppercase, we can go and change the text case as follows:

1. In the Design view, make sure you have the Text tool selected.
2. Select the words **Windsurfing Gear**.
3. Choose **Edit | Change Case | UPPERCASE**. This changes the selected text to all uppercase, as shown in the following screenshot, but it has not changed our paragraph style. We will need to manually select any words that we wish to change to uppercase.

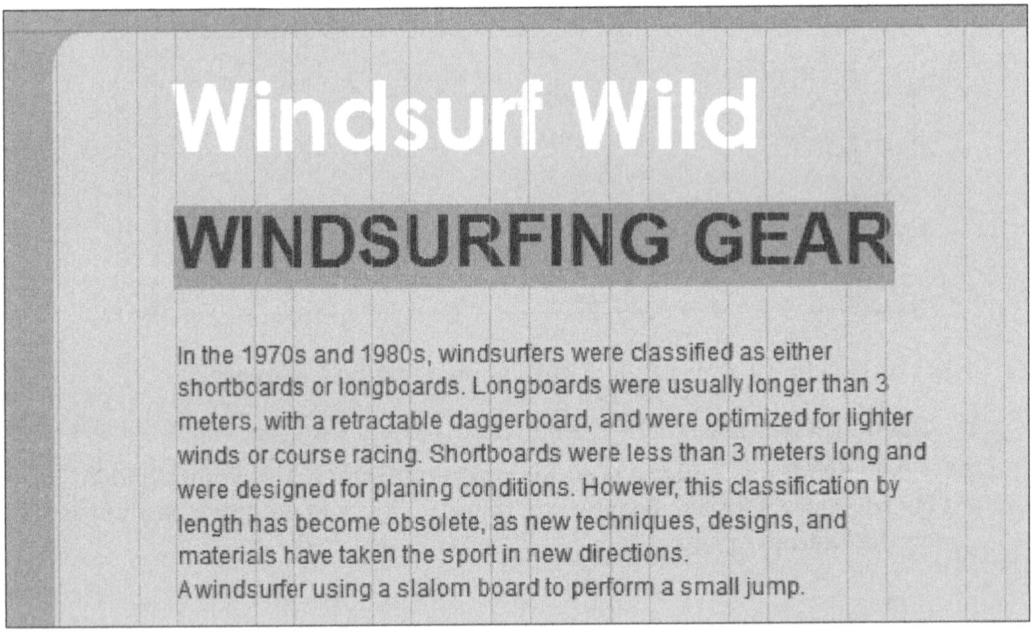

Windsurf Wild

WINDSURFING GEAR

In the 1970s and 1980s, windsurfers were classified as either shortboards or longboards. Longboards were usually longer than 3 meters, with a retractable daggerboard, and were optimized for lighter winds or course racing. Shortboards were less than 3 meters long and were designed for planing conditions. However, this classification by length has become obsolete, as new techniques, designs, and materials have taken the sport in new directions.
A windsurfer using a slalom board to perform a small jump.

Text wrapping

It's not unusual to see boxes of information or images appearing within the text content of a web page. Textboxes within textboxes are sometimes referred to as **callouts** and they supplement the main text with additional information.

Muse makes it easy to create callouts by letting us wrap text around an object such as a rectangle, another text frame, or an image. In the following steps we're going to cut the image currently on the Gear page and paste it inside the text frame we created at the beginning of this chapter. We'll then wrap the text around the image so it flows nicely.

1. Open the **Gear** page in the Design view. Currently it consists of a heading, a text frame, and a rectangle holding an image of two windsurfers.
2. Use the Selection tool to select the image on the right-hand side of the page.
3. Choose **Edit | Cut**, to cut the image from the page and onto the clipboard.
4. With the Selection tool, click on the text frame, then drag one of the handles on the right-hand side of the text frame so that the frame almost fills the width of the page.
5. Then, use the Text tool to define a text insertion point in a text frame. Click once just before the word **In** on the first line of the first paragraph. Paste the element you copied previously (**Edit | Paste**) to insert the object as an inline element in the text frame.

   The image is now inside the text frame but it looks a bit awkward as all of the text has dropped down below it. Take a look at the **Wrap** options in the Control Panel at the top of the screen.

6. Choose between the following wrap options:
   - Inline in text
   - Position left
   - Position right

7. Click on each of the wrap options so you can see how the position of the images changes and how the text wraps around it.

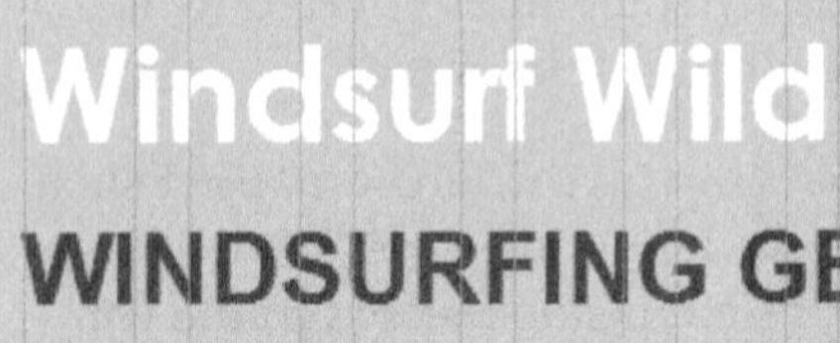

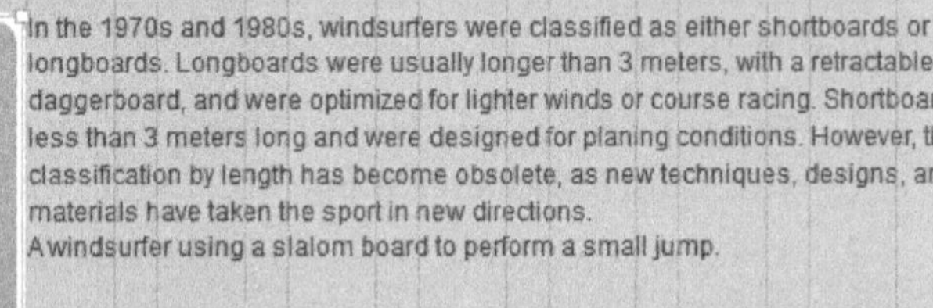

In the 1970s and 1980s, windsurfers were classified as either shortboards or
longboards. Longboards were usually longer than 3 meters, with a retractable
daggerboard, and were optimized for lighter winds or course racing.
less than 3 meters long and were designed for planing conditions. However,
classification by length has become obsolete, as new techniques, designs,
materials have taken the sport in new directions.
A windsurfer using a slalom board to perform a small jump.
Most modern windsurfers (1990s and later) are derived from the shortboard
are intended to be used primarily in planing mode, where the board is mostly
over the surface of the water, rather than cutting through, and displacing the
Planing is faster and gives more maneuverability, but requires a different
the displacement mode (which is also referred to as slogging or schlogging).
smaller (i.e., lower volume, shorter length, narrower width) boards and
are used as the wind increases.
While windsurfing is possible under a wide range of wind conditions, most
windsurfers prefer to sail in conditions that allow for consistent planing with
purpose, not overly specialized, free-ride equipment. Larger (100 to 140 liters)
boards are capable of planing at wind speeds as low as 12 knots if rigged
adequate, well-tuned sail in the six to eight square meter range. The pursuit of planing in lower and lower winds has driven the
spread of wider and shorter boards, with which planing is possible in wind speeds as low as 8 knots, if sails in the 10 to 12 square
are used.

The text runs right up to the edge of the image, leaving it with no breathing space. In order to put a bit of padding around the inline element (the image) we'll add offset values.

8. Click on the **Wrap** drop-down box on the Control Panel. Add 10 pixels of padding to the right of the image and 5 pixels to the bottom.

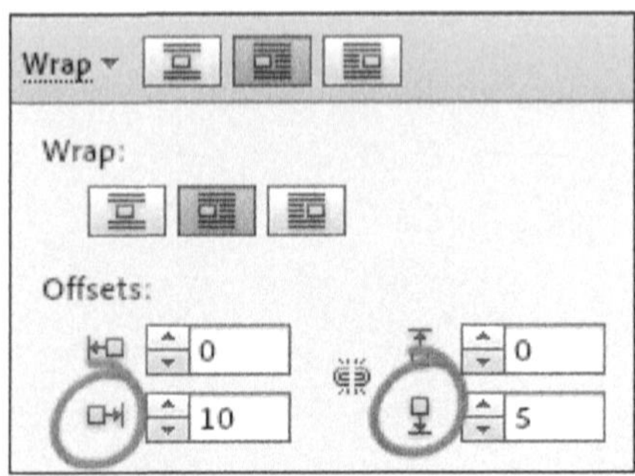

Whenever text flows around an element, make sure that the element is not so wide that it makes the text area too narrow. This can make the text very difficult to read.

Web-safe fonts

There is a list of font families that exists, and this list is known as the **safe list**. It consists of a number of font families that are supported, by default, on Windows PCs and Apple Mac computers.

It is safe to use these fonts on your websites because basically *almost* everyone has them installed on their computers. This means that if you use a font such as Georgia (which is on the list), it is safe to assume that everyone who comes to your website will see your beautiful typography as you intended them to see it.

Times New Roman
Arial
Georgia
Verdana
Comic Sans
Courier
Trebuchet

Now let's say that you've created your own gorgeous font that you really, really, really want to use, but only you and two other people in the world have it, then the problem is that everyone else will not see that font when they come to your website. They will see a replacement or a default font (possibly something like Times New Roman) and all your hard work of choosing fonts will be wasted.

So as a designer, using Muse, you have three choices. You can stick with the web-safe fonts and then you know your visitors will see your site type as you intended. You can use Typekit or (and we really want to avoid this option if possible) you can replace text with images. This means that if you want to use that unique font that no one else has, Muse will convert the text into an image which will be exported when you publish your site or export the HTML.

The disadvantage of the safe list is that it is limited both in the number of fonts and also the variety of styles (bold, italic, regular) within each font category.

The disadvantage of using images instead of type is that the search engines cannot read images in the same way they can read type. So if you want to use this method, only use it for headings. Do not use it for your main body copy.

Metadata – the hidden text on your page

In the previous section we looked at the importance of headings in relation to SEO. Another important factor to consider is your page's **metadata**.

Metadata is data about data. In simple terms, it's the information about the web page. It is invisible to your human visitors but is visible to the search engines that come to your site. Metadata is stored in meta tags that are hidden in the `<head>` of the HTML document. As we're using Muse, we don't need to worry about the `<head>` and `<body>` tags but we do still need to put the metadata into each of our pages.

The two most important Meta tags used in SEO are description and keywords. Here's how we add them:

1. With the **Gear** page open in the Design view, choose **Page | Page Properties**. The page properties dialog box opens.
2. Click on the **Metadata** tab to see a window similar to the following screenshot:

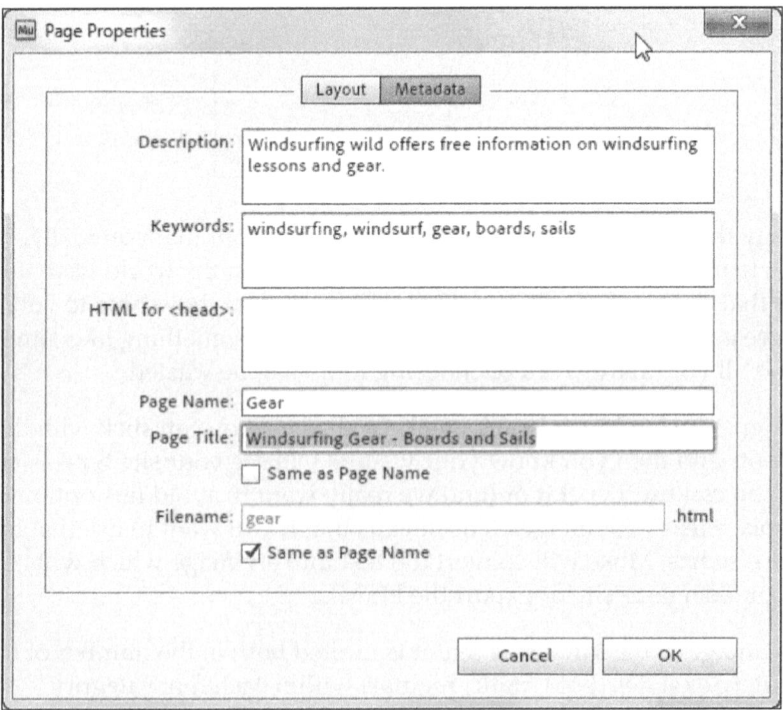

Here's a brief explanation of the options in the Metadata category:

- **Description** specifies the description of your page.
- **Keywords** specifies the keywords for your page.
- **HTML** for <head> allows us to place HTML code into our Muse pages. An example of this would be adding Google Analytics code to track how many visitors the page has.
- **Page Name** is the name of the page as it appears in Muse.
- **Page Title** is the title of the page that appears in the browser. Select the **Same as Page Name** option if you want Muse to use the page name for the page title as well. (It's the default selection.) Using a descriptive page title can help with your SEO efforts while giving your visitors a quick overview of what the page is about.
- **File Name** is the name of the file that will load in a browser. Muse appends the `.html` file extension to the filename by default. Select the **Same as Page Name** option if you want Muse to use the page name for the filename as well. (It's the default selection.)
- You need to add metadata to each of the pages in your website individually. It only takes a minute or two per page and is an important part of your overall SEO efforts.

Summary

In this chapter we looked at how to add and style text on our web pages. We saw how to combine images and text, wrapped together in a text frame. We discussed the importance of headings both from an organizational and SEO point of view, and we saw how to add the hidden (to human visitors) metadata to our pages.

In the next chapter we will learn how to work with images within Muse and how to bring in images from Photoshop.

7 Working with Images

While designing web pages, we use images that are eye-catching and interesting focal points for visitors. Images are used for everything from background images to bullet points. In this chapter, we'll add images to our website, transform them, change their opacity, and look at how Muse is tightly integrated with Photoshop.

In this chapter, you will be learning the following topics:

- Choosing a suitable file format for your images
- Placing an image
- Duplicating an image
- Resizing, rotating, cropping, and positioning an image
- Adding effects to an image
- Setting image opacity
- Pinning an image
- Pasting an image from another program
- Using an image as a background
- Grouping multiple objects together to work with them as a single object

Using images within your content can be a powerful way of capturing visitors' attention and communicating your message. Images can draw people towards parts of the pages they may not have looked at during a quick scan. If used effectively, they are a powerful tool for guiding your visitor's eyes to where you want them.

Hello web-friendly images

When we're designing our websites, it's important to keep in mind that images that are destined for the Web need to be prepared accordingly. Unlike the world of print where we can use huge file sizes at very high resolution, on the Web we need to compromise between a low size of image file and a high-quality image. Before we even open Muse, we make that compromise by following these steps:

1. **Set the correct dimensions and resolution for the image:** You need to decide how big your image should be and save it at that size before you bring it into Muse. While it is possible to resize an image in Muse (and we'll take a look at that shortly), it's good practice to save the image at the correct dimensions in Photoshop, Illustrator, or whatever graphics editor you're using.
2. **Decide which file format you want to use:** Image files used on the Web are saved as JPEG, GIF, or PNG. Almost all the web browsers recognize and are compatible with these file formats. (Each file format has been explained in *Choosing the best file format* section.)
3. **Save and compress the file**: If you're using Photoshop or Illustrator to create your images, choose **File** | **Save for Web & Devices** to scale your images down to the smallest file size possible while keeping the quality reasonably high. If you're using another graphics editor, save your file in either a JPEG, GIF, or PNG format by choosing **File** | **Save As**.

Following these steps will produce images that look good and download quickly.

Choosing the best file format

Before we start going crazy with our images on the website, we need to understand some basics about the type of image file formats we can use on the Web and how to choose the best one for the job. As mentioned, there are three image formats that are supported by nearly all web browsers. The one you pick depends on how many colors are there in your image and whether it has any transparent areas.

They are as follows:

1. JPEG
2. GIF
3. PNG

Here's an overview of each image file format:

JPEG

JPEG (`.jpg`) stands for **Joint Photographic Experts Group** and was developed to store photographic images. This format supports millions of colors, but is known as a lossy format, meaning it throws away fine details to compress the image into a smaller file.

The good news is that we can choose the level of compression when we save an image in a JPEG format. It's possible to set the amount of compression on a scale of 0–100 (0 is the highest compression and lowest quality; 100 is the least compression and highest quality).

Unlike GIF and PNG images, JPEG images can provide fairly small file sizes at 24-bit color. This makes them great for any type of photography or graphics with heavy textures or long gradients.

In order to avoid the visual artefacts that can appear when you save a JPEG image, think carefully about the amount of compression that you apply. There's no point in having a tiny file size if the image looks rubbish. In the next screenshot, you can see an image panel showing how the file looks with no compression (top left-hand side), 70 percent quality, 35 percent quality, and 17 percent quality. The lower the quality, the greater the compression. You can see how the image starts to look pixelated at a lower quality.

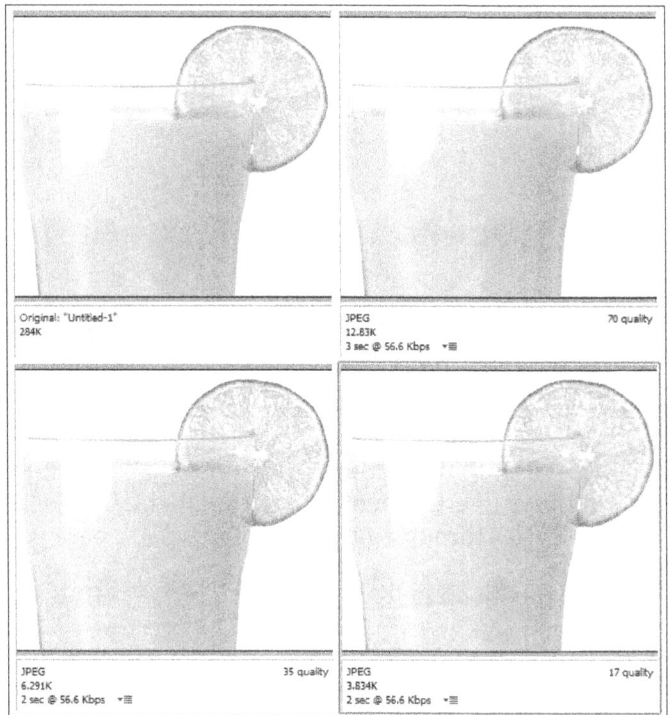

GIF

Graphics Interchange Format (GIF) is a good choice when working with solid blocks of color, a logo for example, or with line art having no gradients. Say you want your logo on your website to blend seamlessly into the background of a web page, you could save the image with no background and save it as a GIF. JPEG won't work in this situation as all graphics editors automatically stick a solid background behind any empty spaces in a JPEG.

GIF only supports 256 colors so it doesn't work very nicely with photographic images which require millions of colors.

GIF can also be a lossy format if you want it to be. The strange thing is, the quality scale works in the opposite way to JPEG, that is, 0 is lossless and 100 is full-on lossy. If you don't want to use lossy compression, you can change the file size by limiting the number of colors included in your image between 2 and 256 colors. Fewer colors results in a smaller file size.

One of the most important features of the GIF format is that it supports transparency. This means you can see through parts of the image, removing the square look or surrounding white box that would appear if saved as a JPEG. In the image in the following screenshot, the checkerboard squares represent the transparent areas of the image:

Another nice feature of GIF is that they support animation. You could create a mini-slideshow or a simple advertisement using animated GIFs. An animated GIF is simply a file that cycles through a number of images, creating the illusion of animation.

PNG

The **Portable Networks Graphics** (**PNG**) format could almost be considered as the offspring of the JPEG and GIF formats. It was developed by the W3C as an alternative to GIF and works with both transparency and millions of colors.

There are two types of PNG images. They are PNG 8 and PNG 24. The number reflects the number of bits saved in each format. PNG 24 supports millions of colors and produces super high-quality images, but the file size tends to be quite large. PNG 8 supports 256 colors. Both file formats support transparency. PNG is a relatively new format. If you know that your web audience is using older versions of Internet Explorer, then it's best to stick with a GIF, otherwise you're safe with PNG on the latest browsers.

In the next screenshot, you can see a photographic image of a t-shirt saved in a PNG format with a transparent background on the left-hand side and a gradient background on the right-hand side:

Web-safe colors – a thing of the past?

In *Chapter 6, Typography*, we discussed the idea of web-safe fonts and how the Web has moved on a little bit from there. The concept of web-safe colors is also going the way of the dodo and is not really a consideration unless you know your target audience is using ancient monitors that can only display 256 colors.

Just to give a very brief history lesson, web-safe colors were a small palette of fewer than 256 colors that would display properly on both Windows computer and Mac computer monitors. Today's monitors can show literally millions of colors; even the phone in your pocket can handle more colors today than those old monitors.

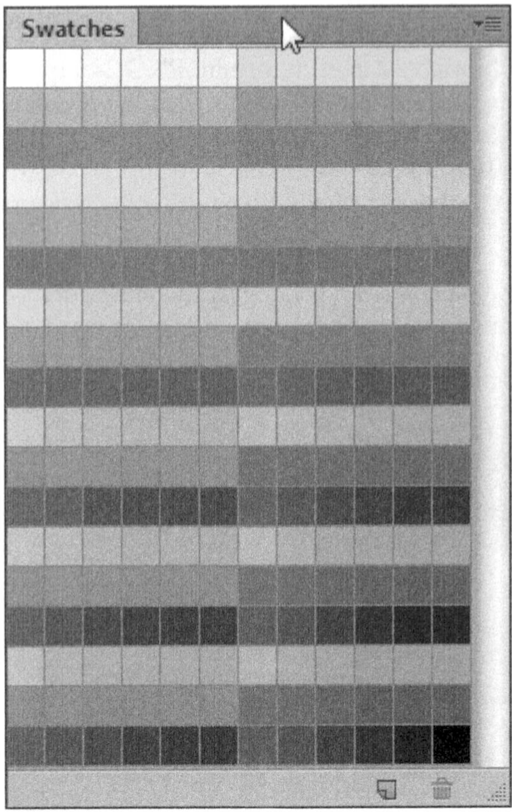

If you're using Photoshop or Illustrator to create your graphics, you'll see that when you choose **Save for Web & Devices**, you can still convert the colors in your image to their web-safe equivalent by using the **Color Table** section. You can also see the web-safe color palette by using the context-sensitive menu on the **Swatches** panel in both of these programs. However, it is highly unlikely that we will ever need to use that option again for web graphics.

Getting images onto your page

Now that we know which kind of images are suitable for the Web, we can go about putting them onto our pages. In Muse, images behave in the same way as rectangles.

Placing an image

In *Chapter 5, The Joy of Rectangles*, we saw how we could insert an image by drawing a rectangle and adding an image to it. Now we'll see how to place an image into one of our Windsurfing pages by performing the following steps:

1. Open your Windsurfing site that we've been working on.
2. In **Plan** view, double-click on the **Sails** page to open it in **Design** view. Turn on the rulers and guidelines to help you position the image on the page.

> Note: If you've been following the exercises in the book, your **Sails** page will have a red background, which we set in *Chapter 4, Powerful Pages*. We'll change it back shortly, so it matches the blue background of the rest of the website.

3. In **Design** view, choose **File | Place**.
4. Browse and select the image or images that you want to place on the page and click **Open** (Windows) or **Select** (Mac OS). You can select more than one image at a time by holding down *Ctrl* button (Windows) or *Cmd* button (Mac OS) while you click. In this exercise, we'll start by adding one image.
5. Choose the `Sails.jpg` image from the folder of this chapter.

6. The cursor changes to a place gun which we use to place the image or images on the page. If you selected multiple images as you loaded the gun, simply click the same number of times to place each image on the page one-by-one.

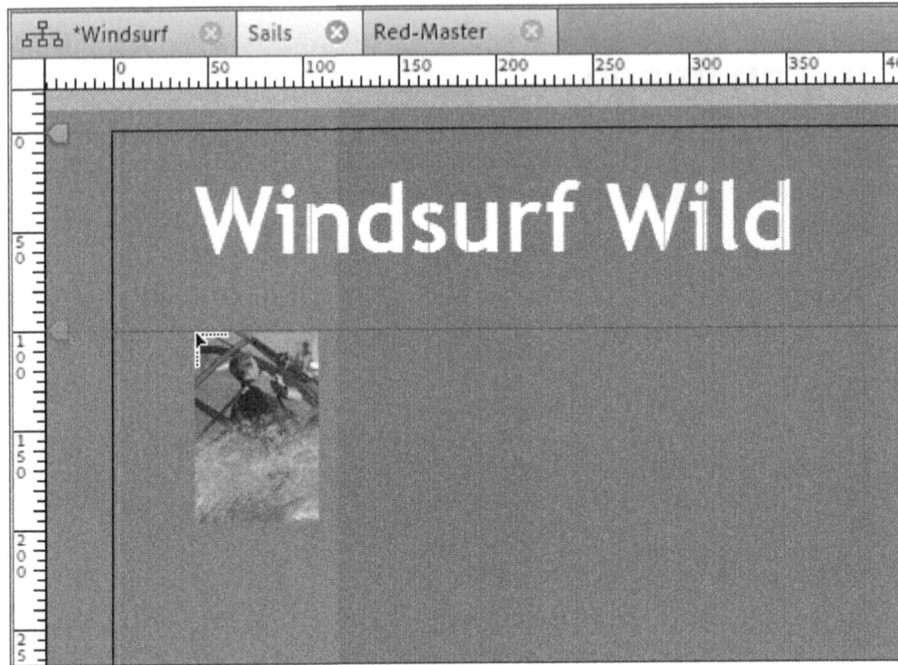

7. For now, click once to place your image on the page at its original size (100 percent) so it lines up under the **Windsurf Wild** text at around 150 pixels from the top of the page. We'll position the image more precisely in just a moment. As soon as you click, your image is placed on the page.

Adding alternative text

It's very important to add alternate text tags to all images on your site. It helps to make the site more accessible for everyone. The alternate text appears in the browser if an image cannot be shown and is read by screen readers. In order to add alternate text perform the following steps:

1. Right-click or control-click the image you've added to the page.
2. From the **Context** menu that appears, choose **Alternate Text**. The **Image Properties** dialog box opens.
3. Fill in a text title and alternate text.

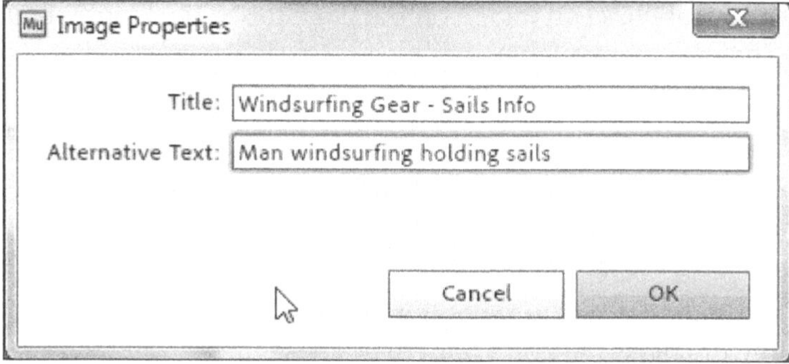

The image **Title** should provide additional information about the image. The title pops up when you hover over an image when using some browsers.

The **Alternative Text** is mainly for accessibility purposes and is read by crawlers.

The image context menu

When we add an image to a page, there are a number of additional options, as well as **Alternative Text** and **Add Title**, available to you through the **Context** menu.

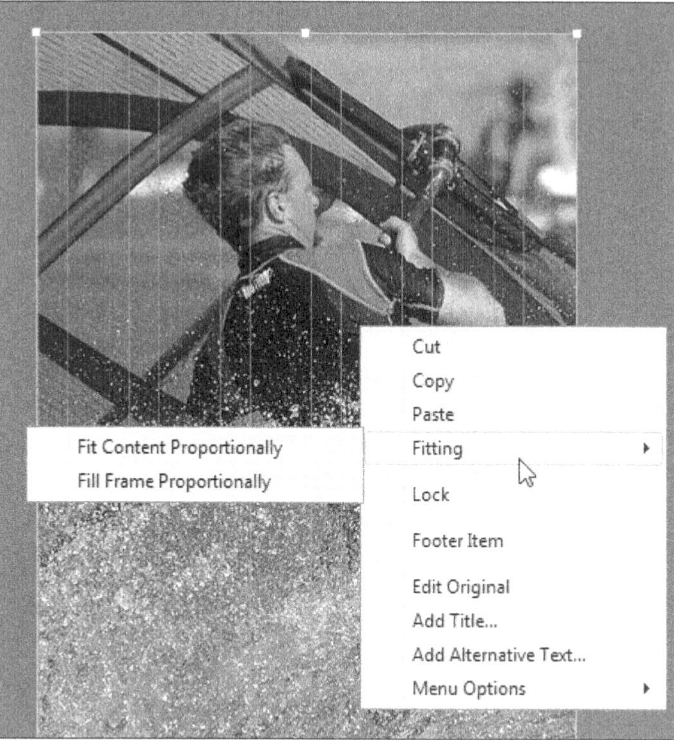

Right-click (or Control-click) an image on the page to see the Context menu appear. The following options are available:

- **Fitting**: You have two choices here: **Fit Content Proportionately** and **Fill Frame Proportionately**. The **Fit Content Proportionately** option scales the image to retain its aspect ratio within the display area. The **Fill Frame Proportionately** option crops the image, if required, to ensure that the display area is completely filled.
- **Edit Original**: This is a great option if you have used a Photoshop PSD file or a Fireworks PNG file on your page. These files could be considered the master source image file and you can click **Edit Original** and make changes to the master version of the file, to keep both copies in sync. This option is not available if you copied and pasted an image onto a page.
- **Lock:** This locks the image into position on the page, meaning the image cannot be selected until it is unlocked. It is not the same as pinning which we'll look at a little later.

Manipulating images

In this section we're going to look at how to manipulate an image once it's on the page. We'll look at resizing, rotating, positioning, duplicating, and cropping. All of these functions are a cinch to do in Muse.

Resizing an image

Resizing an image is always best done by changing the actual size of the image in a graphics editor and then uploading it again to your site. However, if for some reason you have no access to a graphics editor, it is possible to resize it with Muse. The following are the steps to do it:

1. In **Design** view, click on the image to select it.
2. Drag the resize handles to adjust the image's width or height. You'll notice that no matter which handle you choose to drag from, Muse will constrain the image proportionally.

3. An alternative way to resize is to type values for the precise width and height of your image using the **Width** and **Height** options in the Control Panel.

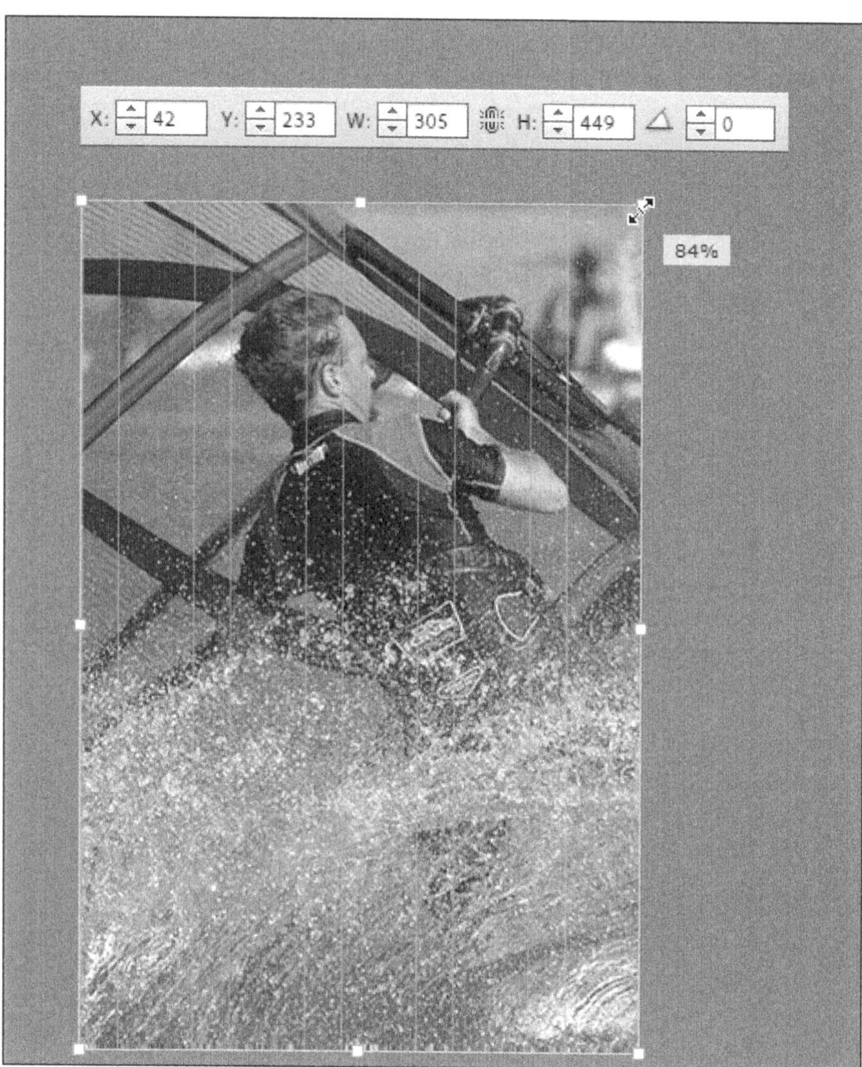

Rotating an image

It's easy to rotate an image. There are two ways to do it. They are as follows:

1. Select the image you want to rotate by clicking on it, then hover the mouse over the corner of the image until you see the rotation icon, and then click-and-drag to rotate the image manually.

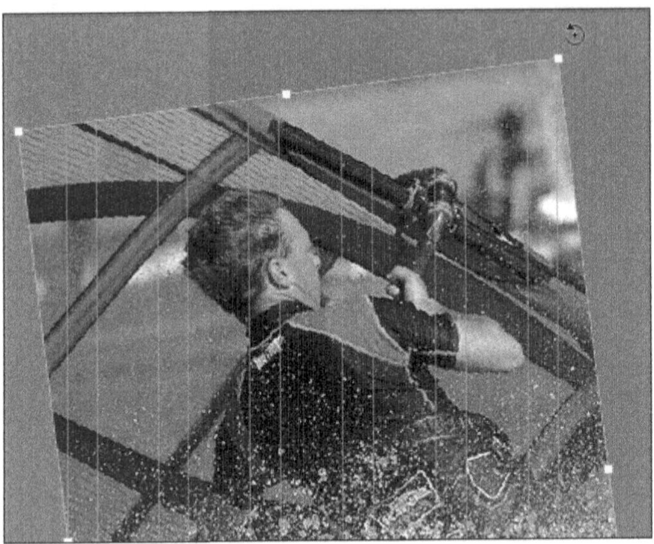

2. With the image selected, increase or decrease the rotation angle in the Control Panel. (The **Rotation Angle** option is the right-most option in the Control Panel.)

Positioning an image

Again, it's very easy to position your image anywhere you want and once again, there are two ways to do it. They are as follows:

1. Select the image you want to position, then simply drag the image to the appropriate position.

2. You can set precise X and Y coordinates for the image using the **X** and **Y** options in the control panel. Set the **X** value to **44** and the **Y** value to **160**.

Duplicating an image

If you want to make an exact copy of an image, you can do it in one of the following two ways:

1. If you are using Windows, click on the image, press the *Alt* button, and drag it. For Mac OS users, click on the image, press the *Option* button, and drag the image.

2. Choose **Edit | Duplicate**. If duplicating to a different page, then **Copy** and **Paste** is another option. If you want to put the image at the exact spot on the second page, choose **Edit | Paste In Place**.

Cropping an image

In some situations, we can create a more interesting image by cropping a photograph. By reducing unnecessary background in an image we can create a greater sense of drama or, by changing the focus of the image we can make it more eye-catching. Ideally, you would do your cropping in a graphics editor and then bring the image into Muse, but sometimes as a timesaver, we can do it all in Muse.

In other situations, the background gives an important sense of context and should definitely not be removed.

In the following exercise, we'll add an image to the **Boards** page, then crop away some of the background by performing the following steps:

1. Open the **Boards** page in **Design** view. Using the steps outlined in the section *Placing an image*, add the `Boards.jpg` image to the page.
2. This is quite a large image and when you place it on the page, the right-hand side will overlap the edge of the page. You find it useful to zoom out to about 75 percent magnification so that you can see the handles on the image when we use the **Crop** tool.
3. With the image still selected, click on the **Crop** tool in the **Tools** panel.
4. Drag the handles on the left and right-hand sides of the image to crop the original into a narrower image, about 420 pixels wide. Drag the handles on the top and bottom of the image to crop vertically to a height of about 600 pixels.

5. Drag the top resize handle downwards to crop away the sky above the board. Check the height on the control bar as you drag and crop the image to 450 pixels high.

6. If you want to, you can reposition the image inside the crop area. To do this, hover over the image until you see the circle icon at the center of the image. Grab the circle and move the image around within the cropped mask, till it looks something like the next screenshot:

7. Finally, position the newly cropped image at X coordinate setting of 44 and Y coordinate of 160 pixels using the fields in the control bar at the top of the screen.

Adding effects to an image

You can add effects, such as drop shadows, bevels, and glows to an image in the same way as we added them to rectangles in *Chapter 5, The Joy of Rectangle*. See the section on *Adding Effects to Rectangles*.

Pasting an image from another program

Let's say you've been working on an image in another program such as Adobe Photoshop or Illustrator and you want to quickly take it into Muse, it's just a simple matter of copy and paste.

You need to perform the following steps:

1. In another program, such as Photoshop, copy your image using the menu options, or press *Ctrl* +*C* (Windows) or *cmd* + *C* (Mac OS) on your keyboard.
2. Open the web page you want to put the image on in **Design** view in Muse and paste the image by choosing **Edit | Paste**, or by using *Ctrl* + *V* (Windows) or *cmd* + *V* (Mac OS) on your computer's keyboard.

Working with background images

We're going to go back and make some changes to the blue master page and then apply that master to our two red gear pages. The blue master page currently contains the temporary logo text **Windsurf Wild** which we'll replace with a semi-transparent logo image.

Adding a logo

Most websites contain a logo in the same place at the top of each page. Usually the logo is also a link to the home page. In the following steps we'll do just that on our site.

1. In **Plan** view, double-click on the blue **A-Master** page.
2. Right-click anywhere on the page and choose **Show Header And Footer** from the context sensitive menu. You'll see additional guidelines appear horizontally to represent the areas at the top and bottom of the page which are the header and footer sections.
3. Click on the words **Windsurf Wild** to select it, then press *Delete* on the keyboard to remove the text.
4. Choose **File | Place** and browse to select the `logo.png` image. Click once to place the image.

5. Using the control bar, set the X position at 44 and Y position at 0.

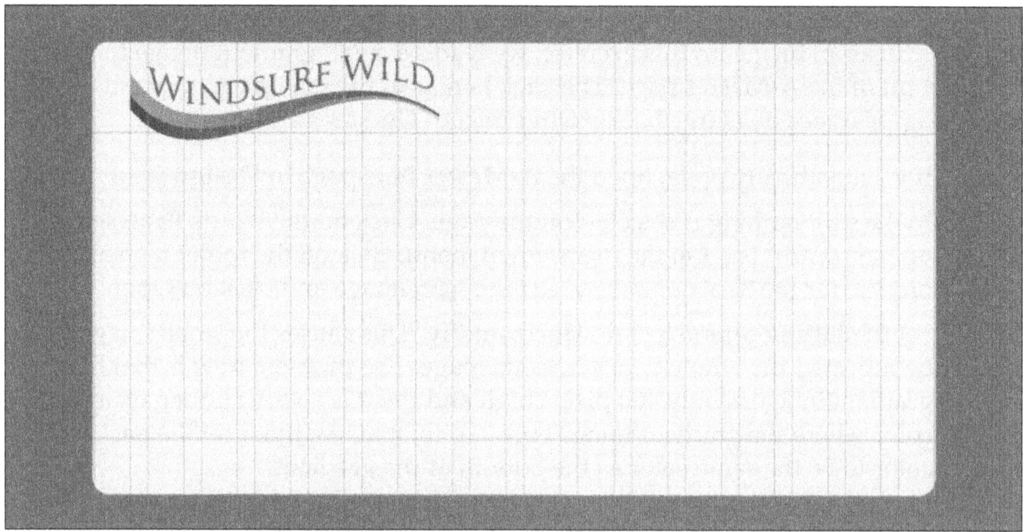

Adding a link to a logo

We want our logo to be a link back to the home page. When someone clicks on the logo, they will always be brought to the home page. This provides consistency on every page.

With the logo still selected, click on the drop-down menu beside the word **Hyperlink** on the control bar. Choose **Home** from the list of pages.

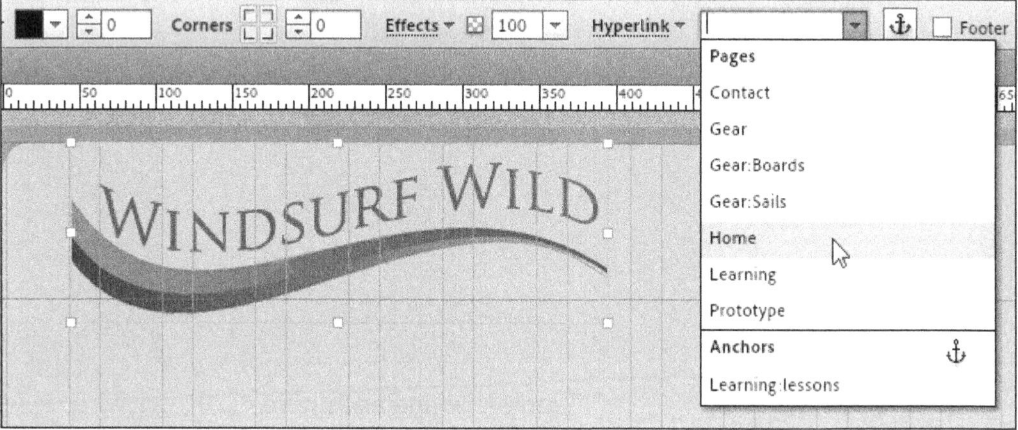

Using a tiled image as a background

To use an image as a background for an object or a page, we need to set the object or page's fill as an image. In this exercise, we'll add a small gradient image to the background of the **A-Master** page. The trick here is to tile the image horizontally to give the appearance of a large background image. The steps are as follows:

1. If it's not already open, open the **A-Master** blue page in **Design** view.
2. Make sure nothing is selected on the page. Click on the words **Browser Fill** on the control bar. On the drop-down menu, click on the folder icon and browse for the `Background-Gradient.png` image and click on **Open**.
3. Set the **Fitting** option to **Tile Horizontally**. This causes the small image to be repeated the whole way across the page. The problem now is that the gradient image is only 400 pixels high and there is a very sudden change in color where the gradient image ends. To fix that, we must set the background color to be the same color as the bottom of the gradient.

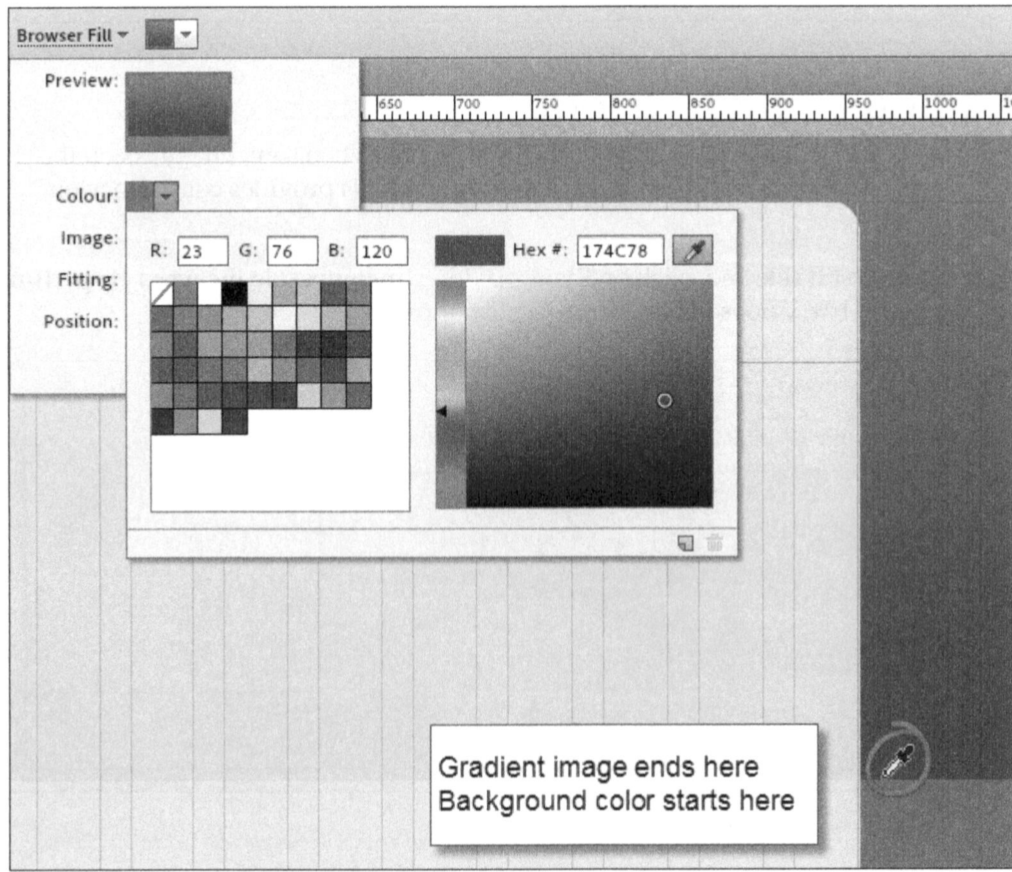

4. Click on the **Colour** swatch. The Color Picker panel opens.
5. Click on the Eye Dropper tool in the top right-hand side of the panel and then click at the bottom of the background gradient image. As soon as you click, the background color changes and we get the illusion of the gradient image continuing down the page. The great thing about this method is that we have used a small image, 30 pixels wide by 400 pixels high, and now have the appearance of a much larger image filling the background of our page.

Using a photographic image as a background image

Photographic images as backgrounds have been popular on the Web for years. As an additional exercise, we'll add a large 1280 pixel wide image by performing the following steps:

1. On the **A-Master** page, make sure nothing is selected, then click on the **Browser Fill** button on the Control bar.
2. Click on the folder icon to choose an image. Choose the `1280RobbieNaish.jpg` image and click **Open**.
3. Click on the centre point in the **Position** grid. Try out top-centre, middle-centre and bottom-centre to see how the position of the image changes.

4. If you want the image to stay in place while allowing the rest of the content to scroll above it, turn off the Scrolling checkbox.

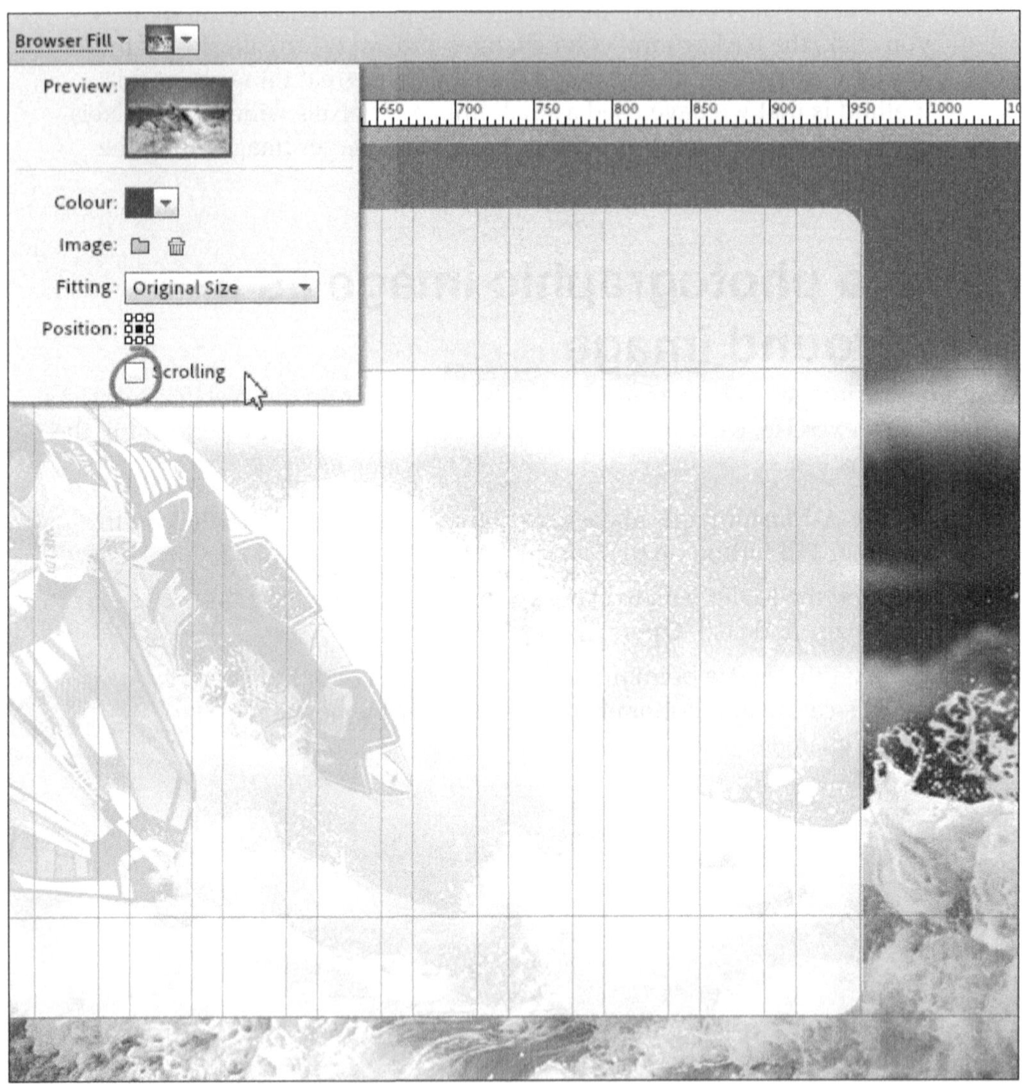

And that's how easy it is to add a large photographic image.

Now that you know how to add a photographic background, as an exercise try out some of your own images as backgrounds and see how well they work.

Check out the following tips on using background images:

- **Make sure your background doesn't distract from the content.** When you create a fixed-width design for your site (and this is currently the case for all sites created in Muse), part of the browser window will display a background. You can choose to have a solid background color or you can add a background image.
- When choosing a background color make sure there is enough contrast between the background and the body text. That means using a fairly dark background color with light-colored text or using a light-colored background with very dark-colored text. The following chart shows examples of bad contrast on the left-hand side and good contrast on the right-hand side:

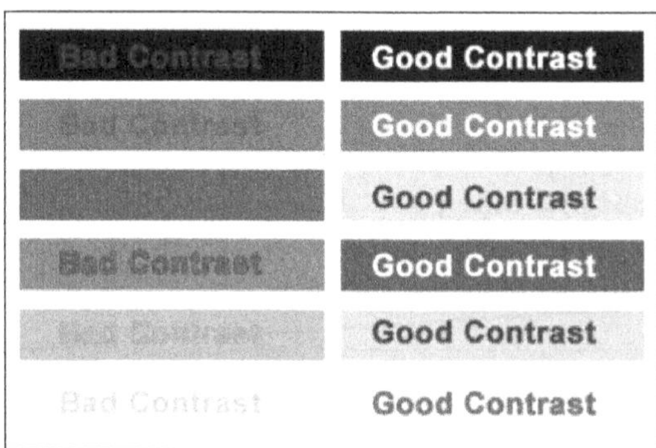

We can also set our backgrounds so they are filled completely or partially with an image. Unless otherwise specified, background images are automatically repeated over and over again by the browser. This is known as tiling, and by choosing an appropriate pattern or image, it lets us give the impression of a huge image filling the background of our website when in fact we are using a small image over and over again.

If you want to use a complex image or photo for your site background, think carefully about how it affects the text above it. Ask yourself whether you are creating clutter by using an image. Patterns in the background can work well if they're subtle or faded and are using only one or two tones. Full color patterns can be highly distracting, so use with caution.

To keep things nice and simple for this website, replace the background image of the Windsurfer with the blue gradient we applied earlier.

Pinning an image

At some stage, you have probably visited a website that carries a little badge or ribbon that floats in a specific location and doesn't move from that point. It sits persistently on the page. This effect is created by pinning the image in place. The ability to pin is a great tool in the designer's arsenal. It allows us to break out of the grid and allow content to flow around the pinned image.

To pin an image to a specific location, you use the **Pin** tool as explained in the following steps:

1. In **Design** view, open the blue **A-Master** page.
2. Place the `PinningWindsurfer.png` image on the page and keep the image selected.
3. On the Control Panel, click a position in the **Pin** tool to specify how you want to pin the image in relation to the browser. Selecting the top-center pin will pin the image in relation to the top-center of the browser. Selecting the bottom right-hand side pin will pin the image in relation to the bottom right-hand side of the browser. The best way to see how the pin works is to preview your content pages in the browser.

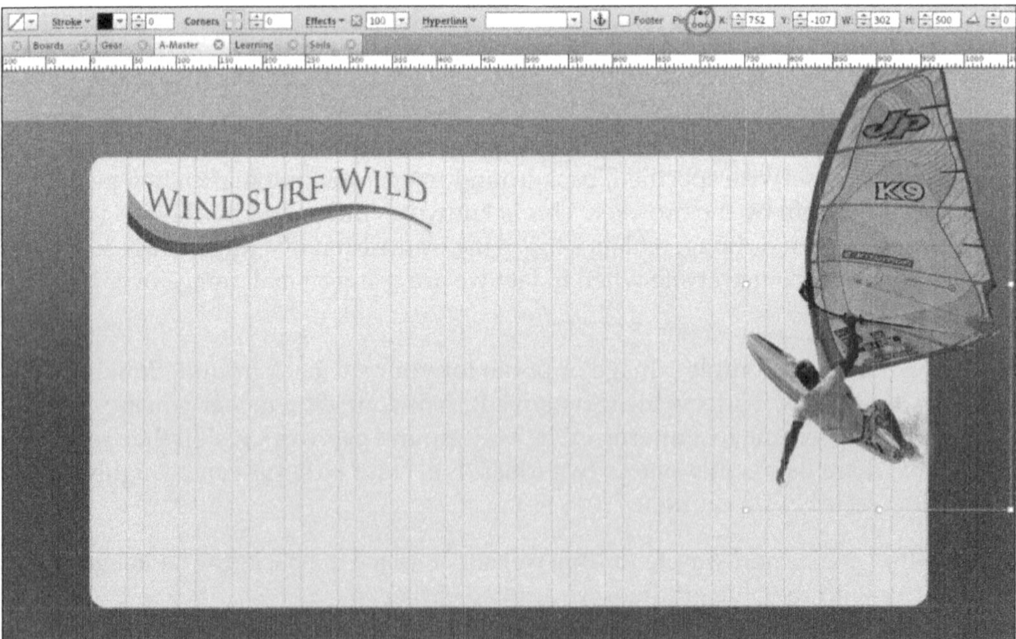

Taking care of site files with the Assets panel

The **Assets** panel show us the filenames of any image files we are using in our website, not just images on the current page. You can open the **Assets** panel by choosing **Window | Assets**. Right-click (or press *Ctrl* and click) on filenames in the **Assets** panel to see the context menu appear. If you've used Adobe InDesign, this panel is called the Links Panel.

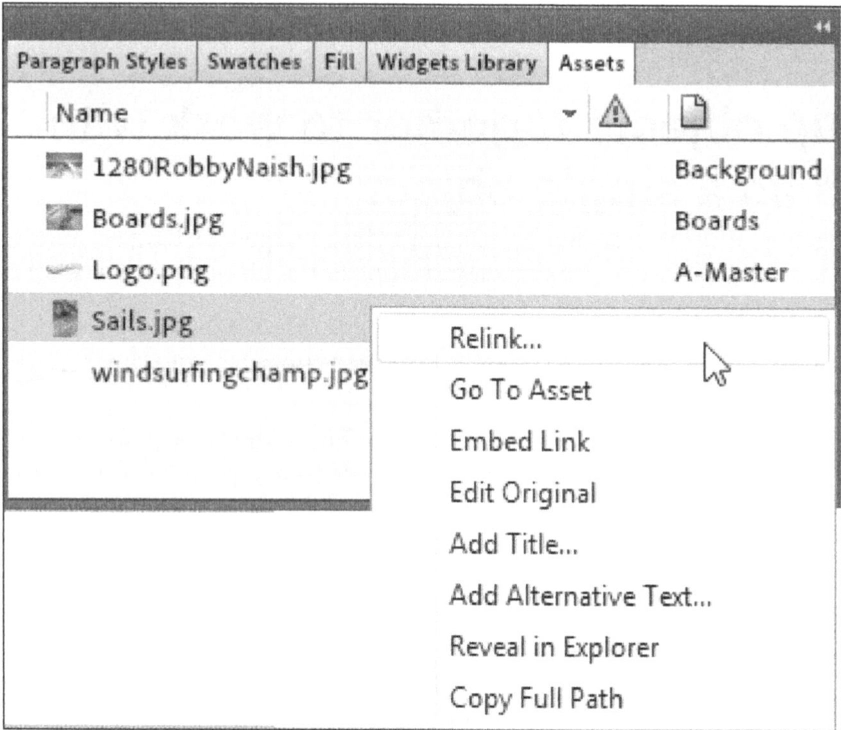

The Assets panel context menu contains the following options:

- **Relink**: This option lets you reconnect files that have been moved after they were placed on the page. When you click on this option, use the **Relink** window that appears, to navigate to the file, and select it to specify its new location to Muse.
- **Go To Asset:** Clicking on this option will take you to the page where the image or asset is located.
- **Embed Link**: Adds a link icon with the path to the asset's location on the local computer.

- **Edit Original:** This is a great option if you have used a Photoshop PSD file or a Fireworks PNG file on your page. These files could be considered the master source image file and you can click on **Edit Original** and make changes to the master version of the file, to keep both copies in sync. This option is not available if you copied and pasted an image onto a page.
- **Reveal in Explorer**: This opens the **File Explorer** (Windows) or **Finder** (Mac) and shows the folder that contains the site's assets, making it easy to locate a specific file.
- **Copy Full Path:** Copies the path to the asset's location on the local computer to the computer's clipboard.

Group objects together to work with them as a single object

You can group multiple selected objects (including images, rectangles, and text frames) as a single group to make it easy to control the placement of a set of items on a page.

1. Use the **Selection** tool to select two or more objects. Hold down *Shift* key to select more than one object at a time.
2. Right-click (or press **Ctrl** and click) and choose the **Group** option from the context menu. You can also choose **Object** | **Group** (or press *Cmd* + *G* for Mac OS).

Grouping objects

Once a set of objects is grouped, a bounding box encircles the entire group. To ungroup the objects, right-click (or press *Ctrl* and click) and choose the **Ungroup** option from the context menu that appears. Alternatively, choose **Object | Ungroup** (or press *Shift* + *Command* + *G*).

Summary

In this chapter, we learned how to add images to our pages and saw how to manipulate them by changing their position, rotating, duplicating, and cropping them. We discussed the type of image file formats that are suitable for use on the Web and how to choose the appropriate format.

In the next chapter, we'll take advantage of Muse's widgets to add extra functionality to our pages.

8
Customizing with Widgets—Menus and Panels

Welcome to the world of widgets. It used to be, not so long ago, if you wanted to add extra functionality or interactivity to your website, you would need a web developer or programmer to create it for you. Things are so much easier now, and extra interactivity in Muse comes in the shape of a widget.

Widgets are the reusable, customizable building blocks of interactivity. Examples include slideshows, panels, and menus. In this chapter, we're looking at how to use widgets to add menus using the Bar, Horizontal, and Vertical menu widgets. We'll also look at panels. These are space-saving panels that can work in a tabbed fashion or like an Accordion.

In this chapter you will learn how to:

- Add and edit widgets
- Create menu bars
- Create Horizontal menus
- Create Vertical menus
- Build an Accordion panel
- Work with Tabbed Panels

Working with widgets

All widgets are found in the Widgets Library. Select **Window | Widgets Library** to see the full complement. The **Widgets Library** panel holds **Compositions** which includes Featured News and Lightbox Display. Also in the **Widgets Library** are **Menus** which are broken into **Bar**, **Horizontal**, and **Vertical** menus. The **Panels** options include **Tabbed Panels** and **Accordion**, while the **Slideshow** options are **Basic**, **Blank**, **Lightbox**, and **Thumbnails**. We'll look at compositions and slideshows in the next chapter. Although each type of widget provides very different functionality, many of the concepts you'll use when working with widgets are the same.

Adding a widget to the page

In the **Widgets Library** panel, expand the widget category by clicking on the triangle to the left-hand side of the widget category. Select the required widget from the list as shown in the following screenshot and drag it onto the page in the Design view:

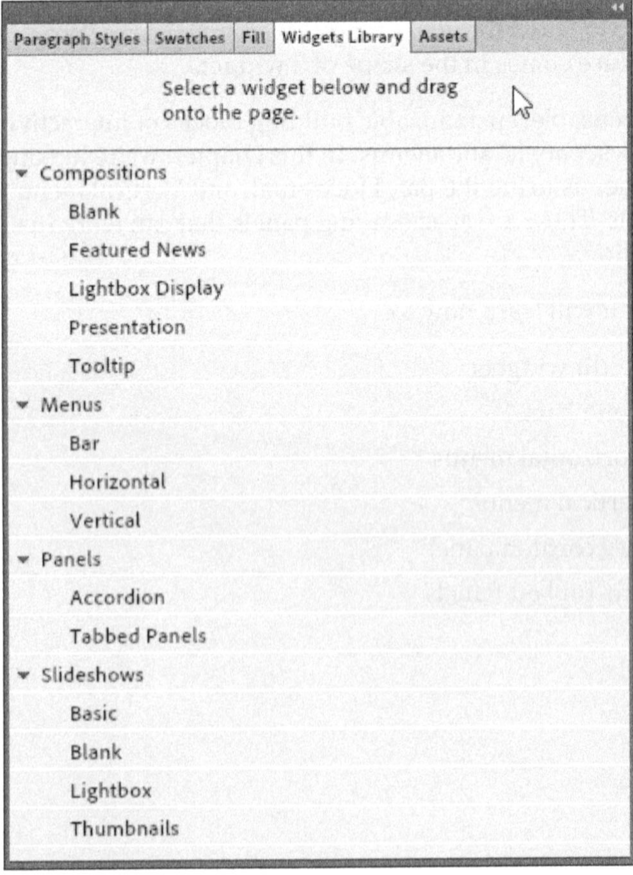

How menu widgets work

Menu widgets display website navigation on a web page. We can choose to let Muse populate the menu with the names of each of our pages using the structure we set up in the Plan view, or we can add links to the menus manually. We can set the menu to a horizontal or vertical orientation.

Menu items which are automatically populated appear with the same name as the page name displayed in the Plan view. Once we've created the menu we can still safely make changes to our website structure and those changes will automatically be updated in the menu to match to the website plan.

When we populate items manually, a plus (+) symbol appears to allow us to add new menu items or submenu items. To delete a menu item, select it and then hit *Delete* on the keyboard. Manual menu items can be rearranged by clicking-and-dragging them to reposition the items within the menu.

Adding a menu bar

Let's start our widget journey by adding a menu bar. The menu bar is something which will appear on every page of our website, so we can add it to our Master Page. As we saw in the *Pages* section of *Chapter 4, Powerful Pages*, we can use our Master Pages to hold any image, text, or object that we want to appear consistently throughout the website.

In the last chapter we made further changes to the **A-Master** panels by adding an image and pinning it to the top right corner of the page. In the next exercise, we'll add a navigation menu with just a few clicks of the mouse. Muse keeps track of all of the pages we add in the Plan view and allows us to quickly add a fully functioning menu bar with links to each of the pages. Perform the following steps to add a menu bar:

1. Open the **Windsurfing** panel in Muse's Plan view:

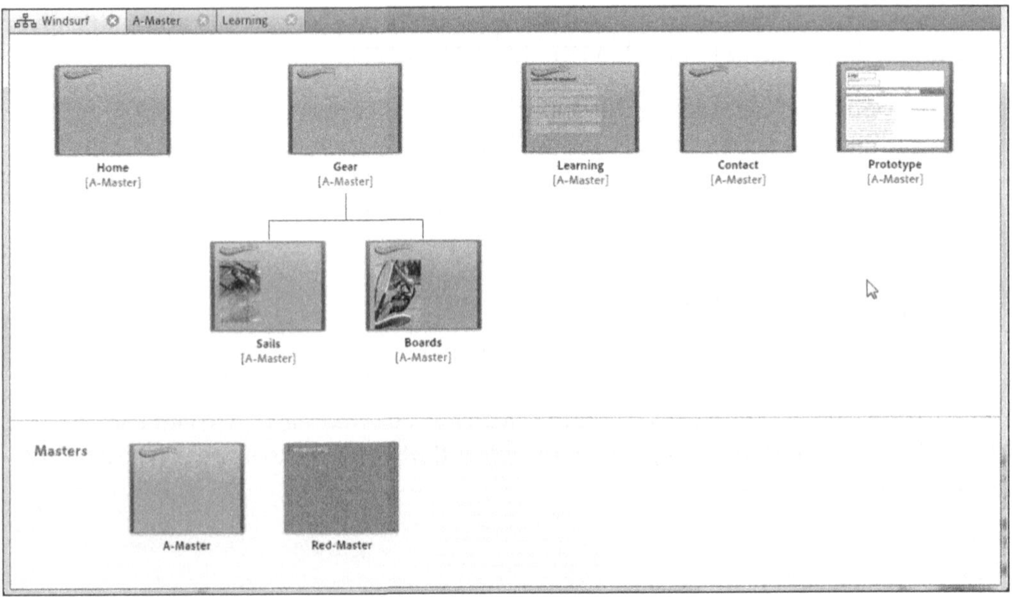

2. Double-click on the **A-Master** thumbnail to open the Master Page in the Design view.

3. From the **Widgets Library** panel, expand the **Menus** list and drag out the **Bar** widget. Place it on the page with X coordinate at 410 pixels and Y coordinate at 62 pixels, so it looks like it's sitting on the header guide as shown in the following screenshot:

Selecting the widget and its subelements

We're going to set up and format our main menu, created using the **Menu Widget** option:

1. To select the entire widget, click on it with the Selection tool. Look at the Control Panel and you'll see it displaying the words **Menu Widget** on the left-hand side.
2. Hover over individual menu items to see their outlines. Click again to select an individual menu item.
3. Click again inside the widget to select the subelements and text of the container. Notice how the name of each subelement appears in the control panel as you click on it and a bounding box on the widget indicates which element is currently selected, as shown in the following screenshot. Each time you click, you are selecting additional nested subelements of the widget, allowing you to edit each item:

When a subelement of a widget is selected, you can format the contents by changing the text, rectangle's color, or background within the boundaries of the widget itself.

Press the *Escape* key to move back up through the hierarchy of nested elements. You can keep pressing the *Escape* key until you have selected the entire widget again. Alternatively click anywhere else on the page to deselect all subelements and the entire widget.

4. Select the entire widget once more. We're going to format the widget and give a new look-and-feel to our navigation bar.

Setting widget options

There are several menu options available to us when working with widgets. Let's have a look at them now:

1. Click on the blue circle icon, to the right of the **Menu Widget** panel to open the widget's **Options** menu as shown in the following screenshot:

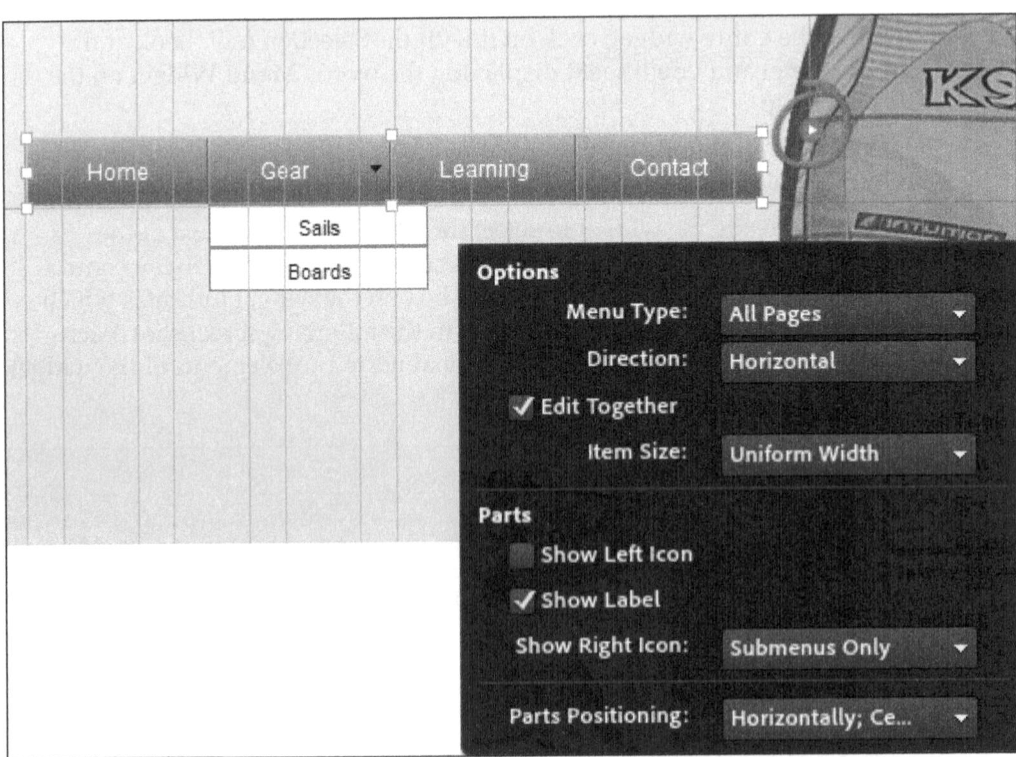

2. Set **Menu Type** to **All Pages**, set **Direction** to **Horizontal**, leave **Edit Together** checked, set **Item Size** to **Uniform Width**, and leave the rest of the options as their default settings.

   Here's an explanation of each option:

   - **Menu Type**: This specifies which items the Muse will use to build the menu. Choosing **Top Level Pages** means a menu item for each page on the top level of your site plan will appear. Choosing **All Pages** means a menu item for each page on the top level of your site plan, as well as submenu items for any child pages will appear. Manual menu types allow you to add menu items manually in the Design view.
   - **Menu Direction**: This lets you pick either horizontal or vertical orientation for your menu.
   - **Edit Together**: When the **Edit Together** option is selected, any changes that you make will be applied to all items in the Menu Bar widget. Deselect this option to make changes to the Menu Bar items individually.
   - **Item Size**: The options here let you specify the type of width for the menu items. **Fit Width** sets rectangles for each menu item that are only large enough to contain their respective words. **Uniform Width** creates menu items of uniform size, based on the largest word in the menu bar.
   - **Left Icon**: Checking this box sets up an image frame to the left of each menu item. You can change the icon in the image frame by using **Fill** and **Stroke** or by adding a background image to it. When unchecked, the image frame is not displayed.
   - **Label**: When checked, the menu items label are displayed. When disabled, the labels are not displayed. The label is the page name of the linked button.
   - **Right Icon**: This works in the same way as the **Left Icon**, except that the image frame appears to the right of the menu item that is displayed. When disabled, the icon is not displayed.
   - **Parts Positioning**: This lets you specify the horizontal and vertical alignment of the menu items.

3. With the entire widget still selected, click on the **Spacing** tab. If it's not visible, choose **Window | Spacing**. Add padding to the left and right and increase the size of the **Gutter**. The **Gutter** is the space between each menu item. On the Control Panel set the **Fill** color to **None**. The following screenshot shows how the changes in the **Spacing** panel makes the menu look:

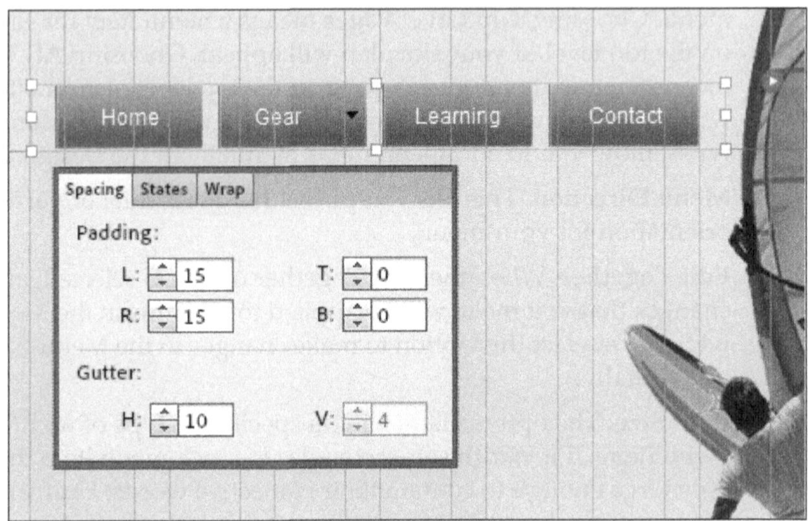

Formatting each menu item

Now that we've made changes to the widget container, we need to select a menu item to change the background color as the current dark gray gradient is a background image on the menu item.

1. With the widget container selected, click once more on any of the menu items. We've now drilled down a level. You'll notice on the Control Panel, that the **Selector** changes to **Menu Item**. You'll also see that the **Fill** for the menu item is set to dark gray.

2. Click on the word **Fill** and from the drop-down menu, set the **Fill Type** to **Solid**, and from the **Color Swatch** picker select **None**. This removes the background color:

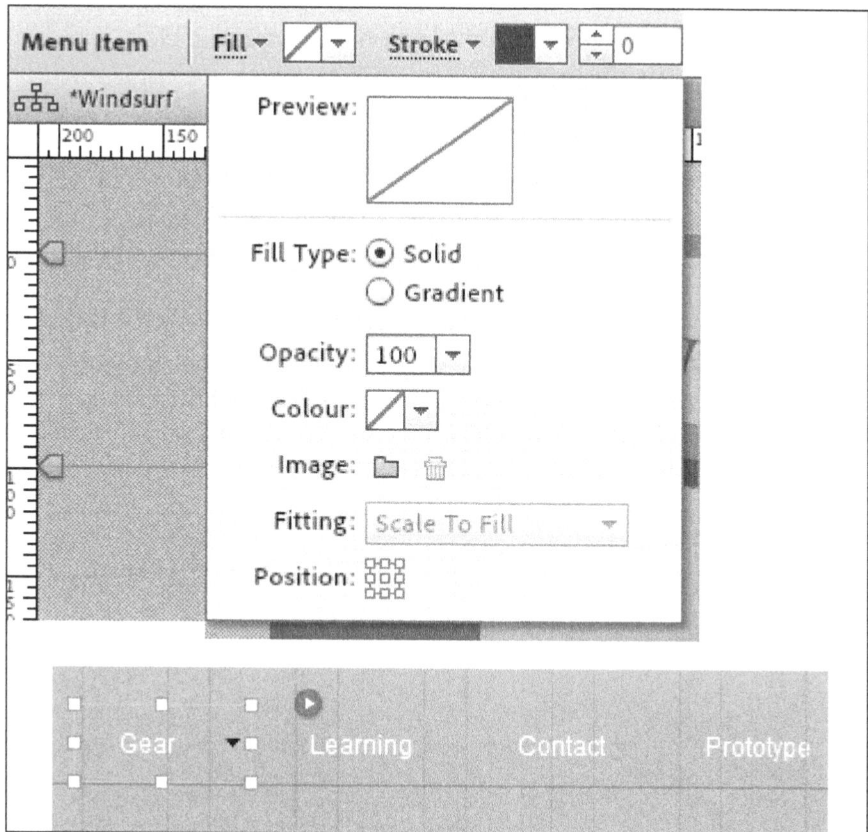

3. Select the **Text** tool, set the **Font Family** to **Arial**, **Bold**, and **Size** to **14**. Set the **Colour** to `#174C78`. Because we set the Menu Widget options earlier to **Edit Together,** all of the menu items change together.

Adding states

We can use the **States** panel to format the appearance of the links in the widget as a visitor interacts with them.

1. With the menu item still selected, click on the **States** panel.

   You'll see four states listed:

   - **Normal**: how the link looks when the page loads
   - **Rollover**: how the link looks when the mouse is rolled over it
   - **Mouse Down**: how the link looks when it is clicked
   - **Active**: how the link looks on the current page

   We've already set up the **Normal** state, next we'll work on the **Rollover** state.

2. Click on the **Rollover** state in the **States** panel and make changes to the background color and text color of the menu item. Set the background color to bright blue, the text color to white, remove any stroke, and set **Corners** to **15**, as shown in the following screenshot:

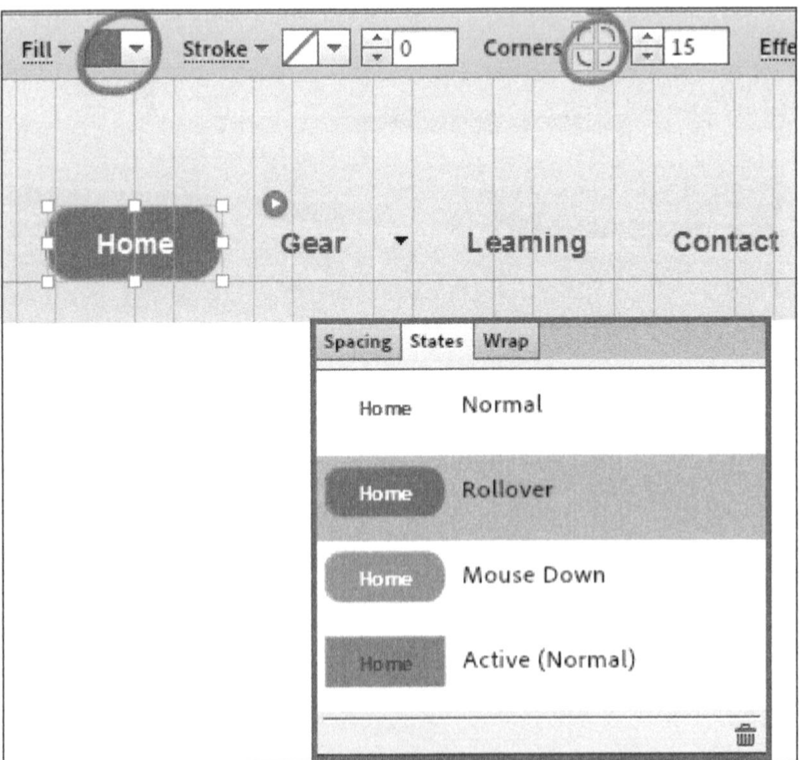

3. Repeat the previous step for the **Mouse Down** and **Active** states. Make each of the states look slightly different from each other. The point here is to provide visual feedback to website visitors. The following screenshot shows the **Mouse Down** and **Active** states:

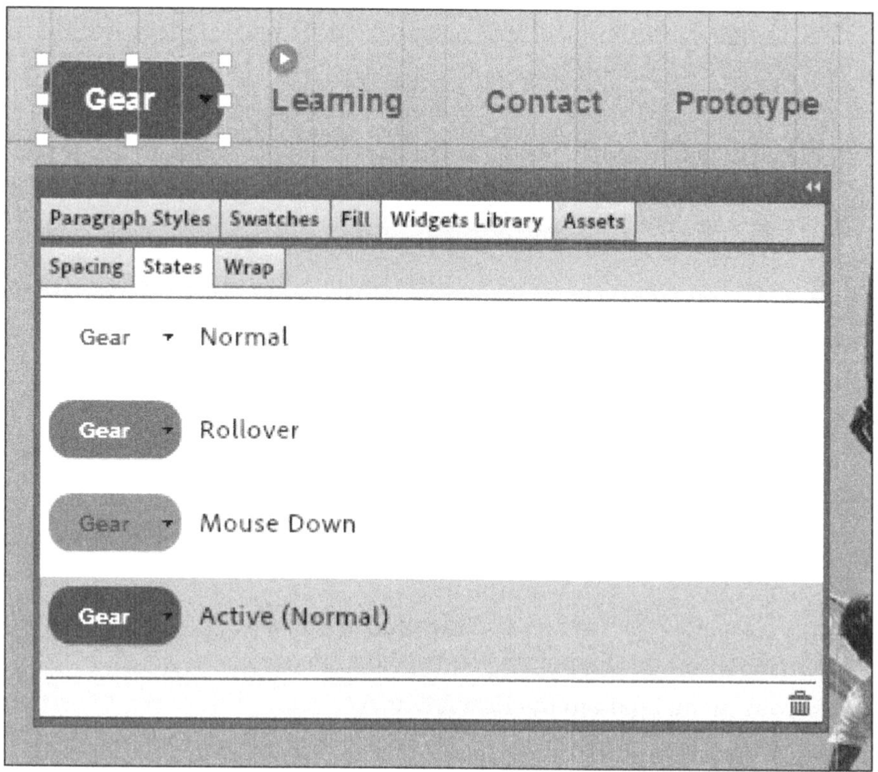

4. We need to test that our menu is working. Because we applied it to a Master Page, it should now appear on all of our pages with that master applied. Click on the **Preview** view and test your menu system to see how each state works. You should be able to click through each page in your site.
5. The **Gear** page has two subpages called **Boards** and **Sails**. We need to apply styles to the submenu for these pages. Open up the Master Page again and click once on the menu bar to select it, and once more on **Gear** to select that individual menu item. This will reveal the submenu items.

6. Click once on the **Sails** submenu item. The concept here is exactly the same as with the top-level menu items. We can set up four states for each submenu item. Notice that the **Boards** item changes style even though the **Sails** item is selected in the following screenshot. Again this happens because we chose **Edit Together** as an option in the **Menu** options:

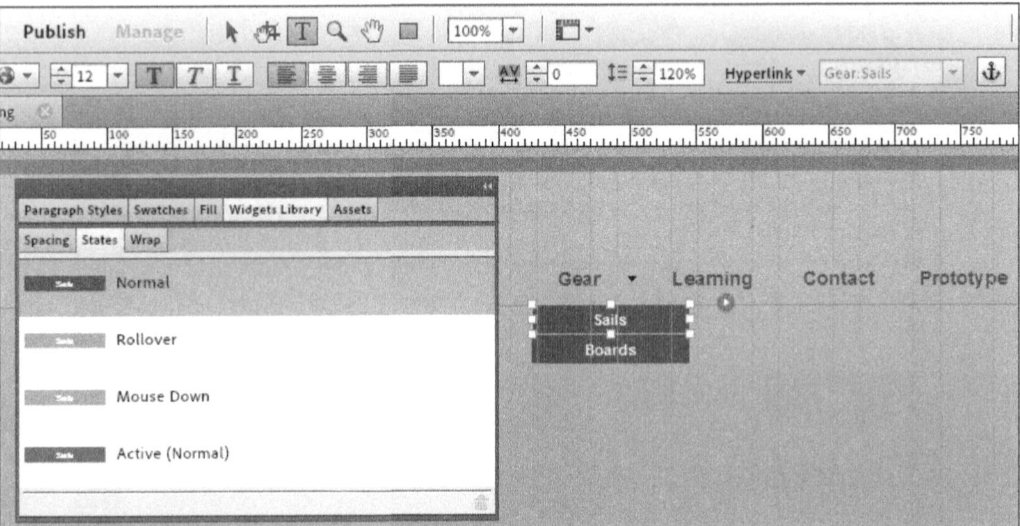

7. Apply a style for each state. Use the blue, navy, and white colors we've worked with so far, to maintain consistency.
8. Test your menu again in the **Preview** view.

Transferring a style

When you've created a style, you can copy it and then apply it elsewhere. Let's say for example, that you wanted to repeat the look-and-feel of the menu we've created at the top of our page, with a similar menu in the footer of the page. Here's how we do it:

> When you have styled the appearance of a widget, make sure the styled widget is selected first, then right-click (or *Ctrl* + click) on the unstyled widget, and choose **Transfer Widget Skin** from the context menu that appears, as shown in the following screenshot. Within a second or two, the new menu will be styled in exactly the same way as the first menu:

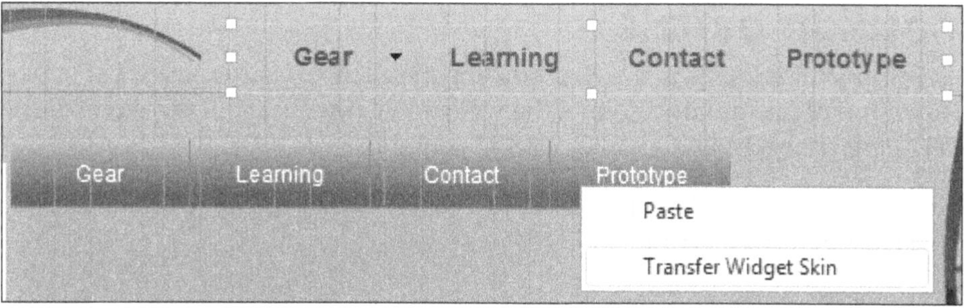

Horizontal menus

Everything we've looked at in relation to a Bar Menu is also applicable to Horizontal and Vertical menus.

To create a horizontal menu, simply click-and-drag it out from the **Menus** section in the **Widgets Library** panel. Once the menu is on the page, you can style it using the same options as the Bar Menu.

Vertical menus

To create a Vertical menu, click-and-drag it out from the **Menus** section in the **Widgets Library** panel. The obvious difference here is that the menu item appears one under the other. The submenus fly out horizontally, as shown in the following screenshot:

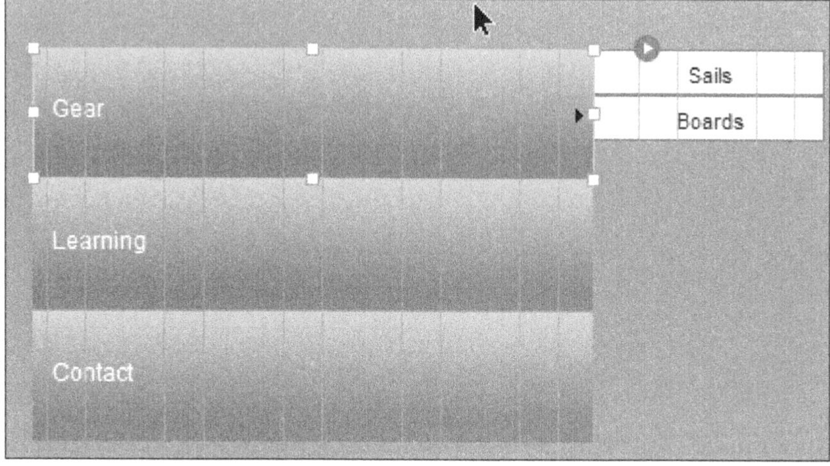

Accordion panels

Next on our list of widgets is the **Accordion** panel. This consists of several panels stacked on top of one another. When the website visitor clicks on the **Accordion** tab, that tab opens a larger panel displaying the content.

This widget allows us to display a lot of text in a small area and adds interactivity to our website.

Adding a panel

Perform the following steps to add a panel:

1. Open the **Boards** page in the Design view.
2. On the **Widgets Library** panel, click-and-drag out an **Accordion** widget. Drop it underneath the **Boards** heading.
3. Drag the right side of the panel to a width of approximately 500 pixels. You can set the width precisely by selecting the **Accordion** panel and then fill in the width field on the Control Panel, as shown in the following screenshot:

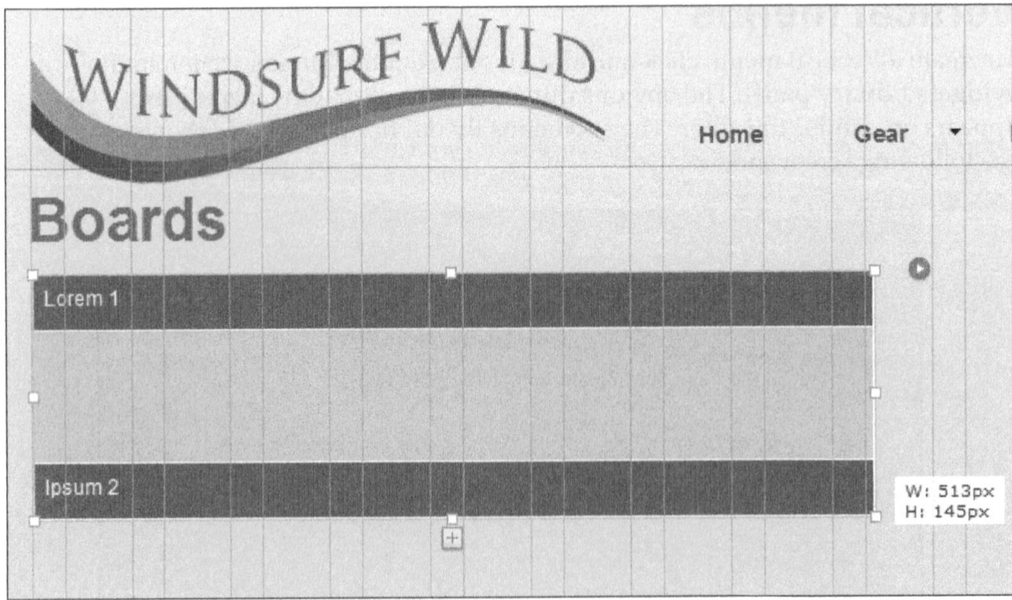

4. Click on the plus (+) icon that appears at the bottom of the widget. This adds another panel to the group. We now have three panels inside our widget.
5. Click on the first panel's name—currently **Lorem 1**. Using the **Text** tool, change the text to read **Freeride**.

6. Click in the large light-gray area underneath the panel to select it and add content. Again using the **Text** tool, draw out a rectangle. Paste in the text from the `Boards-Panel1.txt` file. In this situation, we're adding text but we could add images or other types of content inside the panel either.
7. Choose the **Preview** view so you can see exactly how the panel widget works. Click on each of the panel names and notice how each panel collapses and expands smoothly in an accordion fashion, as shown in the following screenshot:

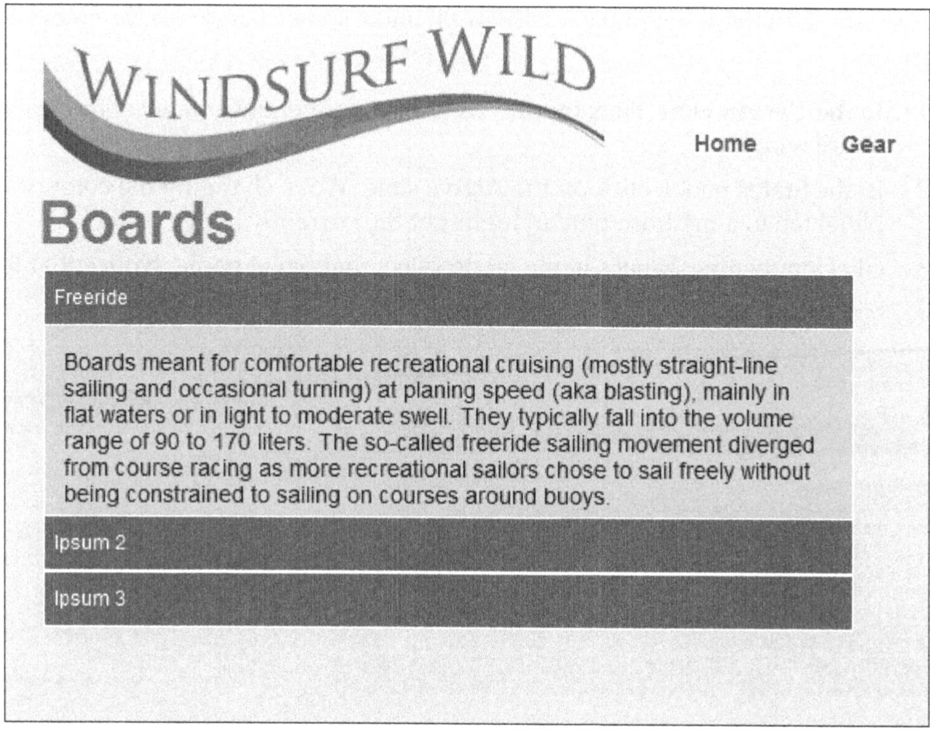

8. Click on the second panel's name—currently **Ipsum 2**. Using the **Text** tool, change the text to read **Wave**.
9. Click in the large light-grey area underneath that panel to select it and add content. Again using the **Text** tool, draw out a rectangle. Paste in the text from the `Boards-Panel2.txt` file.
10. Click on the third panel's name—currently **Ipsum 3**. Using the **Text** tool, change the text to read **Freestyle**.
11. Click in the large light-gray area underneath that panel to select it and add content. Again using the **Text** tool, draw out a rectangle. Paste in the text from the `Boards-Panel3.txt` file.

So that's our content in place. Check it out under the **Preview** view and watch the smooth action of the panels opening and closing. Widgets dynamically adjust their size to accommodate the content placed in them. You will have seen that the text frame you just placed in each panel grew as you added text. Each panel grew vertically to accommodate the additional content you placed inside them.

Editing Accordion widget elements

You can select the entire widget, an entire panel (including its tab), or a single tab in order to edit it. In the following exercise, we'll make some changes to the colors of the panels:

1. In the **Design** view, click on the **Accordion** widget once to select the entire widget.
2. In the **States** panel, click on the **Active** state. We're changing the color of the panel tab to a medium blue to highlight the currently active panel.
3. Click on the first panel's name tab to select that panel name. Notice that the Control Panel selector says **Text Frame**. Set the **Fill** color to `#174C78`:

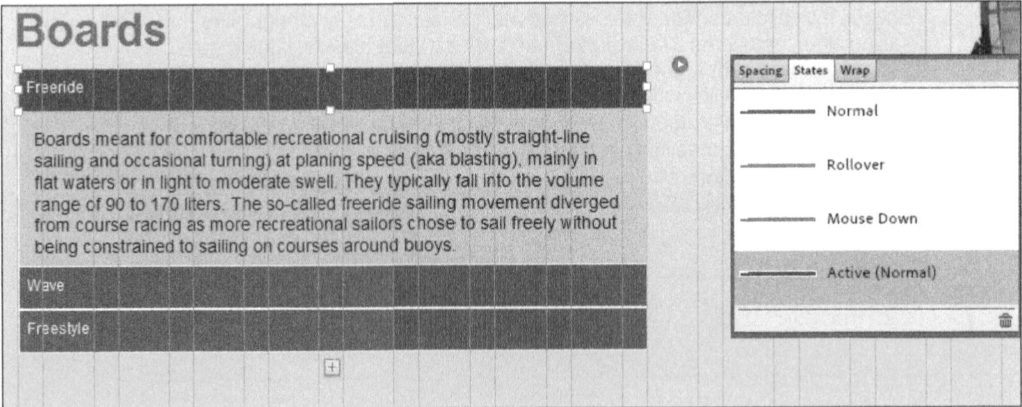

4. Test these changes in the **Preview** view. You'll see that as you click on each panel it changes to blue color as it becomes active.

Editing Accordion widget options

There are a small number of options available for the entire **Accordion** widget. To view them, select the **Accordion** widget you want to edit, and then click on the blue editing options icon, as shown in the following screenshot:

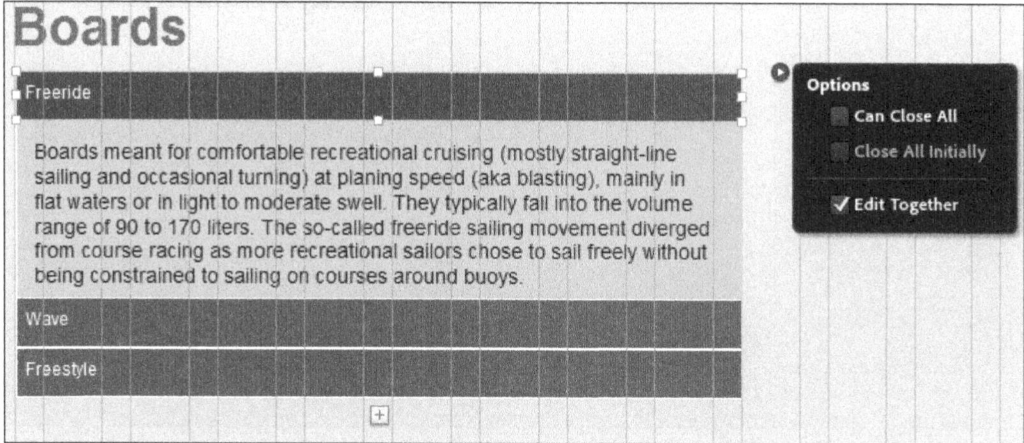

Can Close All: This lets the user close all panels in one go. When this option is not selected, one Accordion panel always remains open.

Edit Together: This means any changes made to one specific part of the panel will be reflected in the same items in the Accordion widget. Deselect this option to make changes to widget items individually.

Edit Accordion widget states: This option lets you edit the various states of Accordion widget panels.

Tabbed Panels

Tabbed Panels are similar to the **Accordion** panels in that they provide a way to put lots of information in a small area on the page. When a user clicks on a tab, the associated content for that tab appears in the box underneath. Perform the following steps to use the **Tabbed Panels**:

1. Start by dragging out a **Tabbed Panels** from the **Widgets Library** panel. Position it on the page by either dragging it with the Selection tool or by using the X and Y coordinates on the Control Panel.

2. By default there are three tabs at the top of the content area. To change the name on a tab, click once to select the widget, then click again on the tab, and once more to edit the tab text, as shown in the following screenshot:

3. To add content to the large area known as the container under the tabs, select the container by clicking first on the widget, then click on the tab under which you want to add content, and then finally click on the container.
4. We can add text by clicking on the **Text** tool and then typing or pasting text.
5. We can add images by placing an image using **File** | **Place**. The image will be automatically resized by Muse to fit within the container.
6. We can add slideshows by dragging them out from the **Widgets Library** into the container.
7. To add or delete tabs, right-click/*Ctrl* + click and choose from the context menu as shown in the following screenshot:

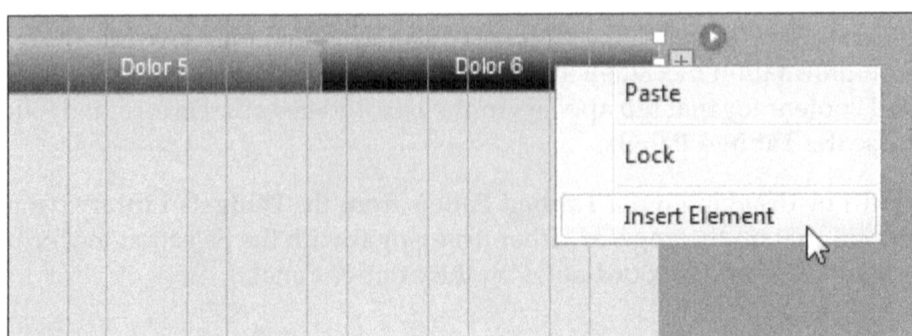

Deleting a panel

If you've added a panel and you want to get rid of it entirely, just select it and press *Delete* on your computer's keyboard.

Summary

In this chapter, we looked at how to create a menu bar for our entire website. We styled the menu and the individual menu items which appear for each page in our website structure. We also used an **Accordion** panel as a way to put a large amount of text on a page without taking up too much space.

In the next chapter we'll again look at widgets, specifically how to use compositions and how to create a slideshow.

9

More Widgets—Compositions and Slideshows

In the previous chapter, we used Muse's widgets to quickly and easily add a menu or navigation system to all our pages and to display a large quantity of text in a small area using an Accordion panel. In this chapter we'll continue to work with widgets to add extra functionality and interactivity to our web pages.

We'll create an elegant slideshow using the Slideshow widget and use the Composition widget to create a simple photo gallery. As well as using widgets to add functionality, we'll use arbitrary HTML to add interactive elements to our pages.

By the end of this chapter you'll know how to:

- Use a Composition widget
- Create a slideshow with a Slideshow widget
- Add an interactive Google Map and feed using arbitrary HTML

Composition widgets

There are several interactive widgets available in Muse which fall under the umbrella term of Composition widgets. They consist of a small container which is known as the "trigger" and a larger container called the "target". When you click on the trigger, something happens in the target. An example of this would be a photo gallery where a user clicks on a thumbnail image and a full-sized version is displayed in the container. For example, you can use a Basic Composition widget to create a photo gallery, with thumbnail triggers that display the full-sized photos when the user clicks on the trigger.

The **Composition** section of the **Widget Library** menu includes the following:

- **Blank**: This widget consists of a number of small thumbnails, which you link manually to the larger container area. When the thumbnail is clicked the content of the large container changes accordingly.
- **Featured News**: This widget is somewhat similar to the Accordion and Tabbed widgets we saw in the last chapter. When the text trigger is clicked, the main content, which can consist of text and images, changes.
- **Lightbox Display**: When a thumbnail is clicked, the rest of the page is dimmed while the content of the target is active.
- **Presentation**: This widget consists of small numbered thumbnails linked to a larger slide or image. By default, the slides swipe in horizontally.
- **Tooltip**: This displays text as a tool tip when the user hovers over the trigger.

Each of these widget types has different display behaviors that allow you to easily add complex functionality to your site, as shown in the following screenshot. Like all of the widgets available in Muse, the Composition widgets are completely editable and customizable:

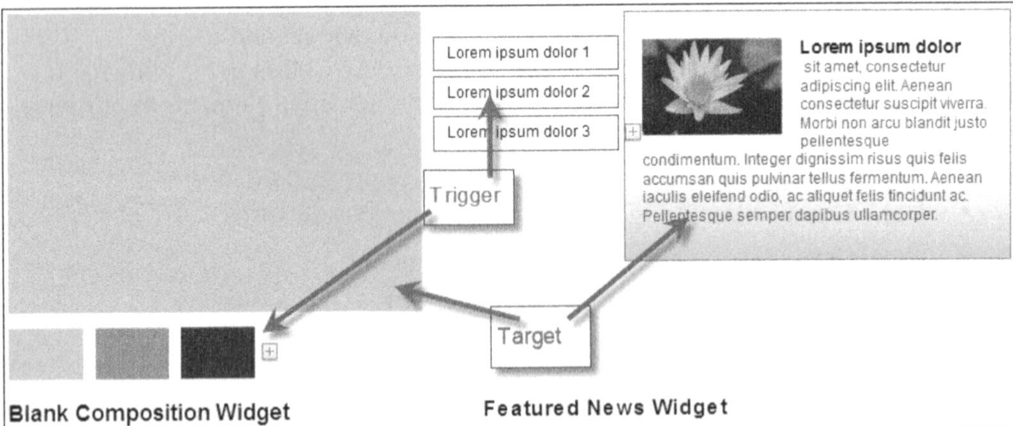

Using Images with Widgets

The images added to your slideshows or composition widgets should be saved in a format suitable for the Web, namely GIF, JPEG, or PNG. It is also possible to use a native Photoshop file `.psd`, as Muse will convert it to the correct web format. Save your images in advance at the size you want to display them in the slideshow. Muse will generate the smaller thumbnails automatically and create an image folder when you're finished with your site and ready to upload. Images can be linked from anywhere on your computer.

Creating a simple photo gallery using a blank composition

We'll create a photo gallery consisting of three images. With a blank composition, we "tell" Muse which trigger matches up to the large image that will appear in the target area. Perform the following steps to create a simple photo gallery:

1. Open your page in the **Design** view and drag out the **Blank** composition widget from the **Widget Library** menu.
2. Click on the **Composition** widget once to select the entire widget. You can now position it anywhere you want on the page.
3. Click on the first light-gray trigger thumbnail under the target area to select it.
4. Click on the **Fill** link on the **Control** bar. From the drop-down menu, click on the Image icon and browse to choose the first Windsurfing image in the **Composite Widgets Images** panel. Set the **Fitting** to **Scale To Fill**, as shown in the following screenshot:

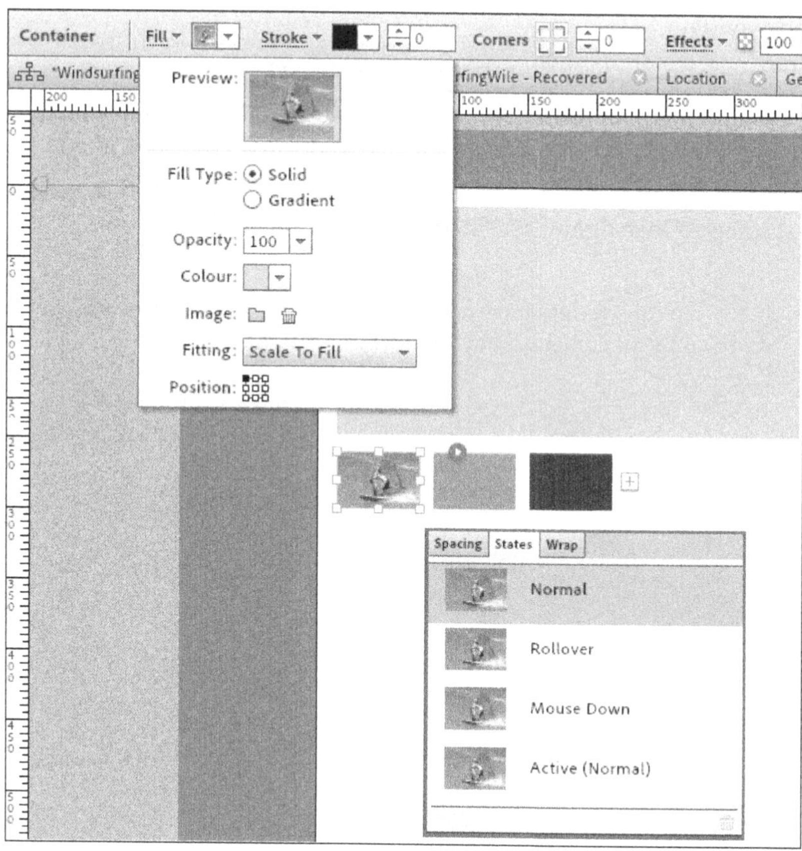

Notice that the thumbnails in the list of states in the **States** widget are now all the same. If you want to create a rollover effect, you could click on the **Rollover** state in this widget and then change the image as we did previously. For this example, we are keeping everything nice and simple, so we'll use the same thumbnail for all four available states.

5. Add two more thumbnail images to the remaining triggers by repeating step 4. Choose the images from the **Composition Widgets Image** folder.
6. If you want to add additional thumbnails, click the plus (+) icon that appears to the right of the trigger elements. If you want to remove a trigger, select it and press *Delete* on your computer's keyboard.

Add content to a target area

Our next step is to add the larger images to the target area using the following steps so that when we click on the thumbnail the correct image appears:

1. In the **Design** view, click on the **Composition** widget once again to select the entire widget.
2. Click once on the first thumbnail to select the trigger.
3. Click on the larger content area to select it. By clicking first on the trigger and then on the target, we are telling Muse that these two are linked.
4. With the content area selected, click on the drop-down **Fill** menu and add the first image. Once again, set **Fitting** to **Scale To Fill**.

In this example, we're adding an image, but you can add any type of content that you like to the target.

5. Repeat steps 1 to 4 to add content to the target for the second and third thumbnails. When you've added the images to both trigger and target, it should look like the following screenshot:

6. Test your photo gallery in the **Preview** view and make sure that your large image matches up with your thumbnail image.

You can change the size of each thumbnail and each target area individually. Simply click once to select the entire widget, click once again to select either a trigger (thumbnail) or a target. Once the element is selected, a bounding box appears with handles in each corner. Dragging on the handles allows you to resize the element.

Changing Composition widget options

Each Composition widget offers several options for setting up how the widget functions. To get to the options, click on the editing options icon—the blue arrow. In the following list, you'll find an explanation of each option available for the blank composition we've just added to our page:

- **Position**: This sets up where the target area is positioned on the page. By choosing **Stacked**, all of the content is overlapped, such as the target content appears in the same place on the web page. By choosing **Scattered**, it lets you position each target container in a different location on the page. Choosing **Lightbox** dims the rest of your web page and puts the focus on your target content.

- **Event**: We can choose to change the content in the target area when the user clicks on the thumbnail - **On Click** or when the user rolls their mouse over the thumbnail - **On Rollover**, as shown in the following screenshot:

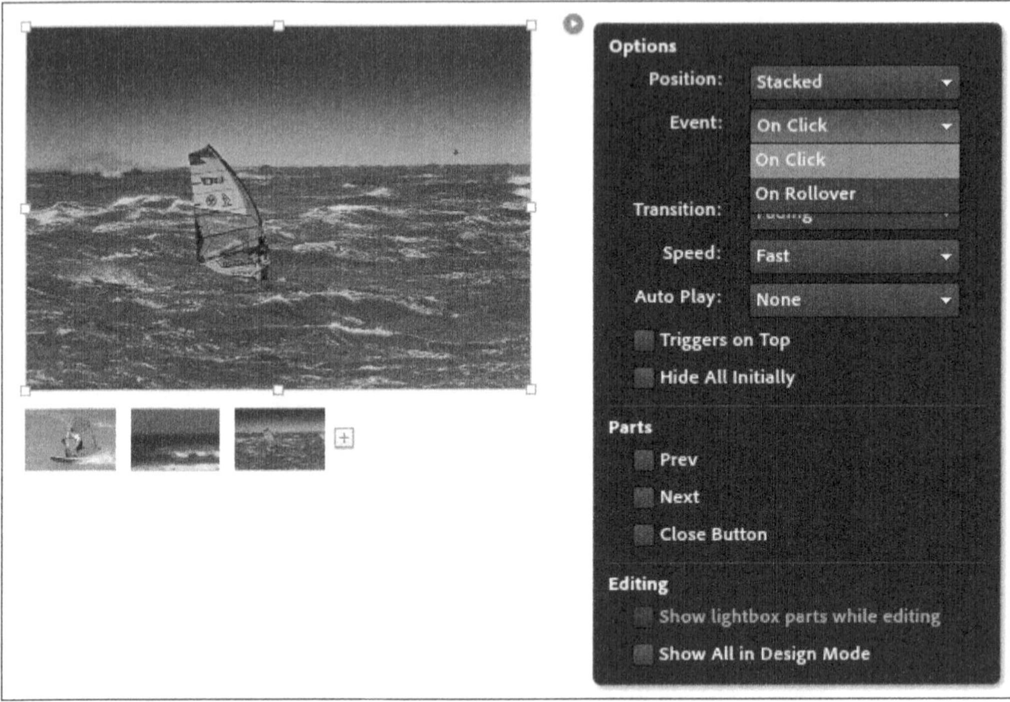

- **Transition**: We can specify how the content changes when the trigger is clicked or rolled over. The choices of animated transitions are:
    - **Fading**: This fades in the new target content while simultaneously fading out the previous target.
    - **Horizontal**: This slides the new target content in, with a horizontal sliding motion.
    - **Vertical**: This slides the new target content in, with a vertical sliding effect.
    - **Speed**: The choices here specify the speed of the transition. If you want an instant transition, select **None**.

- **Auto Play**: This option creates a slideshow requiring no user interaction.
- **Hide All Initially**: This option hides all target areas when the page is first loaded. In order to see the content, the user needs to click on the trigger.
- **Parts**: If you want to add extra user interactivity, you can use these options to show previous, next, or close buttons with the widget.
- **Show Lightbox Parts While Editing**: If you choose the **Lightbox** option under **Position**, you can then hide or display the contents of the target area while editing in the **Design** view.
- **Show All in Design Mode**: This option lets you display all target content areas at the same time when working in the **Design** view. By default this option is deselected, meaning only the target content of the selected trigger element appears in the **Design** view.

Another way to create triggers and targets with multiple images

In the previous example, we manually added images first to the trigger and then to the target area. We set each trigger and target individually. There is another way to add multiple images simultaneously to the target area and Muse automatically creates the corresponding trigger elements for you using the following steps:

1. In the **Design** view, add a new blank **Composition** widget to the page.
2. Click on the **Composition** widget once to select the entire widget.
3. Click again to select the large target area.
4. Choose **File | Place**.
5. Select the multiple images you want to place. Hold down the *Ctrl* (Windows)/*Cmd* (Mac OS) key to select multiple images from the folder.
6. Click on **Select** (Windows) or **Open** (Mac OS).

7. Place the image group by clicking inside the target's content area as shown in the following screenshot. Muse automatically adds trigger elements for each image:

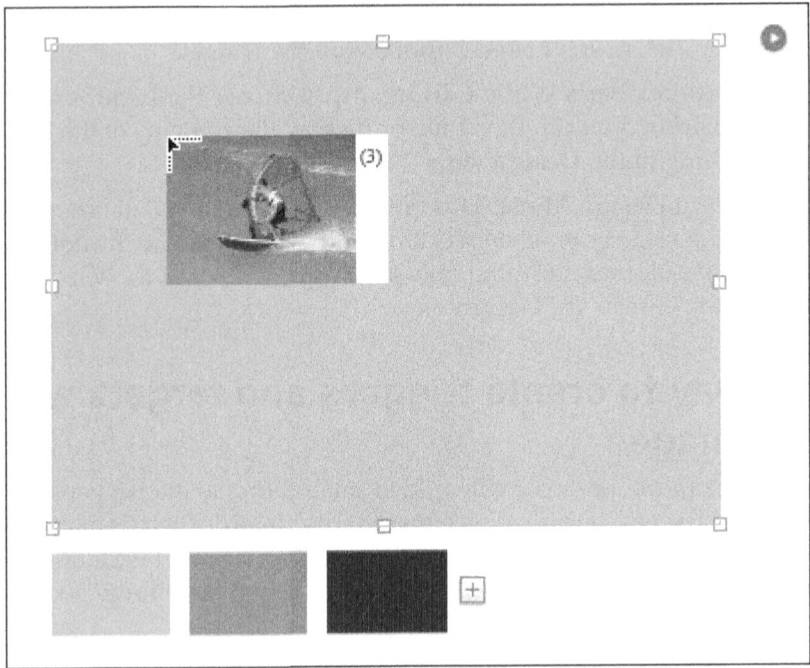

8. Unfortunately, it doesn't add the corresponding images to the thumbnail trigger. If you want to do that, then select each trigger element and place images that match the corresponding target areas to create thumbnail image triggers.

Slideshow widgets

The Slideshow widgets work in a very similar fashion to the Composition widgets, the main difference being the Slideshow widgets work exclusively with images while the Composition widgets can work with any type of content. The types of Slideshow widgets available in the **Widgets Library** menu are:

- **Basic**: The **Basic Slideshow** widget consists of a large content area, surrounded by a dark gray border. Underneath the content area there is a caption area, the number of slides or images which make up the slideshow, and a next and previous button. When you drag out the widget, it comes preloaded with three slides.

- **Blank**: The **Blank Slideshow** widget is similar to the **Basic Slideshow** widget except that it is empty when you drag-and-drop the widget out onto the page.
- **Lightbox**: The **Lightbox Slideshow** widget dims the rest of the page while the gallery element being displayed is active. This is a very popular type of slideshow on the web as it keeps the visitor's focus on the gallery element while reducing other distractions on the page.
- **Thumbnails**: The **Thumbnails Slideshow** widget shows thumbnails, which by default are positioned to the left of the larger content area. As the user clicks on the thumbnail, the image becomes bigger.

The following screenshot shows the different types of slideshows:

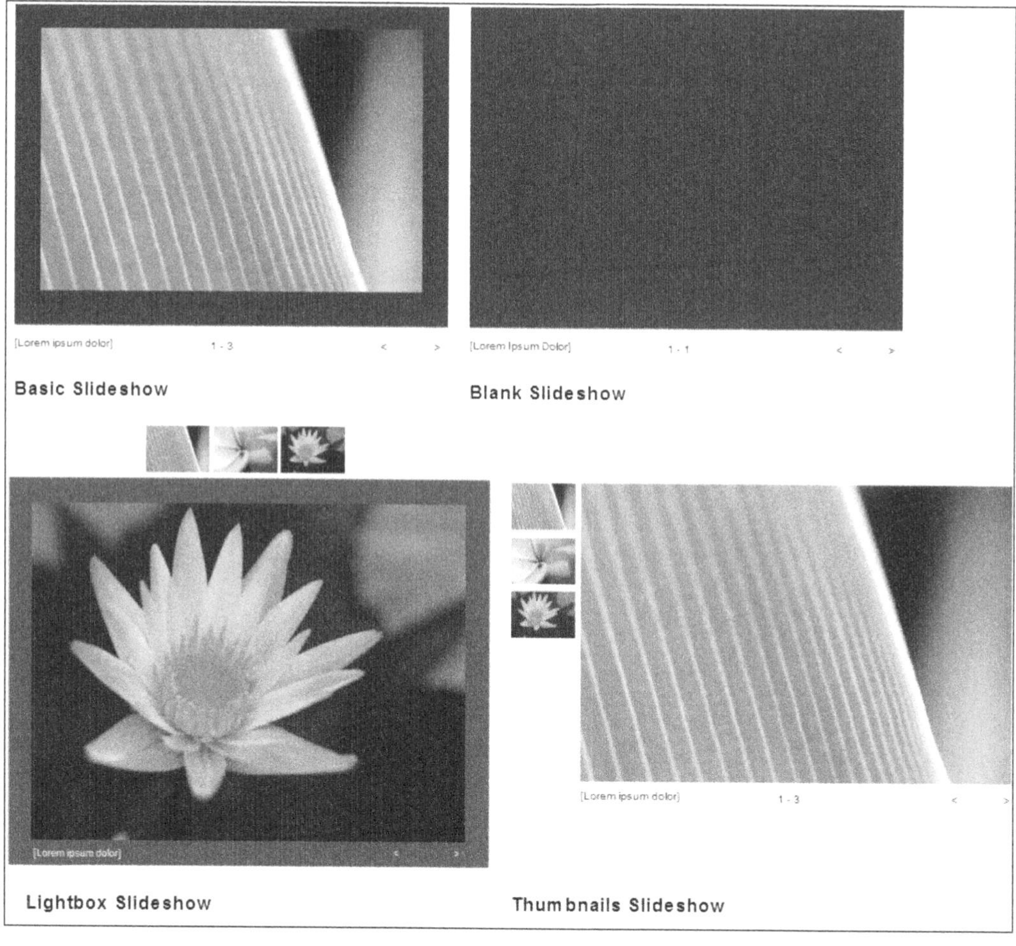

Like the other widgets in Muse, the Slideshow widgets are completely editable and customizable.

Creating a slideshow presentation

Earlier in this chapter we created a photo gallery which required the user to click on a thumbnail to see the larger image. This kind of functionality is also available using the **Lightbox Slideshow** widget or the **Thumbnails Slideshow** widgets. They work in a very similar way to the photo gallery we already created so rather than recreate those steps, in this next example we'll create a slideshow using the **Blank Slideshow** widget. We'll change the settings so that the slideshow plays automatically, running through a series of images. We'll specify the transition effects and the speed at which the slideshow plays. Perform the following steps to create a slideshow presentation:

1. Open your page in the **Design** view.
2. In the **Widgets Library** menu, choose the **Blank Slideshow** widget and drag it onto the page.
3. The Blank Slideshow widget consists of a dark gray rectangle which will hold our large image, a caption area, an image counter, and a next and previous image button for navigation.
4. Click on the blue arrow to access the **Options** menu. Click on the folder icon at the top, next to the **Add Images...** option.
5. Navigate to your `images` folder and choose as many images as you want to add to your slideshow. Hold down *Ctrl/Cmd* to choose multiple images, and then click on **Open**.
6. Your images will be added to the content area and the numbers in the image counter will increase to reflect the number of images in the slideshow. The default images from Muse remain in the slideshow. We simply delete these after adding our own images.

7. Click again on the blue arrow to open the widget's **Options** menu, as shown in the following screenshot:

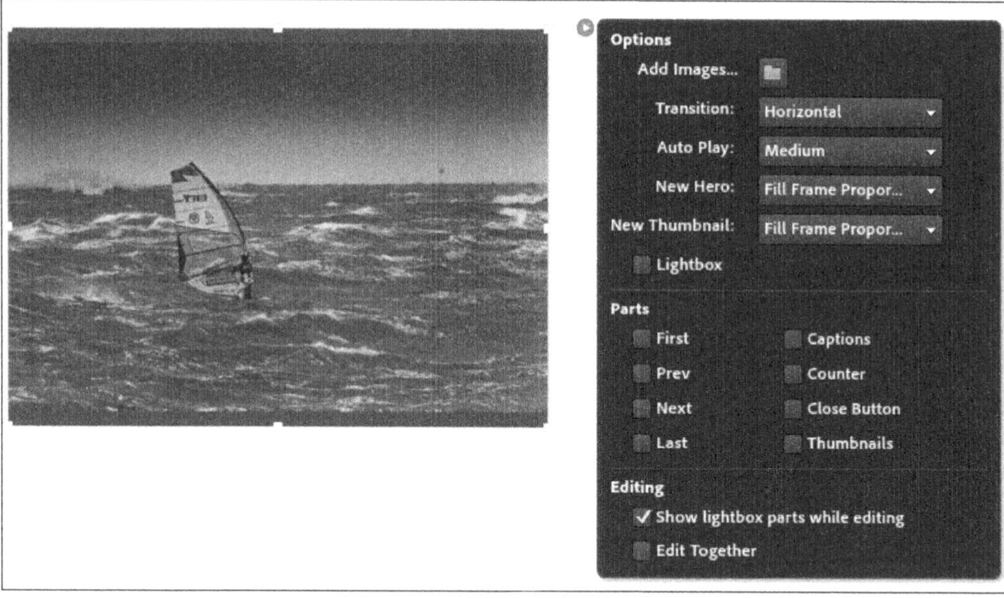

8. Set the following options:
    - **Transition**: **Horizontal**
    - **Auto Play**: **Medium**
    - **New Hero**: **Fill Frame Proportionally** (Hero is just a name for the main image)
    - **New Thumbnail**: **Fill Frame Proportionally**—this is irrelevant here because we're not using thumbnails
    - **Lightbox**: Deselected
    - **Parts**: Deselect all options to hide the captions, counter, next, and previous buttons

    Setting these options leaves us with a single image on the page.

9. Choose **Preview** to see how the slideshow will work in the browser. When all of the images have been displayed, the slideshow will loop around to the first image again and continue to play.

10. If you want to change the size of your slideshow, go back to the **Design** view and drag one of the corner handles of the Hero image frame. Hold down *Shift* as you drag to constrain the proportions of the slideshow. As you drag, you'll see the dark gray area increase in size, as well as the image itself.

    In its current setup, this slideshow requires no user interactivity. If you decide that you want to let the user control the slideshow, click on the blue arrow again to open the options for the widget.

11. To provide thumbnails to correspond with the large images, select **Thumbnails** in the **Parts** section.
12. To provide the next and previous image controller buttons, select those options in the **Parts** section.
13. You can place each part of the widget in different parts of the page. Remember to click once to select the whole widget, and then click on the individual parts of the widget to position them where you want.
14. Select and position the thumbnails under the main image area.
15. Select and position the next and previous buttons at the top and right of the main image, as shown in the following screenshot:

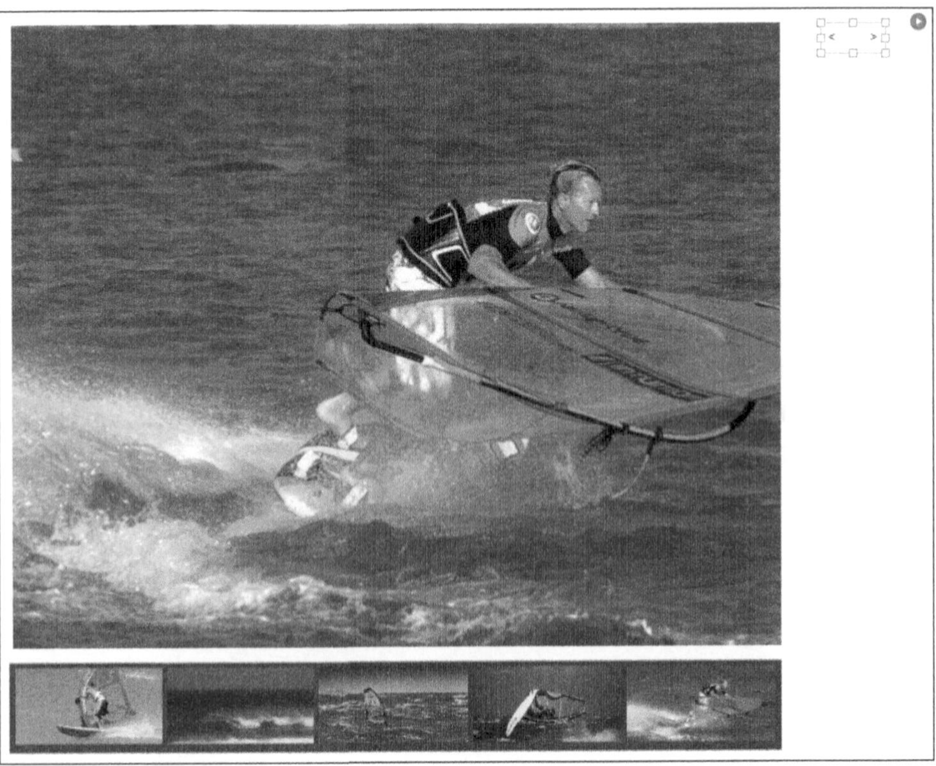

Insert arbitrary HTML

While Muse writes the HTML and CSS for everything we've looked at throughout this book, there may be times when you need to add a little bit of HTML yourself. Don't worry though; you won't have to write this code either. Let's say for example you want to add a Google map to your site to show clients or interested parties where you are based. Google will provide you with the code, you just copy it and then simply paste it back into your page in Muse.

Another example would be if you want to add a YouTube video. You don't need to host the video, you just paste in some code provided by YouTube and the video will appear, embedded in your page. A big advantage of using a service like this is that you don't need to worry about hosting the video content, it's still hosted by YouTube, and it just looks as if it's on your site.

Working with arbitrary HTML on a page in your site allows you to set aside a window in your page where third-party content can appear. As you can imagine, this opens up huge possibilities for you in terms of what you can add to a page without the need to write your own code. You could let your visitors know what the weather is going to be, show them a map of your hometown, impress them with audio and video, or provide them with stock market quotes.

Adding a Google Map to your page

Let's add a map to a new page using the following steps:

1. In the **Plan** view, click on the plus symbol (+) under the **Home** page to add a new page.
2. Rename the new page as `Location`. Notice that the new page automatically takes on the A-Master page because it is a child page or a **Home** page which uses the A-Master page.
3. Double-click on the new **Location** thumbnail to open it in the **Design** view. Add a heading to Location and style it using the Heading style you created in the previous exercise.
4. Open an Internet browser and go to Google Maps at `maps.google.com`.
5. Type in the address or a search term to find the location you want to appear on your map.
6. Click on the **Link** button which you'll see appear at the top left of the interface.
7. Click on the **Link** button that appears in the upper-right part of the interface. Click once again on the option **Customize** And **Preview** Embedded Map.

8. A new **Customize** window appears which allows you to change the size of the map that you'll embed on your page. Select the **Custom** radio button in **Map size** to set **Width** to `800` pixels and **Height** to `400` pixels, as shown in the following screenshot:

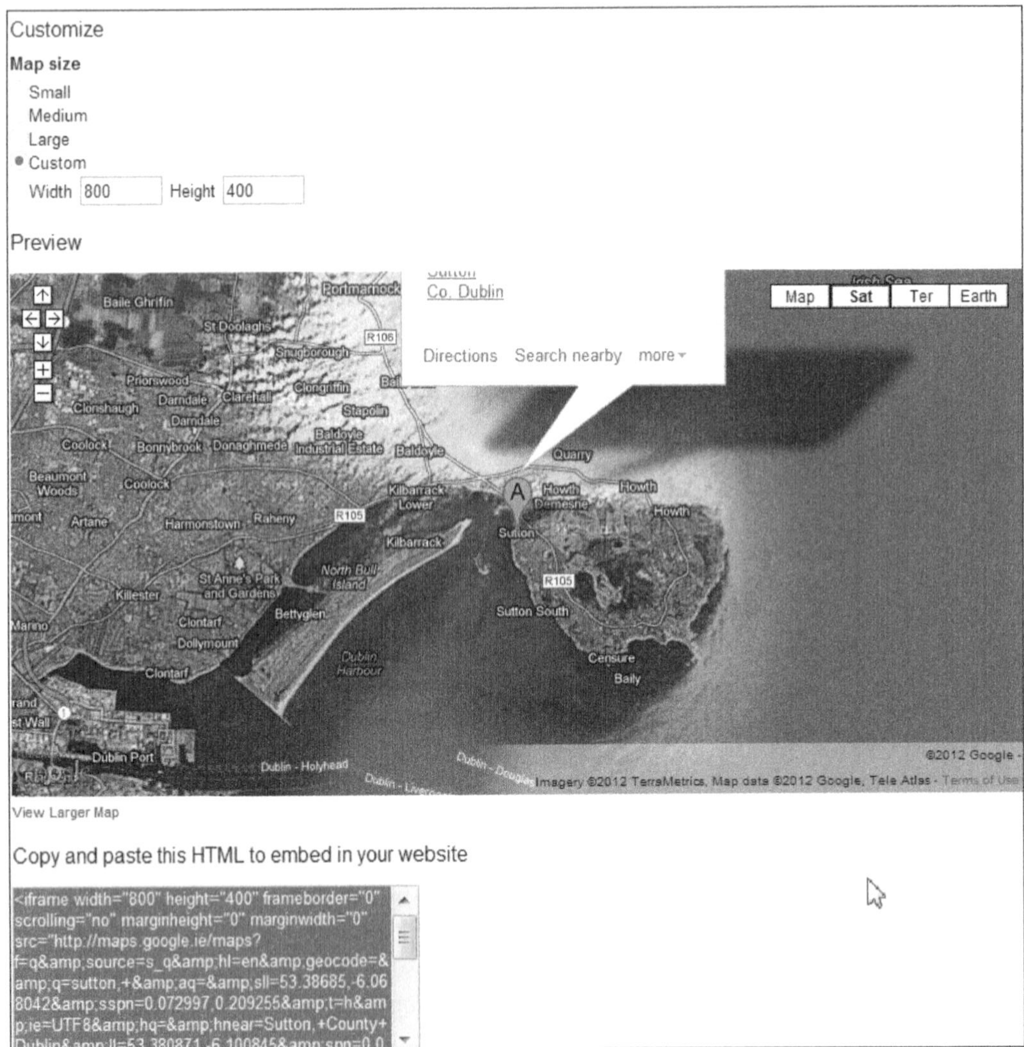

9. You may need to reposition the map within the window to ensure that the pin and address text is fully visible. You can do this by simply clicking-and-dragging the map around until the pin and address are where you want them to be.

10. Google instantly generates the code for the map, which you can select and copy.
11. Go back to Muse. Choose **Object | Insert HTML** to open the HTML code window. Paste in the code you've copied using the keyboard shortcut to paste the code (*Ctrl* + *V* for Windows and *Cmd* + *V* for Mac).
12. Use the Selection tool to position the map where you want it on the page, as shown in the following screenshot:

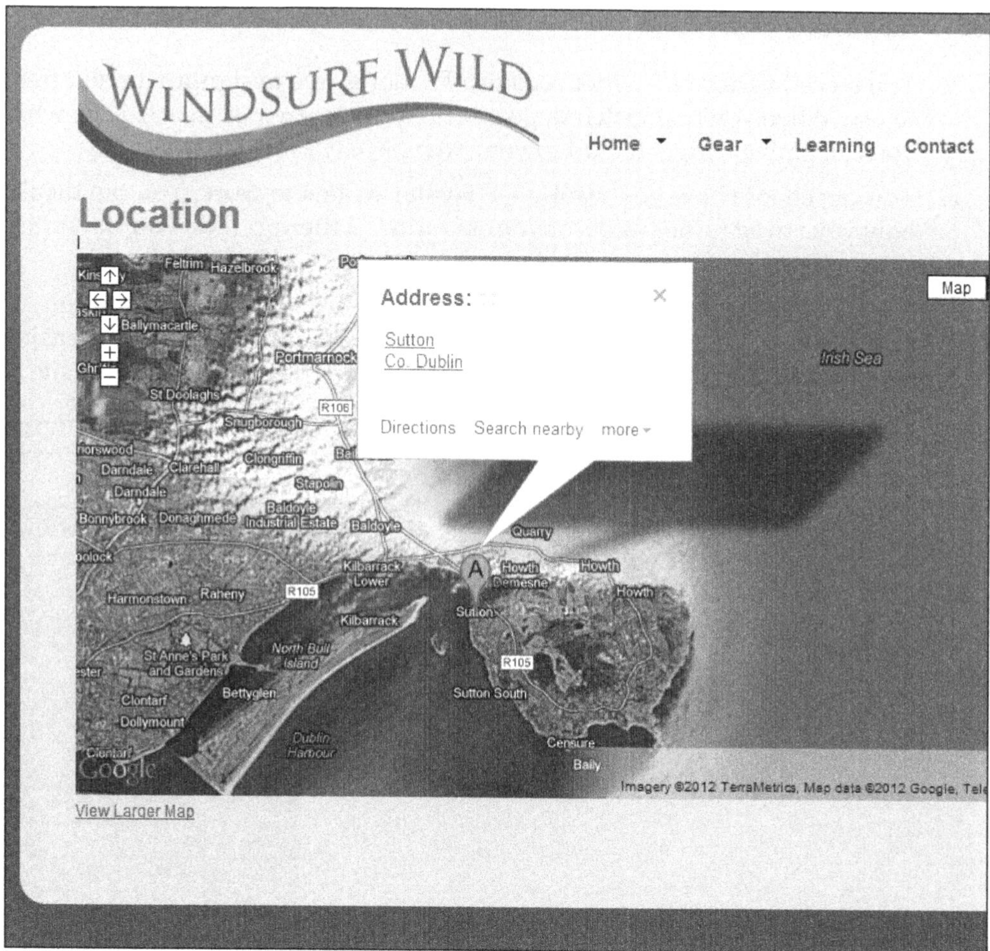

In the **Design** view, you will be able to get an idea of how the Google Map will appear to your visitor. In order to see how the map is working interactively, click on **Preview** to see how it will appear on the live site. You can zoom in and out and move around the map which is embedded on your page.

Adding a Twitter (or any other type of) feed to your site

Unless you've been living in a cave, there is a strong possibility that you have heard of, or use Twitter. Many Twitter users add a feed of their "tweets" to their site or blog and this maybe something you'd like to do with your own Muse-built site. Whether you're adding a Twitter feed or an RSS feed or any other type of dynamic data to your site, the process is essentially the same. The following steps show how to do it for a Twitter feed:

1. You'll need to have a Twitter account. Twitter is free to sign-up for and free to use. When you're registered, go to `twitter.com/goodies/widgets` where you can grab a widget to add to your web page.
2. You can choose how you want your Twitter widget to work. You can display only your tweets, the tweets of your favorite Twitter profiles, your favorite tweets, or a stream of topical tweets about a subject of your choice.
3. Once you've made that choice, you can then set up your widget. You can make changes using the **Settings**, **Preferences**, **Appearance**, and **Dimensions** menu. Choose a color scheme that matches or complements your own site's color scheme.

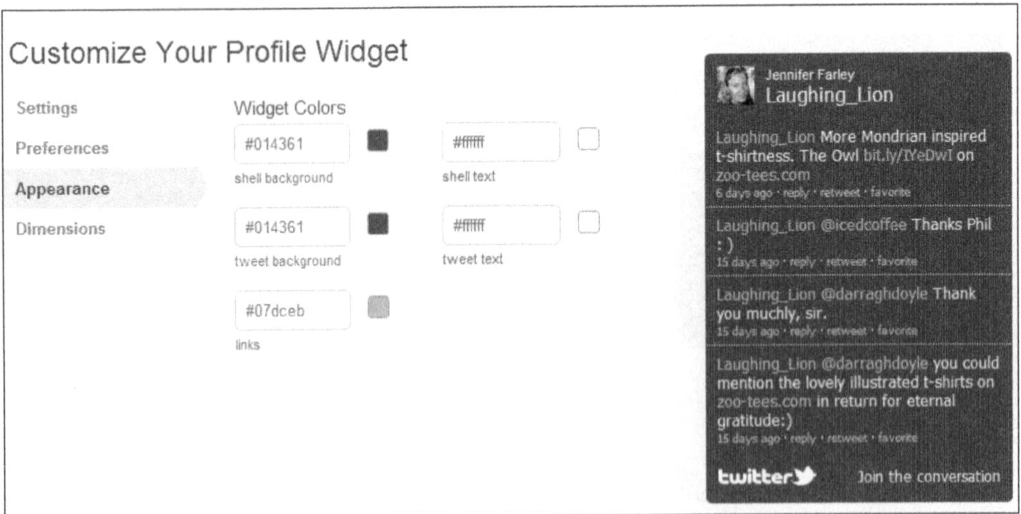

4. When you've set up your Twitter widget's "look and feel", click on the **Finish And Grab Code** button. You'll see a chunk of HTML code which you can copy. Select all the code, copy it using *Ctrl* + *C*/*Cmd* + *C*, then go back to Muse.
5. In the **Design** view in Muse, choose **Object** | **Insert HTML** and paste the code you copied into the dialog box by pressing *Ctrl* + *V*/*Cmd* + *V*. Click on **OK**.

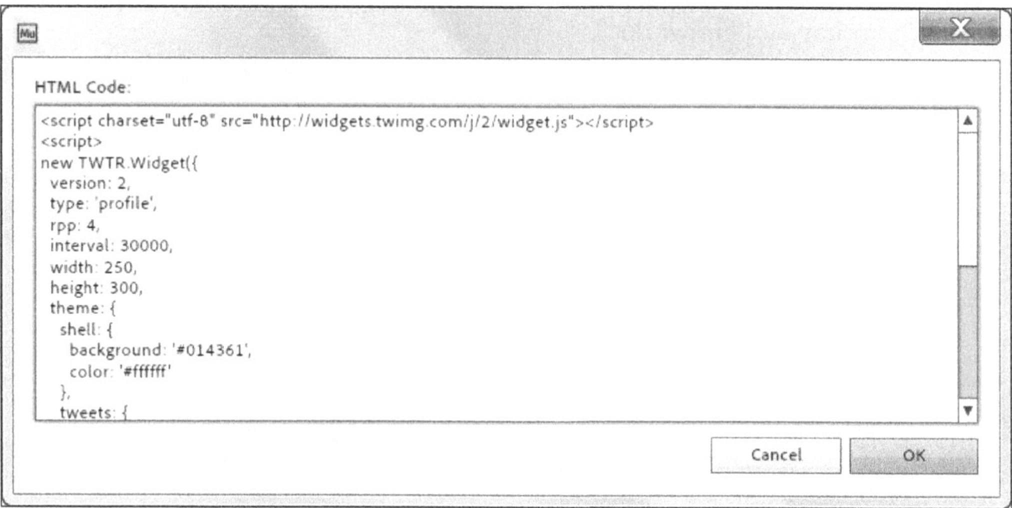

6. Your widget will now appear on the page. Test it by using the **Preview** view.

Summary

In this chapter we've discussed Composition and Slideshow widgets, which allow us to add some very useful interactivity and functionality to our pages without as much as a hint of coding from our end. We also saw how to take code from other websites (such as YouTube, Google Maps, and Twitter) and embed it into our Muse web pages.

In the next chapter, we'll look at how Muse plays nicely with other Adobe products such as Photoshop and Fireworks.

10

Muse, Meet the Adobe Creative Suite

In the previous chapter we used Muse's built-in widgets to add a slideshow to our pages. If you use some of Adobe's other products, such as Photoshop, you will be pleased to know that Muse is tightly integrated with other products in the Adobe Creative Suite. Adobe Muse is not part of the Adobe Creative Suite® 6 release, but it is available as part of the Adobe Creative Cloud membership. However, even if you're using older versions of Photoshop and Fireworks, Muse will work well with the files you create using those programs.

In this chapter, we'll look at how we can use Photoshop or Fireworks to create graphics and easily bring them into your Muse-created websites. We will learn how to:

- Create and add a Photoshop button
- Add Photoshop or Fireworks-based graphics
- Edit images with Photoshop or Fireworks using Edit Original

Adding a Photoshop rollover button

A rollover button is a graphic created by a web designer, which provides interactivity between the page's visitor and the page itself. The term "rollover" comes from the idea that when the visitor rolls their mouse over the button, something changes visually.

Simple rollovers use two images. The first image is what we see when the page first loads. When we roll over that button, the second image is quickly swapped into place. When we roll our mouse off the button, the first image is swapped back into place. This type of interactivity is created using JavaScript, but as always, Muse does the work behind the scenes and writes the code for us.

Rollovers are sometimes referred to as mouseovers.

Rollovers don't have to use images; the simplest rollovers of all use only text. The text may simply change color or appear in bold, italic, or be underlined. We created some text-based rollovers when we added our menu system to the page in *Chapter 6, Typography, Muse, and the Web*. The idea behind rollovers, whether image-based or not, is that the interactivity gives your user some feedback and tells them that this is a button and something is going to happen when they roll over it. And usually something will happen when they click on it too.

States

We can take our rollover button a step further by adding a third image. The third image appears when the user actually clicks on the button. There is also an option to use a fourth image if you want the button to appear in a certain way after it has been clicked.

The way an image appears on the site may change depending on whether the mouse is hovered over it, clicked on it, or moved away from it. Each one of these mouse positions is known as a **State**. We can create buttons in Photoshop or Fireworks (or any other graphic editor) that use the following four states:

- **Up**: The appearance of the button when the user is not interacting with it
- **Over**: The appearance of the button as the user rolls over it
- **Down**: The appearance of the button as the user selects (clicks on) it
- **Active**: The appearance of the button after it has been clicked

You do not have to use four states, or even three if you don't want to, just as long as you know the states are available to you.

In the following screenshot, taken from the Apple website, we can see the three states. When the page first loads, all of the buttons on the menu look the same. They are all in the **Up State**. When the user rolls over a menu item, the button changes to a dark gray. When the user clicks on the button, some shading at the top and right side of the button image gives the impression that the button has been pressed down.

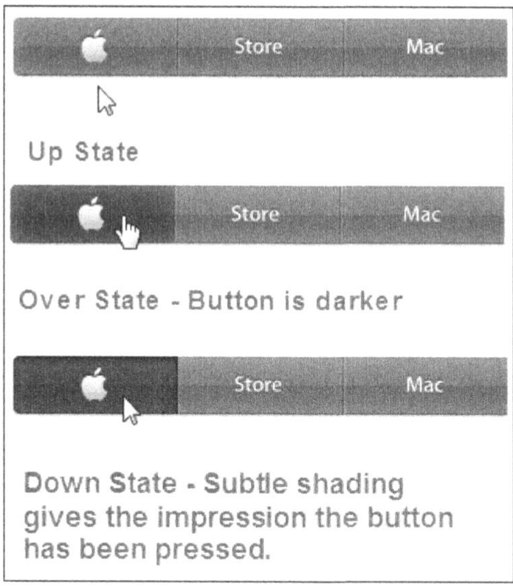

Creating a rollover button with multiple states in Photoshop

In this section we'll create a similar button with three states using Photoshop. If you don't have a copy of Photoshop you can skip to the next section where we'll add the button to the page and you can use the provided `.PSD` file.

1. Open Photoshop and create a new image with a width and height of 200 pixels x 75 pixels, respectively.
2. In your **Layers** panel, click on the **New Group** icon. Click on the new group name in the **Layers** panel and rename it to `Up`.
3. On the **Tools** panel, set the foreground color to red.

4. Select **Rounded Rectangle Tool** (it may be hidden under the rectangle shaped tool). On the tool options bar at the top of the Photoshop interface, make sure that the first icon, **Shape Layers**, is selected. Drag-and-drop a rounded rectangle to the document window.

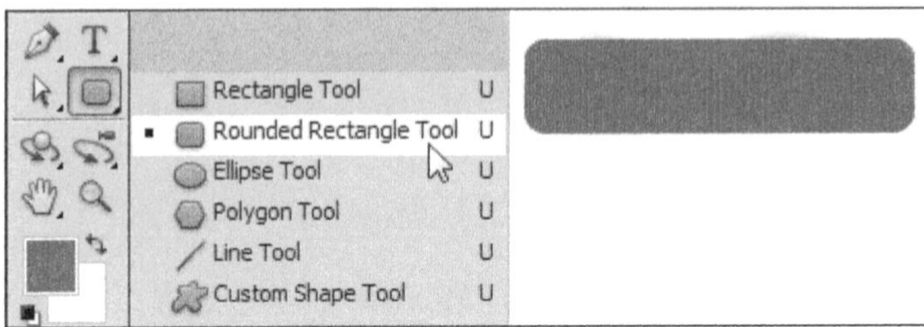

   A new shape layer has been added to the **Up** group. Now we'll add some text.

5. Select the **Type** tool on the toolbar. Set the color to white on the tool's options bar at the top and choose any font you like. Click on the red rectangle and type in `Read More`. A new text layer is added above the rectangle shape layer. Make sure that **Read More** is centered above the rectangle.
6. Now we need to make a similar setup for **Over** and **Down**, but rather than repeating the whole process, we'll simply copy the group structure we have made for the **Up** state.
7. Right-click on the **Up** folder and choose **Duplicate Group**. Name the new group `Over` and click on **OK**.
8. The new **Over** group contains exact copies of the layers made earlier. We're going to make a change to the color of the words in the text layer.
9. Select the **Type** tool again and click on the **Read More copy** layer. Now in the tool's options at the top of the screen, change the color of the text to black.
10. Now let's make one more group. Select the **Up** group you made first, then right-click on it and choose **Duplicate Group**. Name the new group `Down` and click on **OK**.
11. Once again you have an exact copy of your **Up** group. This time we'll leave the text white but we'll add a layer effect so that the button looks as if it has been pressed.
12. Select the **Shape 1 copy** layer in the **Down** group. Click on the **fx** (layer style) icon at the bottom of the layers panel. From the drop-down menu choose **Inner Shadow**.

13. In the **Inner Shadow** dialog box, set the **Distance** to **2 px** and the **Size** to **2 px**. A small dark shadow will appear on the button. If we want to change the direction of the shadow, drag the **Angle** button in a circular motion. Click on **OK**.
14. So after all that, our layers and button should look similar to the following screenshot:

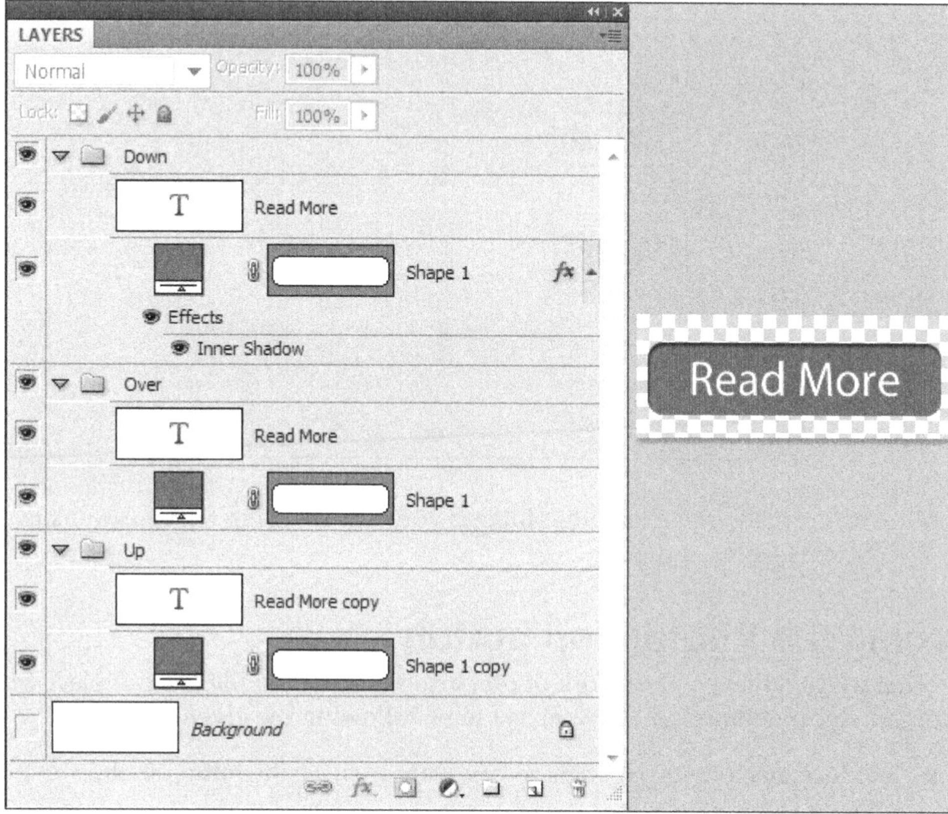

15. We must merge the layers in each of our groups so that each group only contains one layer. Start with the top group (**Down**). Click on the text layer then *Shift* + *Click* on the shape layer so that the two layers are selected. Right-click and from the drop-down menu, choose **Merge Layers**.

    We'll see that our two layers have become one layer.
16. Repeat this process for the **Over** group and the **Up** group so that each group only contains one merged layer.
17. For each of the merged layers, go back and rename the layers **Up**, **Over**, and **Down** as shown in a later screenshot.

18. Finally, we don't need the white background layer. Click on the **Background** layer to select it, right-click and choose **Delete Layer**, or simply press the *Delete/Backspace* button on your keyboard. Our final layer setup should look similar to the following screenshot:

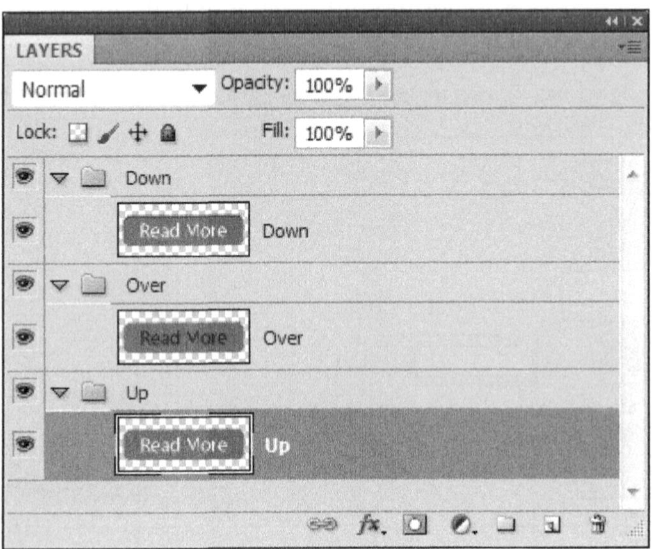

19. Save the file with all the other images you've been using for your website. Name it `ReadMore.psd`.

Placing the Photoshop button

Now that we've done the hard work of preparing our layered file, we can place that button graphic onto the page. You can do so by following the given steps:

1. In Muse, open your page where you want to place the button in the **Design** view.
2. Choose **File | Place Photoshop Button**. The **Place Photoshop Button** dialog box appears. Browse to find your Photoshop file called `ReadMore.psd`. Click on **Select**.
3. The **Photoshop Import Options** dialog box appears. This lets us see a preview of **Normal State**, **Rollover State**, **Mouse Down State**, and **Active State** (or **Up**, **Over**, **Down**, and **Active** as they are often referred to in web designing).

Using the drop-down menus, we can specify which layer in the Photoshop file will show as the button's **Normal State** (or **Up** state), the **Rollover State** (or **Over** state), and the **Mouse Down State** (or **Down** state). The three state menus display the names of the Photoshop layers, and the thumbnail images visually display how each selected layer will appear. You can use the following options:

- For **Normal State**, choose **Composite** from the drop-down menu
- For the **Rollover State**, choose the **Over** layer
- For the **Mouse Down State**, choose the **Down** layer

As we set up a layer for only these three states, we can leave the **Active** state as **None**.

4. You'll probably find that Muse will have correctly selected the layers for you anyway and there is no need to change the menu settings. Click on **OK** to accept the states as they are arranged by default.

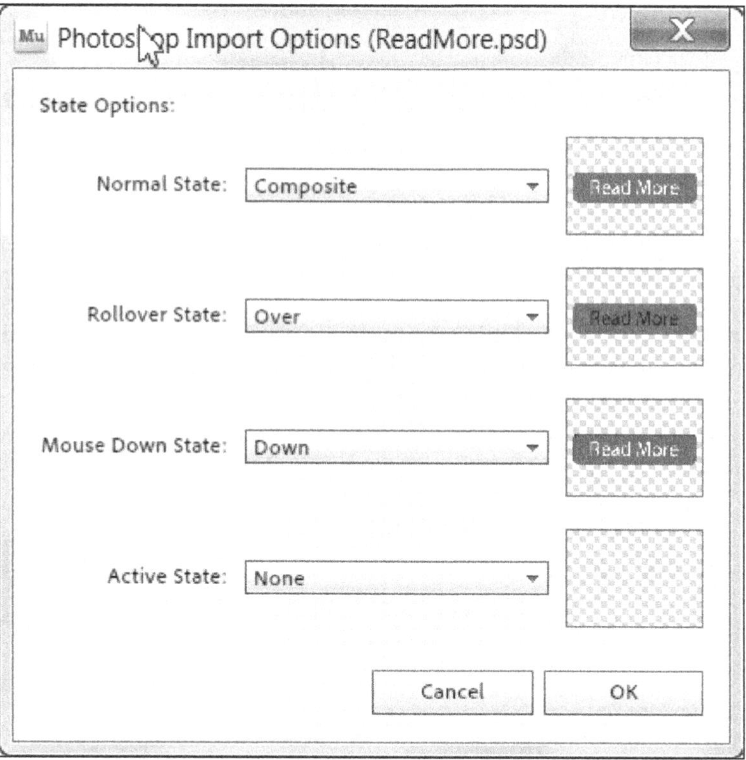

In this example, we used very simple graphics to create three different states for a fairly standard-looking button. However, you are only limited by your imagination when it comes to creating buttons. They don't necessarily even have to look like buttons. Some designers create elaborate designs using many layers for each state. The key to remember is to merge the layers in each group into one layer before finally placing it in Muse.

5. Click once to drop the **Photoshop** button on the page.

   As with most objects in Muse, we can scale, rotate, and position our new Photoshop button as we require.

6. Click on the **Preview** link to test the button. When the page first loads, the Normal State of the button appears. When we hover over the button with the cursor, the **Read More** text changes to black and when we click on the button, the text changes back to white and an inner shadow appears on the button. We can hold the button down for as long as we like and it will keep this appearance.

Adding a Photoshop image that's not a button

Most designers use Photoshop for more than just creating buttons. When it comes to creating images, Photoshop is really only limited by our imagination. When we looked at adding images in *Chapter 7, Working with Images*, we discussed the three main types of image format that can be used on the Web, namely JPEG, GIF, and PNG. So where does a layered Photoshop file (PSD) come into the equation?

Well, the answer is that Muse lets us bring in a multi-layered PSD into our pages, and on saving, it will create a version of that file with a suitable file format to display on the Web. It's still better to have Photoshop do the conversion to JPEG, GIF, or PNG as it does a better job with the compression of the image, but let's have a look at how to bring in a PSD file to Muse:

1. Open your page in the **Design** view.
2. Click on **File | Place**.
3. Browse to the folder where your PSD file is, select it and click on **Open**.

4. The **Image Import Options** box opens. You can choose to import an image as **Composite Image** or to import an individual **Layer**. If you choose **Composite** you will bring in a flattened version of your layered file. If you choose an individual layer, you can select just one layer on a transparent background. Choosing **Clip To Layer Contents** means that the image will be trimmed to remove any extra space around the object on that layer.

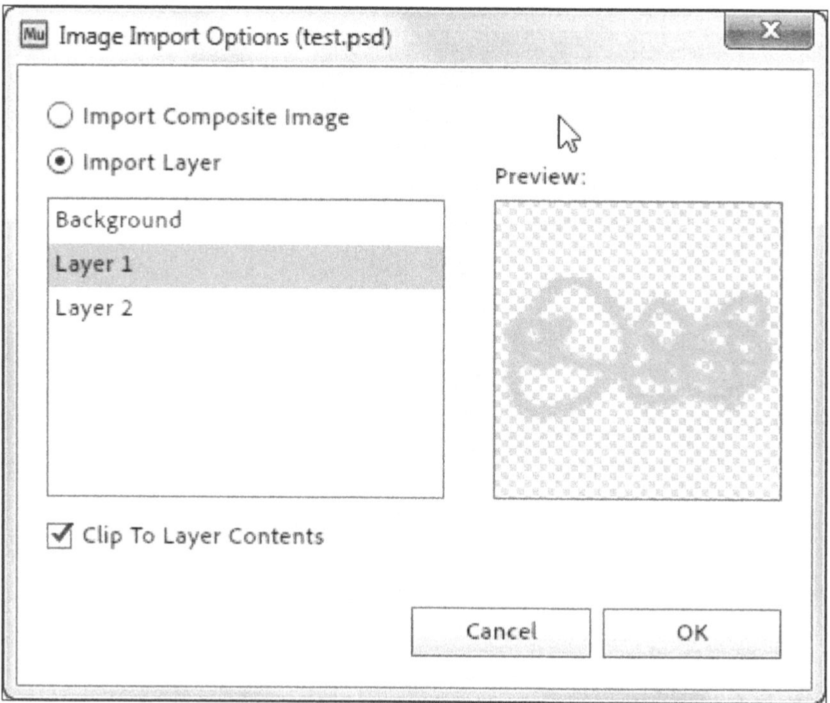

5. Click on **OK** and then position your image where you want it on the page. Again you can scale and rotate the image as you like.

Editing our Photoshop file

One of the nice features in Muse when dealing with a PSD file is that we can easily go back and make changes to our PSD and it will be automatically updated in our Muse web page. Use the following steps to do so:

1. In the **Assets** panel you will see your new image listed as `YourFilename.PSD`. Right-click on its name in the panel to see a list of menu options.

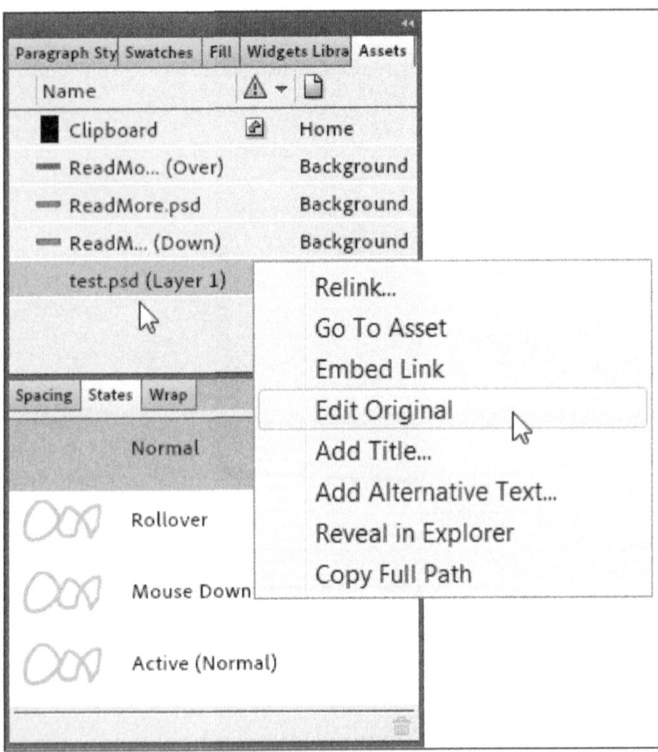

2. If you need to go back and edit your original PSD file, choose **Edit Original**. This takes you back to Photoshop where you can make as many changes as you like.
3. When you are finished editing in Photoshop, choose **File | Save**.
4. Back in Muse, you will see that the changes you made to your PSD are reflected immediately.

If your changes have not appeared, right-click on the filename in the **Assets** panel again and choose **Update Asset**. You should now see the update kick in.

Paste an image from another program

Let's say we've created other images in Photoshop, Illustrator, or Fireworks and we want to take the whole or even part of one of our images directly into Muse. Here's how to do it:

1. In another program, such as Adobe Illustrator, copy the image by selecting all or part of it, then choose *Ctrl* + *C* (Windows) or *Command* + *C* (Mac OS) on the keyboard. In this example, we're copying an image created using many paths in Illustrator.

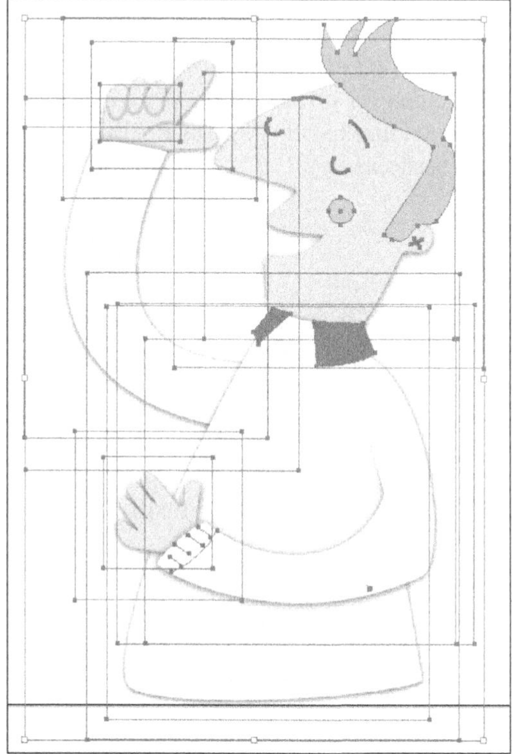

2. Open the web page where we want to place the image in Muse's **Design** view and paste the image by choosing **Edit | Paste**, or by using *Ctrl* + *V* (Windows) or *Command* + *V* (Mac OS) on the keyboard.

   Just like that, the image appears on the page. We can add a stroke or a link to the image, as well as scaling, rotating, or positioning if required.

3. Take a look at the **Assets** panel. Notice there is now an object listed in there as **clipboard**. This is the file we have just pasted in from the other program. When we save our site, Muse will save this asset as part of our site.

Embedding rich media content

If we have some rich media, such as a Flash presentation that we need to add to our web pages, we can do this just as easily as adding an image. Follow the given steps:

1. Open the page you want to add the media file to in the **Design** view.
2. Choose **File | Place**. In the **Import** dialog box, navigate to the folder with your media files and choose the one you need. Muse supports Adobe Flash SWF files.
3. Click on **OK** and place the object where you want it on the page.

If we want to add a video file to our page, it's highly recommended to upload the video to a service such as YouTube. YouTube hosts the video so we don't have to worry about bandwidth for our website. We can simply add the arbitrary HTML code provided by YouTube to our page as outlined in *Chapter 9, More Widgets – Compositions and Slideshows.*

Summary

In this short chapter we examined how we can create a layered image in Photoshop and then place it as a Photoshop button in Muse. This allows us to create buttons with multiple states, which is a useful way to give feedback to our web visitors. We also saw how easy it is to take an image created in another program and copy-and-paste it into Muse.

In the next chapter we'll look at previewing and testing our whole site before publishing it.

11
Previewing and Testing Your Site

Once you've done all the hard work of putting the site together, the final hurdle is to test, test, and test. This is a very important part of the web design process that involves previewing your site in various browsers to make sure it all works ok. You have already been doing some testing as you made your site by previewing your pages as you go.

In this chapter, we'll look at how Muse Preview uses WebKit to render previews, and we'll discuss how to rigorously test your website. We'll examine how to:

- Preview a single page in Muse
- Preview a single page in a browser
- Preview an entire site in a browser
- Export HTML and all associated assets of your Muse site
- Follow a set of steps for testing your site

Previewing pages

Adobe Muse uses WebKit as its rendering engine for Previews. WebKit is an open source layout engine, which was created to allow web browsers to render web pages. It powers the Apple Safari and Google Chrome browsers. It is also used as the basis for the experimental browser included with the Amazon Kindle eBook reader, as well as the default browser in the iOS, Android, BlackBerry Tablet OS, and webOS mobile operating systems.

This means that when you preview your page or your site from within Muse, you'll get a pretty good idea of how it will look on all the browsers mentioned previously.

Completing the site

To complete the site we have built so far, add text to the **Home** and **Sails** page, which is provided as `.txt` files. Add a fictional address and e-mail link to the **Contact** page.

The completed windsurfing site is also provided as `Windsurf-CompleteSite.muse`, as shown in the following screenshot:

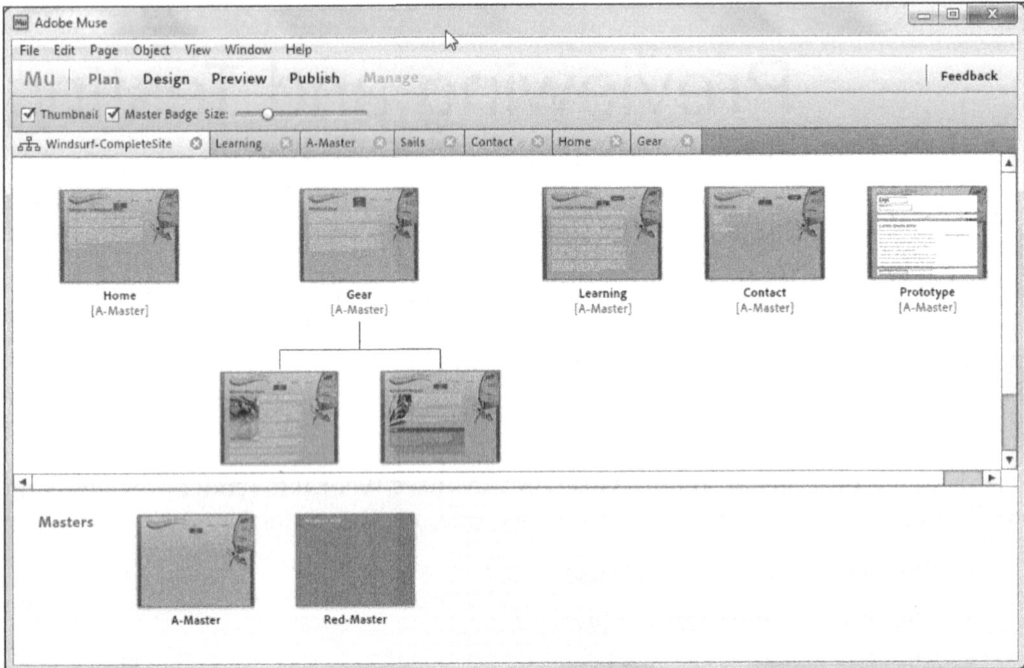

Preview a page in Muse

You've done this many times now if you've been following along, but here's a quick refresher on how to preview a page in Muse:

1. Open the page that you want to preview in the **Design** view.
2. Click on the **Preview** link on the upper-left corner of the Muse interface.

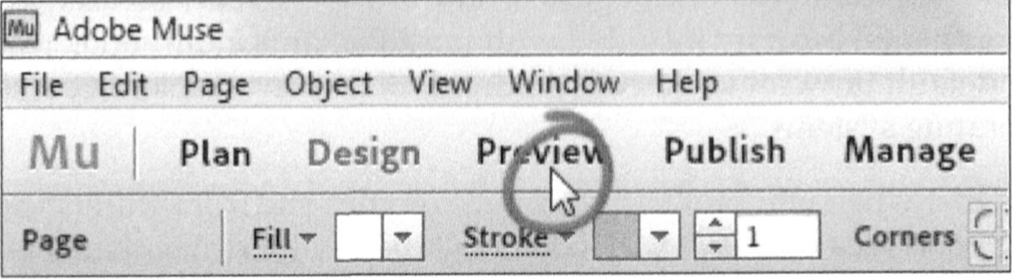

Preview a page in a browser

While it's obviously very convenient and quick to preview from Muse, you should, as part of your testing routine, preview the web pages created in Muse in external browsers. Follow the given steps:

1. Open the page that you want to preview in the **Design** view.
2. Select **File | Preview Page in Browser**, as shown in the following screenshot:

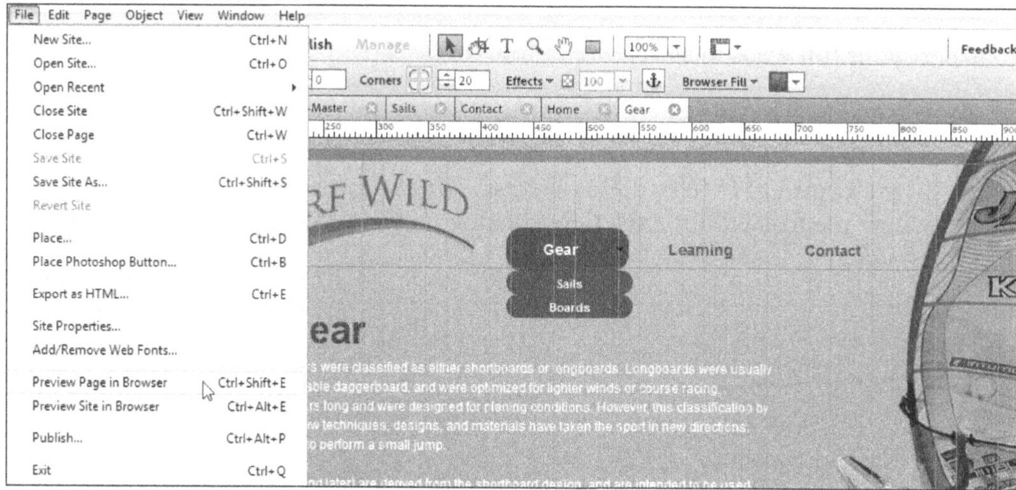

Preview the entire site in a browser

If you want to test links while previewing, you'll want Muse to create preview files for the entire site.

To preview the entire website, beginning with the home page, select **File | Preview Site in Browser**.

Export HTML for browser testing

In *Chapter 12, Publishing Your Site*, we'll look at how to publish our site and the various options available to us. However, as part of our testing, we can export the HTML files and examine the assets that have been created by Muse. Exporting the HTML files means that the files are stored locally on our computer where we can access them and take a look at what has been generated by Muse.

When you export your site, Muse slices and optimizes the images and creates a folder that holds these images, HTML, Cascading Style Sheets, and the scripts required to make the site work its magic.

If you're at all interested in code, you can open up the HTML files in any text editor and see the tags used to build your pages. If you're not interested in the code, and most people who use Muse will not be, you can just open up `index.html` (your home page) in any of the browsers you have installed on your machine and test them locally.

To export your full website as HTML, follow these steps:

1. Select **File | Export as HTML** or press *Ctrl* + *E* (Windows) or *Command* + *E* (Mac).
2. In the **Export to HTML** dialog box, specify the location on your computer where the files will be saved, by clicking on the folder icon, and then click on **OK**.

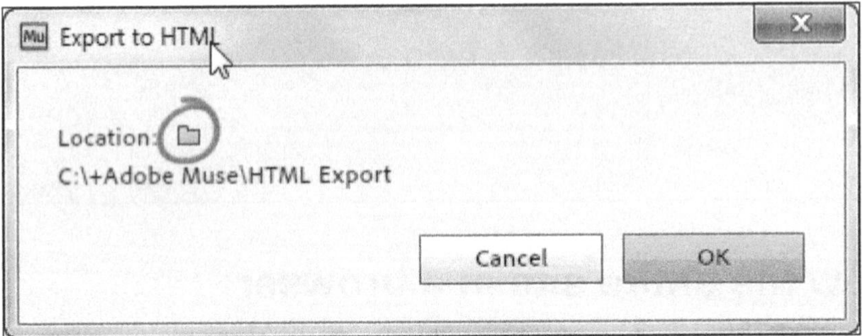

Your files will appear in the folder you specified and should look similar to the following screenshot:

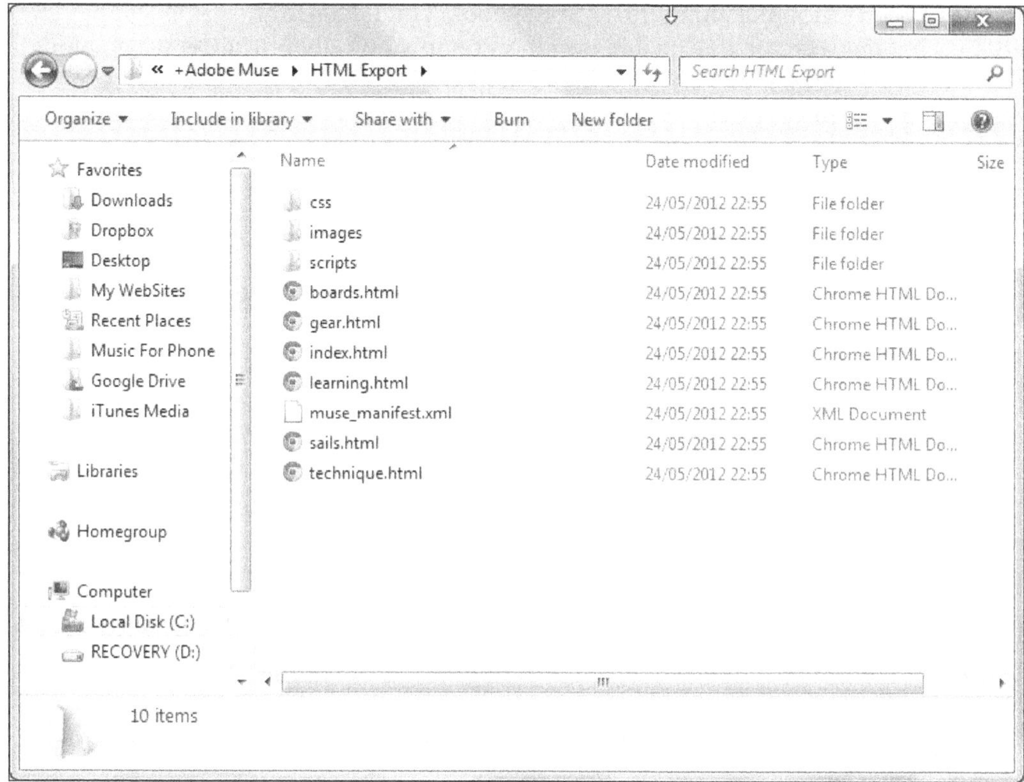

On the computer from which this screen grab is taken, Chrome is set up as the default browser; that's why the Chrome icon appears beside each of the HTML files that have been generated.

Viewing your home page on an installed browser

You can open the home page in any browser you have installed on your computer by right-clicking (Windows)/*Command* + click (Mac) and choosing **Open With** from the menu, and then choosing the browser in which you want to see the HTML page.

What to test for?

Testing should be completed during each phase of a site's development. Two mistakes new designers often make are waiting until just prior to launch before testing, or not testing at all.

If you've been following along through the book, you'll have done some testing after each page is created by clicking on the **Preview** link. By testing as we go along, we reduce the number of bugs and errors that could appear if left until just before the launch. The message is, keep testing and previewing throughout the entire Muse project.

So what do we need to test for?

Test your website on multiple browsers and platforms

Even though your website looks good and works well in Muse, doesn't mean it will look as good or function as well on other browsers and/or platforms. Adobe has created a product that *should* create web pages that look good on all browsers and platforms but it is part of your job to check and test that they do.

Which browsers and platforms to test?

In *Chapter 2, The Muse Workflow*, we discussed the challenge of web design compared to print design. The major challenge is that there are several platforms and many Internet browsers, which your visitors could be using to visit your site. There are many popular operating systems and browsers on which you might test your site.

The following is a list of the operating systems:

- Macintosh OS X
- Macintosh OS 9
- Windows 7
- Windows XP SP1 and SP2
- Windows 2000
- Windows 98
- Linux
- Android
- iOS
- Windows Mobile

The following is a list of popular browsers:

- Safari
- Mozilla
- Firefox
- Chrome
- Opera
- Internet Explorer
- Browsers for Mobile Devices

There are several online tools available to help with cross-browser testing, as it is unlikely that you would have access to all the browsers on every type of platform. Check out the following websites to see how you can test your site on multiple browsers in one go:

- Browsershots: `http://www.browsershots.org/`
- Browsercam: `http://www.browsercam.com/`
- Browserlab: `http://browserlab.adobe.com/`

Only Adobe Browserlab offers a free service.

Test page optimization

Optimizing your pages right from the start can help ensure that your site design and images support fast page load times, and that the site's development is smooth and efficient. We've discussed the importance of optimization of images in *Chapter 7, Working with Images*, a compromise between the best quality possible with the lowest file size.

There are also free online tools that calculate document weight, composition, and page load times, and even offer recommendations for optimizing web documents. Check out Website Optimization's web page analyzer at: `http://www.websiteoptimization.com/services/analyze/`.

View pages on a variety of displays

Visitors will be accessing your site from desktop computers, laptops, tablets, and smartphones. Your lovely design may not stand up on each of these displays, so it's important to try out your pages on as many of these displays as possible.

View pages on different screen resolutions

Unlike designing for print, not everyone will be viewing your site at the same resolution. A useful tool for testing your site at various screen resolutions is Firefox's Web Developer plug-in. This includes a customizable window-resizing tool.

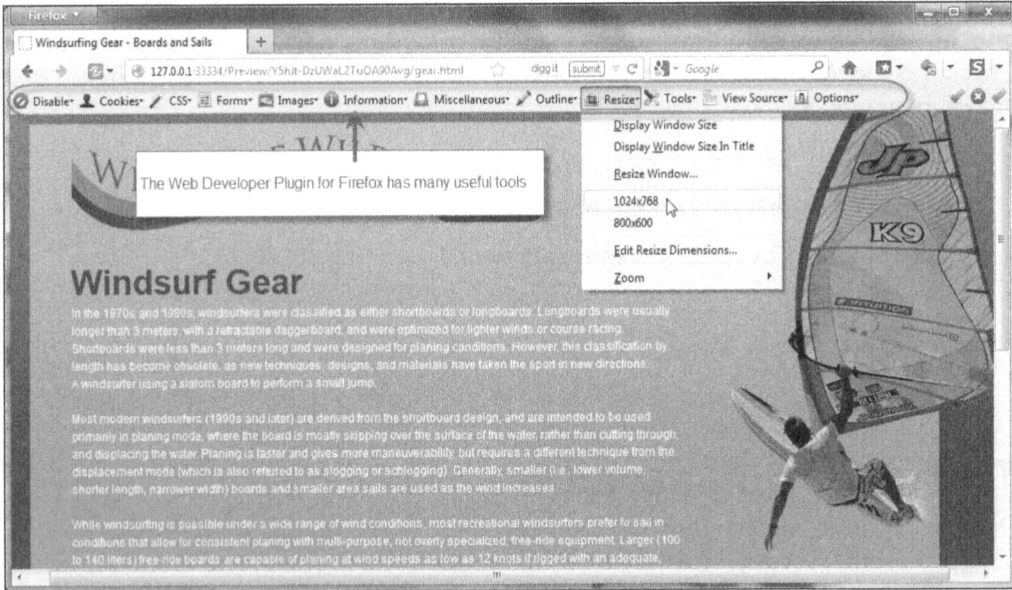

Check for adequate color contrast

Make sure it's easy for people to see your content by providing good contrast between the text and the background. A useful tool that can be helpful for checking your design's color contrasts is Vischeck (`http://www.vischeck.com/`), which simulates colorblind vision, allowing you to see your pages as a colorblind user might.

Test the functionality of all your widgets

If you've added some of the handy widget functionality provided by Muse, make sure it works. It *should* work, but don't forget to test. If there is a problem, it will be with older browsers, which will not support some functionality. If you find that a large portion of your visitors are using an older browser (and this is something you will discover over time by using website logs or Google analytics), then you may need to provide an alternative to that functionality.

Test all links, including navigation

Make sure all the links work properly. Links in your main navigation are created automatically by Muse, so check that it includes all the pages you want, and that it doesn't include any pages you don't want.

Check all links to external sites and check your anchor links to ensure they are taking the visitor to where they should be.

Test all downloads

If you have added a link to a download such as a PDF file, make sure that your download links point to the correct files, and that the download files exist.

Test the site's accessibility conformance

Use at least two different accessibility evaluation tools. A useful list of tools is available on the W3C accessibility initiative website: `http://www.w3.org/WAI/RC/tools/complete`.

Proofread all content

Spelling errors are a major turn-off for visitors to websites. Make sure you spell check and read through each page of your site to check that all the text is clear, simple, and appropriate for your website's target audience.

Usability testing

The tests and checks listed so far are something you can do yourself, but to really test your site, you need a fresh pair of eyes; ideally, several sets of eyes. The main goal of usability testing is to make sure your final version, your live website, is user-friendly and works well for your visitors.

You will have to test the following:

- **Effectiveness**: Testing to see if the user can accomplish the desired tasks
- **Efficiency**: Testing to see how much effort is involved in accomplishing the desired tasks
- **Satisfaction**: Testing to see if the user has a satisfactory experience and will return

You may be surprised that what seemed completely obvious to you, may leave an independent tester scratching their head, wondering what to do on your website.

For tons of information on website usability, visit Jakob Nielsen's website at: `http://www.useit.com/`.

Mr. Nielsen is recognized as one of the pioneers of usability testing on websites. You might also be surprised at how plain the site is.

Some of these tests will only be possible once you upload your site to the server (which we'll cover in the next chapter), but many of them are possible by testing locally on your machine.

If you were creating a very large site you would need to do additional testing, but for a small personal site created with Muse, testing everything that's been mentioned so far would be a good start.

Creating a device-friendly website

While Adobe does not officially support mobile device designs in Version 1 of Muse, there are a number of things you can consider when designing your site to make it mobile friendly, as follows:

- Adobe Flash technology is not supported on iPhones and iPads. This was the source of some antagonism between Apple and Adobe. If you put Flash on your website, it will not be visible to users of iPhones or iPads.
- Apple does not like pinned images either. On the iPhone and iPad, your pinned images will not stay pinned where you want them.
- Some embedded HTML that you added to pages using **Object | Insert HTML** can produce unexpected results on smart phones and tablets. You should test the site on a mobile device and if there is a problem, you should remove the embedded HTML to see if the rest of the page behaves normally.

- There is no Rollover/Hover state on touch devices. On many devices, the first touch is treated as a hover, with the second touch acting as the Click or Down state. Again, testing on a mobile device is required to ensure that your menu widgets and other links work correctly.
- Aim for a good user experience for all of your visitors. At this point, it is very difficult, if not impossible, to duplicate the experience on a mobile device as on a desktop or laptop computer. So keeping your site simple and easy-to-use is one way to ensure that your site performs well on a mobile device.

Summary

In this short chapter, we saw how to preview your page within Muse and in a browser, how to preview the entire site in a browser, and how to export the site as HTML and its associated assets. We also discussed testing and what you as the designers should be checking for, and we saw some tips on making your website mobile device friendly.

In the next and final chapter, we'll learn how to publish our site on the Web.

12
Publishing Your Site

You've built your site from scratch, added text, images, and interactivity, and now it's time to unleash your hard work on the Web. The final (and exciting) step is to publish your site. In this chapter, we'll look at how to get your site up there, onto the Web for all to see. There are two ways to host your site that you've created with Muse and we'll look at both of these. In this chapter, you will learn the following topics:

- Publishing a temporary site
- Publishing your site with Business Catalyst
- Publishing your site to a third-party hosting provider

Adobe ID

When you first download and install Muse, you are required to create an Adobe ID. If you have previously created an Adobe ID (on `www.adobe.com` to access other Adobe services), you can use the same password with your Muse account. The following screenshot shows a **Sign In** window.

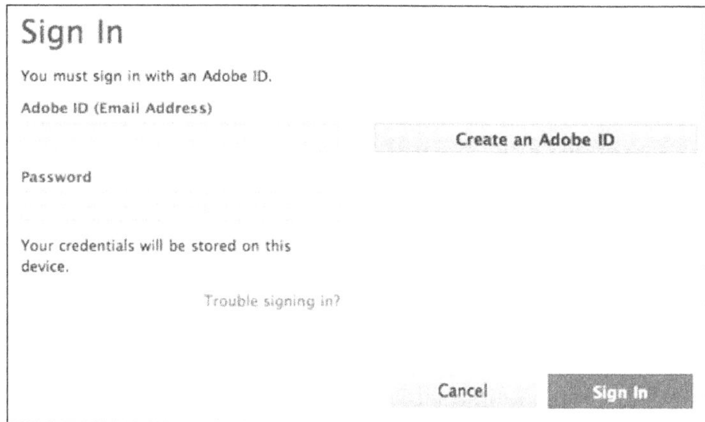

If you purchased a subscription with Adobe Creative Cloud, you'll use the same password to log into Muse when you first install it.

If you previously created a Business Catalyst account and used the same login email to create your Adobe ID, the system will detect that the e-mail address you entered matches a record in the Business Catalyst database.

Whichever way you first set up your ID, you will need to know that username and password when it comes to publishing your site.

Publishing a temporary site

When you use Muse, you can make and publish as many temporary sites as you wish. Every temporary site you create is active for 30 days. This gives you plenty of time to upload your sites, test them, and share them with your clients before going for a final launch. If you want to, you can publish one original form of your site, publish a second version as a temporary site, and make changes to that one. This allows you and your client to compare the before and after iterations of the same site.

If a temporary site you're working on is active for more than 30 days, you can extend its life by simply publishing the site again from your `.muse` file.

Remind me what the .muse file is again

When you design, build, and save your site in Muse, a single file with the extension `.muse` is created. This is very different from the situation where you may have handcoded or used a program like Dreamweaver to create your website. In that situation, you would have a folder which would contain the following files:

- HTML files for each page
- At least one CSS file for styling your pages
- All of your image files
- Any other files you might use on your site, such as a Flash movie.

The advantage of a single `.muse` file is that all your links, pages, styling, and images are in this file. If you're working collaboratively, you can send a `.muse` file as well as the placed images to your work partner and they can open it safely with the knowledge that everything required for the site is in this one file.

When you publish to a temporary site, you upload this single `.muse` file.

Let's now look at how to publish a temporary site; later we'll learn how to permanently publish your site to its final spot on the Web.

When you publish a site, it automatically takes the site name that your project started with, and adds the Business Catalyst domain name. So for example, the temporary site's URL for our Windsurfing site would look like this:

```
http://windsurfing.businesscatalyst.com
```

Remember, this is only temporary, so when you are going for the final site launch, you can assign a domain name of your choice to it. The following steps have to be performed to publish a temporary site from Muse:

1. Click on the **Publish** link at the top of the Muse workspace.
2. The **Publish** dialog box appears. Enter the name of your temporary site in the **Site Name** field. This should be a descriptive name that will help you to identify the site. For example, you could enter `My windsurfing site`.

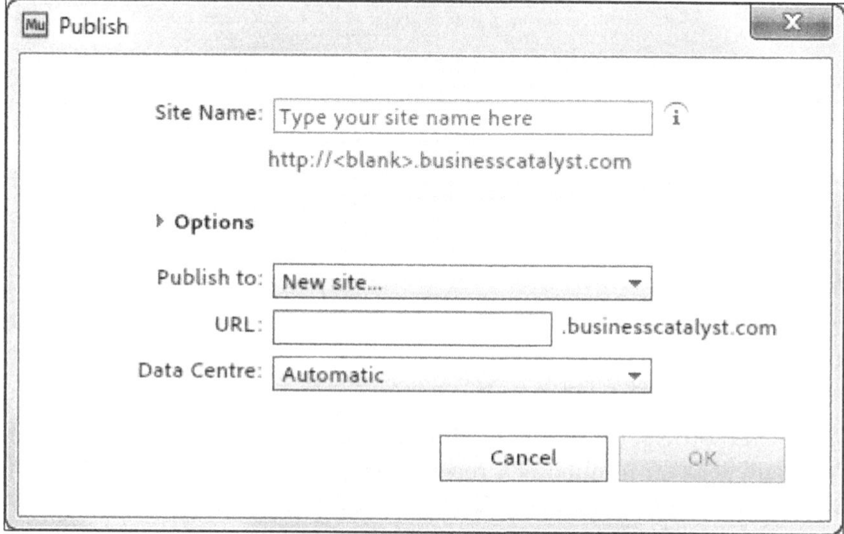

3. If they are not already visible, click on the **Options** link to see more options for your temporary site.
4. Leave **Publish to** as **New site...**.
5. The site's **URL** field in the **Options** section will automatically remove spaces and special characters and spaces that were entered in the **Site Name** field to create a suggested URL for your live temporary site. You can edit the contents of the **URL** field to change the automatically generated URL, if you want to.
6. The **Data Centre** field selects the data centre where the site files will be hosted. Muse will detect this automatically, but if you want to be specific, you can choose from United States, European Union, or Australia.

7. If you don't live in any of these three options, you can choose the **Data Centre** closest to your client's location.
8. When completed, the dialog box should look something like the following screenshot:

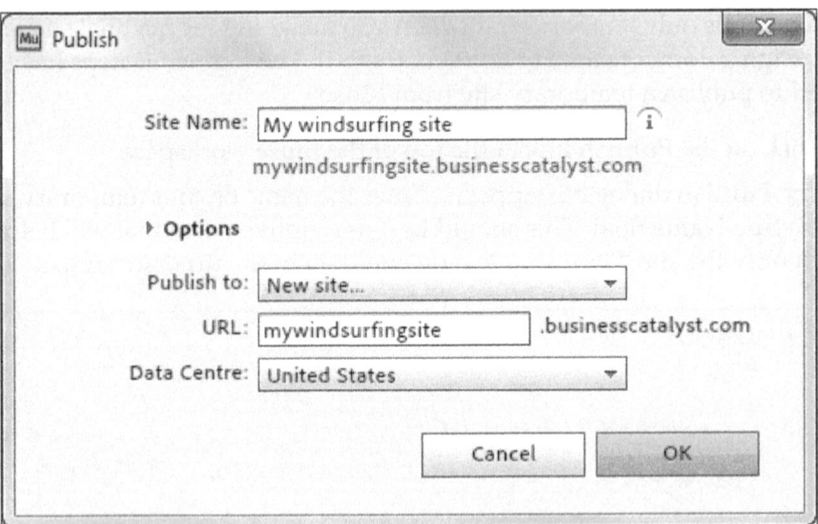

9. Click on **OK** to publish your new temporary site.
10. Muse will upload all of your pages and assets, and when uploading is complete, you'll get a confirmation message telling you that your temporary site is now hosted. Click on **OK**.
11. Your Web browser will open automatically at the temporary site address. You will also simultaneously receive an email to your Adobe ID address congratulating you on publishing your temporary site with a link to the temporary URL.

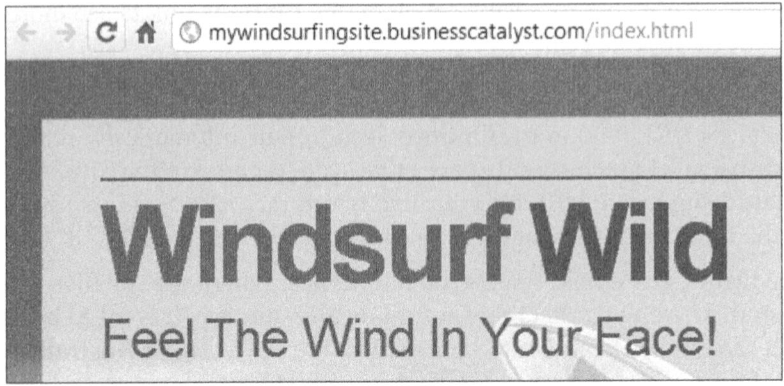

If you want to make more changes to your Muse site and upload them to the same location, click the **Publish** link in Muse again. You'll see that the link to your temporary site is displayed automatically below the **Site Name** field. Click on the link to launch your temporary site in a new browser window and test it.

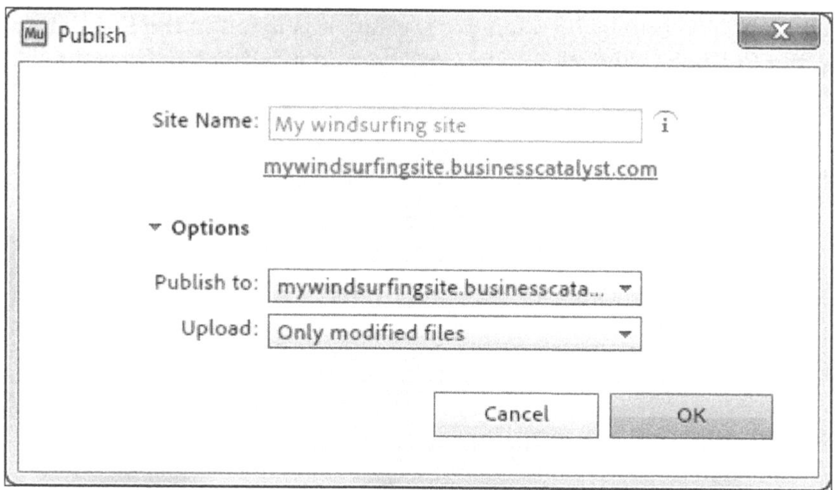

The URL of the temporary site can be copied and sent to your clients for review. You now have an excellent opportunity to go through all of the testing we discussed in the previous chapter. Also, you'll be testing a working, online website but without having to worry about the general public wandering onto the site.

Once you've published the temporary site, the **Manage** link will now be available and active. We'll use this shortly to publish the final site.

Editing and updating a site

You have now published your site and spoken to your client, but you may find that there are some changes required. In order to edit and update your site, apply the following steps:

1. Open the same `.muse` file in Muse.
2. You have two options now:
    - Make changes in the existing `.muse` file and then choose **File** | **Save** and click on the **Publish** link again.
    - Choose **File** | **Save As** to create a new copy of the site. Make the changes required in the Muse workspace and then click on the **Publish** link again.

3. You can now publish over the existing temporary site by leaving the options as they are in the Publish dialog box, or you can create a new temporary site. This makes it easy for your client to compare the before and after changes.
    - By choosing **File** | **Save As**, you are keeping your original site safe.
4. When you've published a temporary site, it is listed in the **Publish to** menu in the **Publish** dialog box. You can select an existing site from the list, or choose to create a new site.

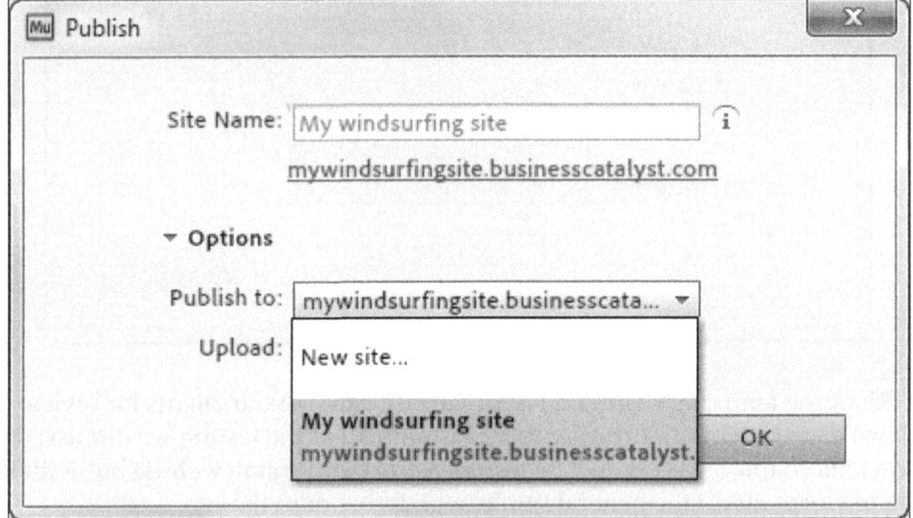

5. You can upload all the files, or only those that you've modified. If you have a very large website, it's a good idea to upload only the modified files. When Muse is upgraded, it may be a good idea to republish the entire site.
6. Repeat this process until you and the client are happy with the site. Hopefully that won't take too many iterations.

Upgrading and launching

The final steps involve "upgrading" your site and publishing it. When you get to this stage, you will need to pay for hosting fees. You will also need to register a domain name for your site and this is done through a third party.

Register a domain name

You will need to contact a domain registrar in order to buy the domain name that you want to use for your website. There are many sites offering this service online and you should be able to buy a `.com` domain for less than $10 online. Buying a domain name is very straightforward and is generally completed very quickly. We will return to the domain registrar after we complete a few more steps.

Upgrade to a published site

The following steps will tell you how to upgrade your site and publish it:

1. In Muse, with your previously published temporary site open, click on the **Manage** link. The **Manage** link is only available once you've published your temporary site.
2. After clicking on the **Manage** link, the **Business Catalyst** admin console opens in your Web browser window. You'll see the **Dashboard** where you can manage your Muse sites hosted by **Business Catalyst**. You'll also be able to view your site's statistics.

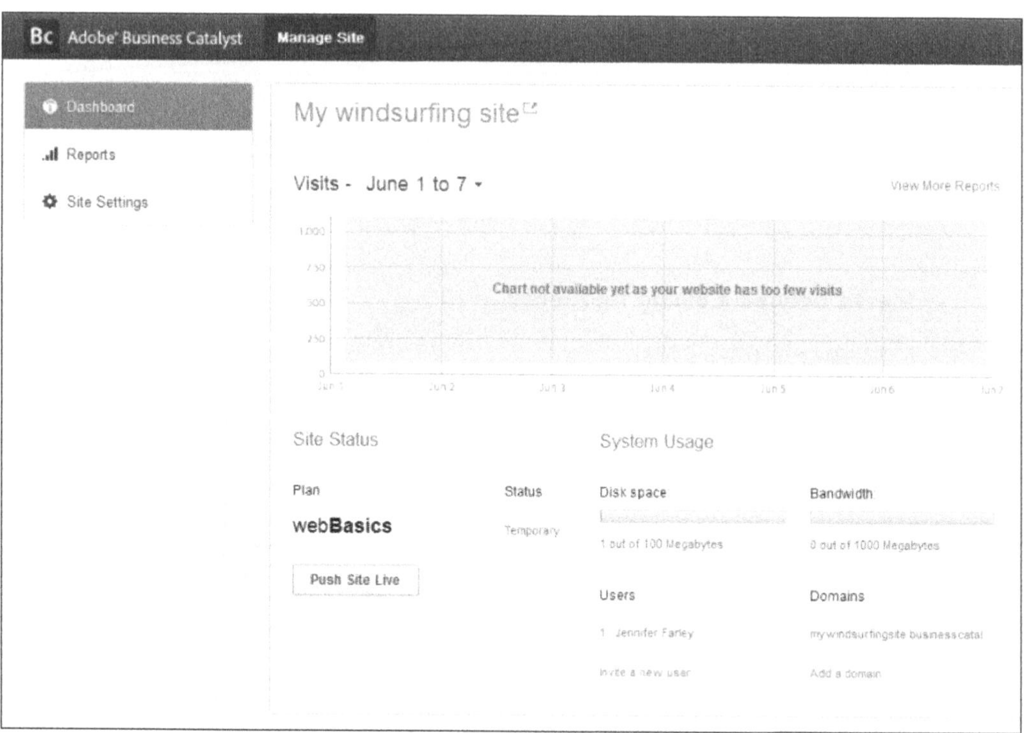

3. Click the **Push Site Live** button on the **Dashboard**.
4. The **Site Upgrade** window appears. Click on **Proceed to checkout**. You'll need to enter your credit card information to complete the upgrade.
5. Leave the default settings for the first two options:
   - Site hosting plan: **webBasics**
   - Billing option: **Invoice Me Directly**

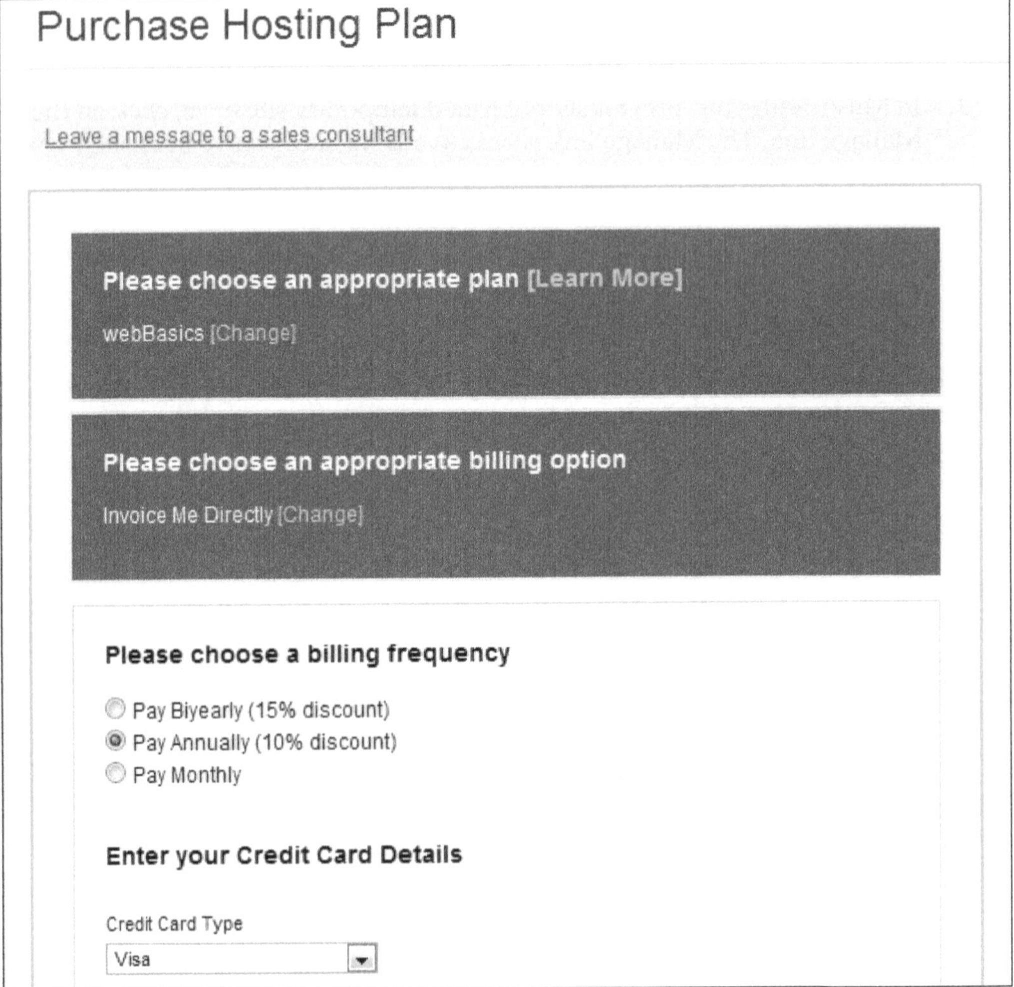

6. Choose how frequently you want to be billed, fill in your credit card details and click on **Make Payment**.
7. Your credit card payment is processed instantly, based on your selection.

8. You will be returned to the **Dashboard** and the **Site Status** is now **Live**.

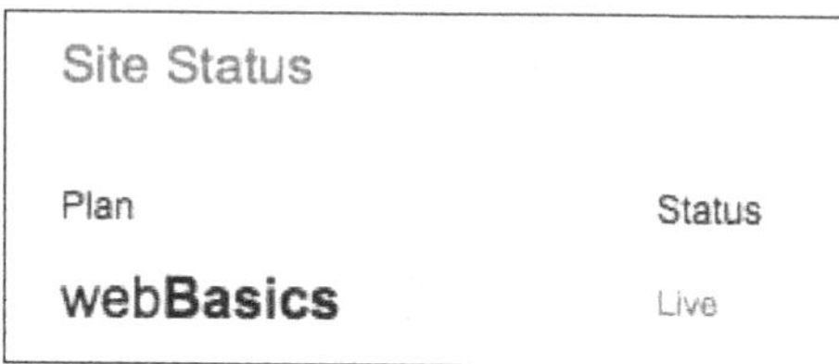

Associating the domain name with your Muse site

Our temporary site is now upgraded and is hosted commercially by **Business Catalyst**. This upgrade means that we can associate our domain with the site name we bought from the domain registrar.

Before an upgrade from a temporary site, the site address looks something like this:

`http://my_site.businesscatalyst.com`

(for example, `http://mywindsurfingsite.businesscatalyst.com`)

After the upgrade and launch of a site, we can add our domain name so it looks more like this:

`http://my_domain_name.com`

(for example, `mywindsurfingsite.com`)

In this section, you'll use the interface in the **Dashboard** of the admin console.

1. Click on the option in the **Dashboard** and then click on **Add a domain**.

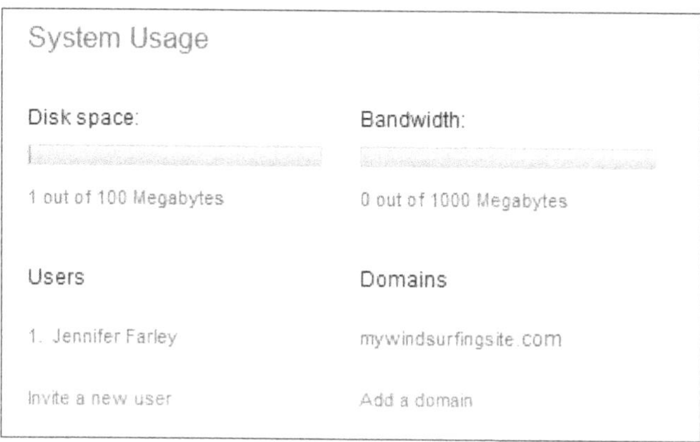

2. When the **Site Domains** dialog box appears, click on the **New Domain** option.
3. Type in the domain name you registered in the **Domain** field. Do not include the `www.` prefix before the domain name, but do include the domain's extension (such as, `.com`, `.org`, or others); for example: `my_domain_name.com`.
4. Select the **Home Page** on the **Start Page** menu. Set the **Country** and **Culture** for the site. Leave all other default settings and click on **Save**.

5. You'll see a confirmation message. Click on **Close** to close the **Add a New Domain** dialog box and return to the admin console. Your domain name that you added to the site is now listed.
6. Click the **Dashboard** link in the left sidebar to return to the **Dashboard**.
7. In the **Domains** section, the domain name you entered is now listed.

Re-delegating your domain name

You are nearly there. There is only one more thing to do and that's re-delegating your domain name. This just means making sure that when you type in your domain name in the browser, it goes to the right place.

Unfortunately, this is not something you can do either through Muse or through the **Business Catalyst** dashboard. Here's how to do it:

1. Go to the website of the registrar that you bought your domain from.
2. Most registrars have a Control Panel which you can use to re-delegate your domain. You'll need a username and password supplied to you by the registrar.

3. Using your account information, log into the registrar's website. You need to find the option to update the **Domain Name System**(**DNS**) settings. You need to update the name servers on the registrar to the following:
   - `ns1.worldsecuresystems.com`
   - `ns2.worldsecuresystems.com`
   - `ns3.worldsecuresystems.com`
4. This process can vary from registrar to registrar. If you are having problems finding where to change the DNS settings, contact them directly.
5. When the name servers have been changed you may need to wait for 24 hours for the settings to kick in. When they do, your domain name will bring you directly to your muse-created website. Congratulations!

Alternative hosting

You are not tied to using Adobe's Business Catalyst hosting. You can use any hosting service of your choice. The only difference is that firstly you will need to export your site as HTML, as seen in *Chapter 11, Previewing and Testing your Site* and then upload the folders and files using an FTP program to your host.

File Transfer Protocol (FTP)

File Transfer Protocol (**FTP**) is a method of uploading files to your hosted Website. After you export your site as HTML, you can use the FTP software to transfer your files to your host.

You will need to pay for hosting and for a domain name. There are some amazing offers out there for packages of hosting and domain names, so do some checking before buying the first hosting package you see.

When you have arranged a host for your site, you will receive an email with FTP details, or a link to where you can find your FTP details on their website. As a minimum, you will need a username, password, and FTP address. You cannot guess these; they need to be provided by the hosting company. FTP is a method that verifies you've entered the correct username and password to connect to a specific site.

FTP clients

There are loads of free FTP clients (software) available online and they work perfectly. You don't need to buy one for straightforward uploading or downloading. Here are a few well-known FTP clients:

- FileZilla used in Linux, Mac OS X and Windows operating systems
- SmartFTP used only in Windows operating system
- SimpleFTP used only in Mac OS X operating system
- CuteFTP used in Mac OS X and Windows operating systems

When you use FTP, you can upload files from your local computer to the host server and download files from your host server to your local computer.

When you enter your FTP details into the client, click on the **Connect** button. If all your details are correct, the FTP client will connect with the host computer. On one side of the FTP client's interface, you will see the files on your local computer; on the other side you will see the files on your remote or host computer.

By following the instructions from the hosting provider, you will be able to upload your local files (which you exported as HTML) to the remote host. Uploading is the same as publishing your files from the **Business Catalyst** dashboard.

When your files have been uploaded, your site is live on the Internet. If you need to make changes to the site, make those changes in Muse and then export your files again. Upload only the files that have changed. When you are finished uploading, click on **Disconnect**.

Summary

In this chapter, we discussed how to publish and launch your site. You can publish using Adobe's own hosting with Business Catalyst or you can export your site as HTML and then upload it to a host of your choice.

That ends our trip through Adobe Muse together. I hope you have enjoyed learning about the program and will go on to produce beautiful websites of your own.

Index

Symbols

D

E

F

N

O

P

U

V

W

X

Z

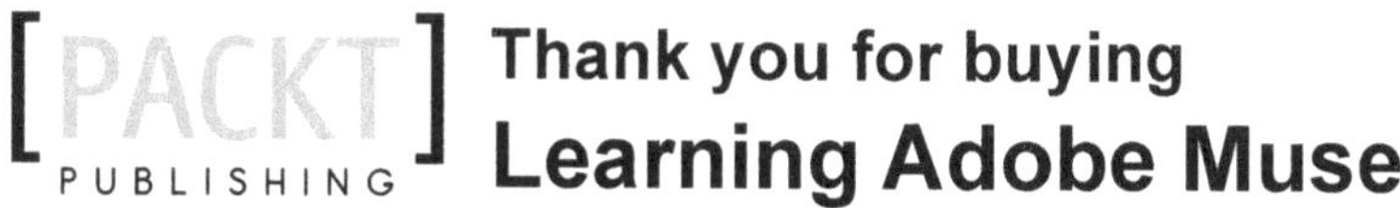

About Packt Publishing

Packt, pronounced 'packed', published its first book "*Mastering phpMyAdmin for Effective MySQL Management*" in April 2004 and subsequently continued to specialize in publishing highly focused books on specific technologies and solutions.

Our books and publications share the experiences of your fellow IT professionals in adapting and customizing today's systems, applications, and frameworks. Our solution based books give you the knowledge and power to customize the software and technologies you're using to get the job done. Packt books are more specific and less general than the IT books you have seen in the past. Our unique business model allows us to bring you more focused information, giving you more of what you need to know, and less of what you don't.

Packt is a modern, yet unique publishing company, which focuses on producing quality, cutting-edge books for communities of developers, administrators, and newbies alike. For more information, please visit our website: `www.packtpub.com`.

Writing for Packt

We welcome all inquiries from people who are interested in authoring. Book proposals should be sent to `author@packtpub.com`. If your book idea is still at an early stage and you would like to discuss it first before writing a formal book proposal, contact us; one of our commissioning editors will get in touch with you.

We're not just looking for published authors; if you have strong technical skills but no writing experience, our experienced editors can help you develop a writing career, or simply get some additional reward for your expertise.

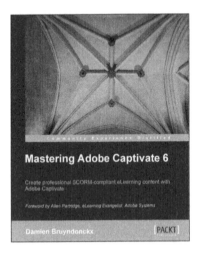

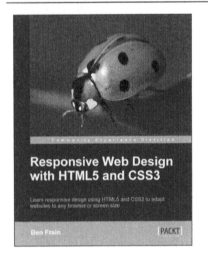

Dreamweaver CS5.5 Mobile and Web Development with HTML5, CSS3, and jQuery

ISBN: 978-1-849691-58-1 Paperback: 284 pages

Harness the cutting edge features of Dreamweaver for mobile and web development

1. Create web pages in Dreamweaver using the latest technology and approach
2. Add multimedia and interactivity to your websites
3. Optimize your websites for a wide range of platforms and build mobile apps with Dreamweaver
4. A practical guide filled with many examples for making the best use of Dreamweaver's latest features

---

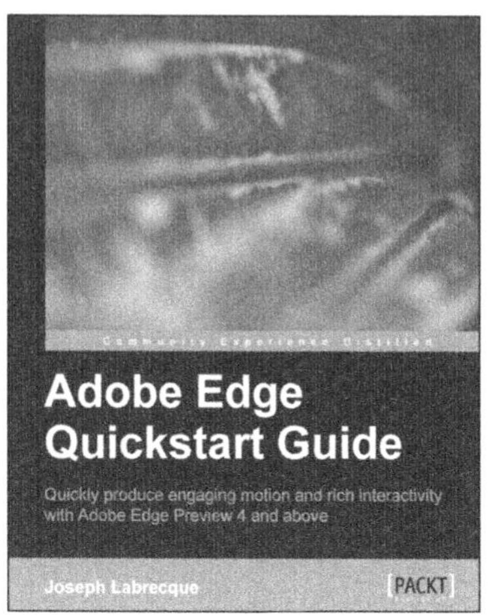

Adobe Edge Quickstart Guide

ISBN: 978-1-849693-30-1 Paperback: 136 pages

Quickly produce engaging motion and rich interactivity with Adobe Edge Preview 4 and above

1. Learn to use Adobe's newest application to create engaging motion and rich interactivity
2. Familiarize yourself with the Edge interface and unleash your creativity through standard HTML, CSS, and JavaScript
3. Add motion and interactivity to your websites using Web standards
4. A quickstart guide for creating engaging content with Adobe Edge

Please check **www.PacktPub.com** for information on our titles

Lightning Source UK Ltd.
Milton Keynes UK
UKOW07f0042170615

253619UK00004B/237/P

9 781849 693141